The Economics of Professional Team Sports

Do dominant teams kill public interest in professional sports?

Do spectators relish close contests and unpredictable results?

Are sports stars overpaid?

Will recent changes to sports broadcasting undermine the traditional organisation of professional team sports?

To address these and other issues, Paul Downward and Alistair Dawson offer a detailed survey of the economic literature on sporting leagues, the demand for professional team sports, and the players' labour market.

Amongst the topics discussed are the US system of franchising and draft picks, and the chances of their being adopted elsewhere, the implications of player strikes, the onset of pay-per-view and digital television, and the relatively new notion that sport is a business like any other.

This book is unique in that it constitutes the first truly rigorous application of economic principles to its subject. It will be of great interest to students and practitioners within the field of sports and leisure economics.

Paul Downward is Reader in Economics at Staffordshire University and is a founding member of the Board of the new *Journal of Sports Economics*. **Alistair Dawson** is Senior Lecturer in Economics at Staffordshire University and is the Business Manager of the journal *Economic Issues*.

Economics/Business Studies/Sports and Leisure Management

The Economics of Professional Team Sports

Paul Downward and Alistair Dawson

London and New York

First published 2000
by Routledge
11 New Fetter Lane, London EC4P 4EE

Simultaneously published in the USA and Canada
by Routledge
29 West 35th Street, New York, NY 10001

Routledge is an imprint of the Taylor & Francis Group

© 2000 Paul Downward and Alistair Dawson

Typeset in Times by Steven Gardiner Ltd, Cambridge
Printed and bound in Great Britain by Clays Ltd, St Ives plc

British Library Cataloguing in Publication Data
A catalogue record for this book is available from the British Library

Library of Congress Cataloging in Publication Data
Downward, Paul, 1964–
The economics of professional team sports / Paul Downward and Alistair Dawson.
    p.   cm.
Includes bibliographical references and index.
1. Sports teams – United States – Economic aspects – 20th century. 2. Professional
sports – Ecnomic aspects – United States – History – 20th century. 3. Sports teams – Great
Britain – Economic aspects – 20th century. 4. Professional sports – Economic aspects –
Great Britain – History – 20th century. I. Dawson, Alistair, 1940– II. Title.
GV716.D69   2000
338.4′7796044′0973 – dc21   00–029116

ISBN 0–415–20873–4 (hbk)
ISBN 0–415–20874–2 (pbk)

Contents

Figures

Tables

Acknowledgements

This book has grown out of considerable experience teaching and researching in the fields of sports, leisure and recreation economics at Staffordshire University. Identifying particular individuals, groups of academics or students to thank is thus not generally attempted. However, we would like to note our appreciation on a couple of counts. The first is to the scores of Sports and Leisure Management students over the years that, often unwittingly, acted as experimental subjects in our attempts to teach economics to non-economics specialists. Sitting alongside Economics students, their efforts are to be commended. They have helped to shape this book immensely. Moreover, we think that a particular word of thanks should be made to Dr John Bridge, our former Head of Division, and (the late) Dr Basil Ashford, the former Head of the Sport, Health and Exercise Division. Both had the foresight and originality of mind to bring together the teaching of economics and sport at the university.

Writing a book can, at the best of times, though rewarding be an arduous task. This is not only in terms of academic issues such as being unsure about whether the book really meets its objectives, or is argued well, etc., but also in terms of the sheer administration involved. In the climate of the 'new' universities in the UK these burdens are somewhat magnified given increasing teaching loads, administration and the expectation that research targets are met. Books as academic vehicles of discourse are, indeed, in some cases frowned upon with the drive to produce journal articles. Given these pressures we fully acknowledge that any errors in the book are our own.

More particularly, PD is grateful to the patience of his wife, Cathy, and children, Sarah-Louise and Joseph, for putting up with the long hours of work associated with this project (among others!). No doubt in their eyes these hours could have been better spent engaging in sports actively with them, running, learning to do 'tumble-turns' or scrummaging-down respectively. AD is looking forward to more mountains – Tal y Braich – and to retirement.

1   Introduction

Why are professional team sports of interest to economists?

As members of the public, there is no especial reason why economists should be interested in professional team sports. This book is thus not simply based on the interest of the authors who happen to be economists. On the contrary, this book is based on a belief that sports, and particularly, professional team sports, lend themselves to economic analysis. Consequently, some of the topical issues in professional team sports regarding, for example, the Bosman Ruling, the rise of the Premier League in association football (soccer), the effectiveness of salary caps in sport, we argue, can be understood from an economic perspective. There are two main reasons for this. The first comprises the nature of professional team sports as opposed to sports generally. The second is the world-wide growth in the commercialisation of sport.

Professional team sports comprise leagues of clubs who compete on the sporting field by arrangement through a fixture list and according to rules of the sport, which are set by leagues. Success in sporting terms is essentially defined in terms of the rank order of clubs in the league at the end of a season after points have been allocated for their performance in the set of fixtures. This, of course, is something that applies to all team sports – whether of an amateur or professional status. The *production* of team sports *per se* is not in itself something that naturally lends itself to economic analysis. Schoolchildren can produce team sports! What matters as well is that money changes hands in the production, distribution and consumption of the sport; money, of course, being the mechanism by which key sporting resources such as athletes are obtained by, and allocated between, the various teams to use in competition against their opponents on the field. Clearly professionalism in sport is an integral aspect of this development.

The purchase and sale of players as well as payment to them to perform, for example, require financing decisions. Thus, gate revenues need to be earned to pay players' salaries. Clubs must co-ordinate match schedules since they cannot produce in isolation, and potential spectators must be informed where and when matches are to occur. In turn, spectators need accommodation and a means by which payment can be extracted from them while restricting access to the sport to non-payers. Thus, *enclosed* stadia are necessary features of professional sports supply. Characteristics like these clearly indicate that, rather like the production, distribution and consumption of other goods and services, professional team sports can be viewed as an economic process. Inputs such as labour – the athletes and manager/coach – are combined with capital – the sporting field, equipment and so on – to produce, along with another team in the league, a product – the fixture – that is sold to consumers – spectators and supporters – typically in a stadium.

Of course, professionalism is not something that is confined to team sports. Golf, tennis and boxing are long-standing professional sports. Athletics is now professional as well. However, we would argue that these lack some of the above essential characteristics of professional team sports. The first is a league structure. In contrast we would argue that athletes who compete in boxing, golf and tennis do so under conditions that could be better described as tournaments. As such the regularity of contact between opponents is less and typically of a 'one-off' nature. Knock-out cup competitions organised by sporting leagues share these characteristics. Participants and supporters recognise their distinctiveness compared to league fixtures. Second, we would argue that these athletes essentially compete as individuals despite 'team' membership in such events as the Ryder cup in golf or the Davis cup in tennis. Consequently, the economic need to organise the production process through the co-ordination of labour in the team is naturally less. Thus substitutes do not appear in boxing, tennis or golf as part of the natural order of play. Moreover, athletes are not bought and sold between competitors.

Of course, there is an element of semantics in this distinction. There are similarities between professional team sports, professional sports such as golf, boxing and tennis, as well as amateur sports and sport in general. Consequently, it may well be that many of the ideas discussed in this book apply to such sports and, indeed, we would expect this to be so. However, we leave extending the analysis of these sports to the future.

The second main reason for the interest by economists in professional team sports is that the commercial nature of sports in general has radically increased over the century. For example, the TV rights for the Olympics in 1948 were £27,000. In 1996, this had risen to $900m and is forecast to rise to $3.6bn by 2008. Similarly, BSkyB will have paid over £600m to Premier league association football clubs between 1997 and 2001. Contracts for the next period are estimated to exceed £1bn. Opel sponsor A.C. Milan association football team for approximately £6m per year and Nike are currently sponsoring the Brazilian national association football team by approximately $200m over a ten-year period. In the US, approximately 94 million spectators watch the Superbowl annually and Michael Jordan earned $25m in 1996. These point to the growing economic impact of both sports generally and professional team sports. There is thus considerable impetus to study these developments.

The need for a textbook

Having made these comments, we should be quite clear that there is nothing absolutely new in these sentiments. As the reader will become aware, there has been some long-standing interest in the economics of professional team sports in the US and a number of very readable volumes exist. Those particularly worthy of mention are the contributions by Quirk and Fort (1992) and Scully (1989; 1995). These academics can, in many respects, be seen as the pioneers of the economic analysis of professional team sports, particularly in the US. We strongly encourage readers of this book to read these volumes. As the reader will see, their work is referred to extensively in this book.

In the UK there are no comparable volumes. The work of individuals, such as Peter Sloane, has been influential through journal papers. Other than this, texts such as Gratton and Taylor (1985) and Cooke (1994) are seminal manifestations of attempts to apply economic analysis to sports, recreation and leisure generally.

The literature on professional team sports, however, has tended to follow two disparate trends. On the one hand, the number of periodical articles has increased. The *American Economic Review*, *Applied Economics*, *Applied Economics Letters*, the *Bulletin of Economic Research*, *Economic Issues*, the *Journal of Economic Literature*, the *Scottish Journal of Political Economy* and the *Southern Economic Journal* are some of the economics journals that have published papers on the economics of professional team sports. Indeed, to help meet a growing demand a new periodical – the *Journal of Sports Economics* – of which one of the authors of this volume is a founding member of the board of editors – has been launched. Other journals that have published papers on the economics of professional team sports include: *AREA*, a geographical journal and, naturally enough, sports and leisure journals such as the *Journal of Sports History*, the *Journal of Sports Management*, *Sports History Review*, and the *Journal of the Philosophy of Sport and Leisure Studies*.

This said, the technical content of the economic journal papers is usually high, which limits their readership to economic specialists. In contrast, recent texts, for example, in the UK, though eminently accessible and well written have adopted a business strategy perspective and have tended to focus on association football. Szymanski and Kuypers (1999) and Hamil *et al.* (1999) are examples. Without debating the relative importance of economics versus business strategy, which is a meaningless debate, suffice it to say that many of the concepts and literature referred to in these books draw upon the economics literature. Necessarily, however, their business strategy approach makes some of their treatment of the issues superficial in an *economics* sense. As will become apparent, for example, we argue in this book that the uncertainty of outcome hypothesis that is widely cited in such literature, as an integral component of the success of sporting leagues, has been somewhat overworked. Examination of the details of the economic research on this matter reveals this to be the case.

This said there is, of course, a compelling reason for the approach adopted in these texts. Without question, economics as a single-honours discipline is contracting radically in the UK, coupled with a tremendous growth of interest in business and management courses. To be somewhat crude, one can argue that students are interested increasingly in discussing economic issues but not necessarily exploring the underlying economics. Nonetheless it remains that there is a need to explore these economic issues robustly.

Taking all of these considerations into account, therefore, we perceive there to be a gap in the market for a text that presents economic issues in economic language and approach but in an accessible manner. Moreover it is clear that there is a need for a text that helps to link developments between US professional team sports and the *variety* of UK sports. Importantly, our experience of teaching identifies this gap.

It is also reflected in the pedagogic approach adopted in the book. The book is based on a set of final-year undergraduate lectures to students at Staffordshire University. The lectures have been developed over the last ten years as part of a broader package of study in sports and leisure economics provided by the Division of Economics. This package of study is undertaken by students of Economics, Business Studies and particularly Sports and Leisure Management. Consequently, it has the explicit intention of engaging with the logical rigour of economics but in an accessible way. Accordingly, it is fully intended that the book will be of use to students who have only an elementary knowledge of microeconomics but will also be useful to students with a more formal economic training. Primary exposition is verbal reasoning with support from diagrammatic apparatus. All concepts are both developed and discussed in the context of professional team sports. We do, however, also present some details of key statistical methods when it is deemed necessary in order to understand the details of an aspect of the literature or why we criticise it as we do. Our experience is that providing these methods are introduced *in situ*, and through focusing on the interpretation of results in studies of professional team sports, students without technical backgrounds very quickly make good sense of many of the journal articles on the economics of professional team sports.

Also, students with more technical training get the opportunity to think about the *application* of the concepts they are familiar with both generally and in an area that is, perhaps, unusual for them but of general interest. For such students we also include among the appendices to the chapters some more technical discussion of techniques and concepts used in the analysis of professional team sports. Some of the appendices, moreover, are simply extensions of discussions in the chapters. It remains that the book is designed without the *need* to access these appendices. Thus, led by the tutor, a judicious combination of the textual material, the appendices and further readings based on the bibliography we feel offers a flexible study resource. Some discussion questions that we have used in the past are included with each chapter.

Finally, we would like to remark that as active researchers in the economics of sport and leisure, it is hoped that other academics will find the book useful and interesting. For those unfamiliar with the study of sport from an economic perspective, we hope the book will provoke their interest. Moreover, at all times in the book we adopt a critical perspective on the literature and raise research issues where necessary – some of which we are currently addressing. We hope that academics also researching into the economics of sport will find the book stimulates their research. It remains that we are pleased to receive any feedback from academics and students alike.

Economic methodology

Because of the wide variety of intended readership for this text, we feel that it is incumbent upon us to outline some of the main characteristics of economic methodology. These are important in understanding how economists research issues and are implicit in discussions throughout the book. Those readers who are familiar with this approach could well skip this section.

The economic approach to understanding the world – and consequently professional team sports – is somewhat different from many academic disciplines. Thus, unlike the anthropologist, sociologist or historian who might focus on the context and detail of particular issues, economics, in the main, adopts a very different perspective. Indeed this is implied in the above discussion in which it was remarked that one aspiration of this book was to draw parallels between a variety of professional team sports both within and across countries. Economic epistemology – that is, theory of knowledge – is based on the use of simple models to produce predictions about general relationships covering events. Consequently, it is entirely 'natural' for the economist to try to generalise about developments in professional team sports and to look for simple ways to generalise on this behaviour.

The main characteristics of this approach, which the reader will see employed throughout the book, are perhaps best argued in an influential essay written by Milton Friedman in 1953. Although this is a complicated essay, and has been subject to much discussion, it does illustrate the main emphases of conventional economic methodology. The first of these emphases is that economic theories should be viewed, first and foremost, as instruments of prediction. Consequently, the assumptions used to construct or structure a theory, and upon which predictions are based need not be realistic nor have descriptive relevance. What matters in judging the theory, thus, is the correspondence of the theory's predictions with actual events.

Moreover, Friedman argues that theories that are 'fruitful' or exhibit 'simplicity' would be best. Somewhat ironically this is really an argument about efficiency – which as shown in the text is of paramount importance to economists. This efficiency argument for theories has become known as 'parsimony'. It suggests that the best model is the simplest model that can accommodate most predictions.

Friedman's arguments have been referred to as 'instrumentalist'. However, an instrumentalist position essentially does not hinge on referring to notions of truth or falsehood. In this respect, in methodological terms instrumentalism lies in contrast to realism. Comprising a variety of philosophical doctrines, realism maintains that there is a real entity that is referred to by the theory though not necessarily in a realistic way. Consequently, this 'ontological' commitment – that is, theory of the nature or essence of things – suggests that the world is at least partially independent of human knowledge and as such has objective elements. Friedman does not necessarily suggest that his theories do not refer to real things or that he is not interested in truth or falsehood *per se* despite his comments on the role of assumptions in theory. On these bases it is clear, moreover, that economists eschew postmodernism which suggests that the world we theorise about is essentially subjectively constructed. Further justification for this argument comes in the second major characteristic of economic theorising.

The mainstream approach to economic theorising has an implicit ontology that comprises the constant conjunction of events. Theories and empirical claims thus essentially comprise statements of the form 'if event X occurs then event Y follows'. This is, of course, a necessary if not sufficient condition for the aspiration of offering theories that predict events. Postulating the existence of a law and observing it are two different tasks! More generally, the economic approach appeals to 'covering laws'. These are relationships that transcend particular contexts in time or space. It is in this respect that economics looks to reduce a variety of economic behaviours in a variety of contexts to the same basic theoretical explanation.

It is worth noting that this emphasis has not always been the case and there is disagreement about economic methodology. Nagel (1963) provides a critique of Friedman. More generally, for the interested reader Mair and Miller (1992) is an excellent introduction to such debates between 'schools of thought' in economics. The reader should be aware that it uses a particular methodological framework, due to Imre Lakatos, to characterise the various schools.

We would also like to note that we share some of these concerns. Consequently, we do feel that the insights generated by this book should be thought of as open to debate between different disciplinary traditions. Indeed we sincerely hope that debate is encouraged by the book.

Summary of chapters

In Section A of the book, which comprises the first three chapters, we discuss the main economic characterisation of sporting leagues. In Chapter 2, we begin our analysis of the economics of professional team sports by outlining some of the key economic theories and concepts that are referred to throughout the book. In discussing the appropriate definition of the firm in professional team sports, the chapter also introduces a tension that exists between the economic characterisation of professional team sports and usual economic policy recommendations. It argues that the 'uncertainty of outcome hypothesis', a central theme in the economics of professional team sports, is based on a market failure – known as an externality – and has been presented as central to the success and evolution of sporting leagues. In turn, this has generated a preoccupation with institutional arrangements in professional team sports that lie outside economists' usual emphasis on free markets.

In Chapter 3, thus, it is argued that a sports league is a cartel of sporting firms as a manifestation of imperfectly competitive behaviour. This implies that predictions of the overall evolution of sporting leagues can be understood as manifestations of monopoly power, but that the explanation of the mechanisms by which leagues operate and develop is enhanced relative to describing sporting leagues as monopolies *per se*. To illustrate these arguments some broad empirical developments in sporting leagues are sketched. A discussion of club objectives is also undertaken.

Chapter 3 argues that it probably does not matter too much what objectives team owners are assumed to have. This is when, consistent with the methodological discussion above, economists are able to derive useful predictions about the markets in which they operate. A prime example of this is whether league management policies have helped to preserve uncertainty of outcome on the field. The results of such investigations are discussed in Chapter 4.

In this chapter the economic rationale for cross-subsidisation in team sports leagues is examined and a widely cited model of team sports leagues is presented, as well as key empirical results associated with the model. Together with a discussion of the limitations of the model and analysis it is suggested that, despite the theoretically assumed centrality of the uncertainty of outcome hypothesis to the team sports literature, various policies of cross-subsidisation do not appear to have had the desired effects. An economic explanation of this result is discussed. Importantly, it is argued that the resultant impact of these policies is primarily in the players' labour market. As a result these policies produce conflicts of interest between clubs and players over the distribution of profits, which is further discussed in Chapters 9 and 10.

In Section B of the book, four chapters examine the demand for professional team sports. In Chapter 5, a critical discussion of the basic underlying economic theory of demand is outlined, together with the central features of the statistical method employed by economists to measure the demand for professional team sports and, for that matter, most economic relationships. The results of an investigation into the demand for Scottish association football are reported to exemplify this material.

In Chapter 6, the empirical literature on the demand for professional team sports is discussed. Based on a critical review of the literature it is suggested that while there is a diversity of findings concerning the determinants of demand, nonetheless some significant patterns can be understood. As far as economic factors are concerned, while the traditional literature argues that market size is a ubiquitous determinant of demand, price and income effects are identified as weak influences. Moreover, as far as sporting factors are concerned, seasonal success, though not the traditional notion of uncertainty of outcome, and team and player qualities appear important determinants of demand. Significantly, it is argued that the traditional literature suffers from a short-run aggregate and average emphasis. In contrast, as longer time horizons are adopted for empirical studies then traditional economic determinants of demand, such as prices and incomes, appear to be more significant determinants than previously had been argued to be the case – though heterogeneity of findings remains. An additional finding is that the uncertainty of outcome hypothesis receives little support in studies on the demand for professional team sports.

Because of the assumed centrality of this hypothesis for the economics of professional team sports, Chapter 7 re-examines some theoretical and empirical issues associated with the measurement of uncertainty of outcome in more detail. Nonetheless we conclude that while there are several problems associated with measuring this concept, nonetheless, in sympathy with the discussions of the last chapter and Chapter 4, long-run domination in sports through evolution into a traditionally acceptable form of competition seems to have been the pattern in sports league development. We therefore question the previously assumed centrality of this hypothesis to making leagues work effectively.

In contrast, in Chapter 8 we argue that this situation *could* change with the growth of TV revenues in sport. This is through such revenues changing the underlying structure of demand and the feedback effects of this demand upon the supply of professional team sports. In Chapter 8, a brief history of the origins of televised sport in the US and the UK is presented. Broad economic reasons explaining these developments are offered, together with an analysis of the economic consequences of these changes. In particular, it argues that more research needs to be done on the effects of TV on sports generally. It is suggested that the evidence that is available implies that the impact of TV coverage of fixtures on attendance is not likely to affect traditional fixtures. However, the feedback effects of TV through the financing and supply side of professional team sports could be profound. The advent of huge increases in TV revenues in, for example, the UK has produced an 'exogenous' shock to historically more stable relationships. It is argued that whatever the precise outcome it seems that such vast skewed TV revenues will change the structure of leagues at a previously unknown speed. Competitive balance, or uncertainty of outcome, will thus change at a previously unknown speed, and may thus matter much more in the future than in the past.

Perhaps more than before, the future of professional sports leagues will reflect the relative bargaining power of a variety of constituents. It is this more than anything else that makes predicting these developments more difficult. Having began these discussions by contemplating the demand for professional team sports, the growth in the bargaining power of players as a key component of the supply of professional team sports is thus discussed.

In Section C of the book, having alluded once more to the supply of professional team sports in the last chapter, we examine what we perceive to have been the major impacts of leagues' attempts to manage uncertainty of outcome. Chapter 9 outlines some of the key economic concepts associated with the economic analysis of labour markets. In particular the idealised labour market is outlined illustrating the close relationship between product and labour markets. The theory of monopsonistic competition that has figured prominently in the traditional literature is then outlined. The theory is exemplified by exploring, in some detail, some of the early studies of monopsonistic exploitation in US baseball.

In Chapter 10, we examine the key institutional changes that have taken place in both the US and European sporting labour markets. The changes involve the movement to free agency in both US and UK sports. In the UK context, the 1995 Bosman ruling, made by the European Court of Justice, is explored. It is argued that these developments reflect increased player power in the labour market. As a result players are now more able to bargain over their salaries and contracts. To provide an economic understanding of these processes, the chapter also explores bargaining theory and examines the application of this theory to sporting labour markets. It is argued that there is evidence in the US that player salaries are now more in line with marginal revenue products, that typical contract lengths have increased and there has been a widening dispersion of salaries. In the UK, transfer fee determination is discussed and it is noted that there are differences of opinion as to the correct characterisation of the labour market. Finally, it is noted that the implications of increased player power for league policy really hinge upon players transferring wealth back to themselves and away from clubs. Labour market restrictions are probably indefensible in terms of policies to protect competitive balance in leagues. This implies that the other options, discussed in Chapter 4, remain the most relevant for league management policies. As discussed in Chapter 8, moreover, targeting sources of revenues directly, that are increasingly generated by TV contracts, may be more apposite for future policy.

The market, industry and firm in professional team sports

2 The market structure of professional team sports leagues

General themes

Introduction

In the introduction it was argued that professional team sports lend themselves to economic analysis. In this chapter we begin our analysis of the economics of professional team sports by outlining some of the key economic theories and concepts that are referred to throughout the book. As well as being a reference point for some of these concepts, the chapter also sets the scene for a tension that exists between the economic characterisation of professional team sports and usual economic policy recommendations.

As the book will show, the history and economics of professional sporting leagues is replete with institutional arrangements that lie outside economists' usual emphasis on free markets. In contrast, because of the 'uncertainty of outcome hypothesis' it has long been argued that league authorities should intervene in the allocation of resources in sporting leagues in order to ensure the survival and success of the league.

In the next section, we briefly review the theoretical reasons for the economic argument that free markets allocate resources efficiently. The market structure of perfect competition and monopoly is outlined to illustrate what is meant by efficiency in a particular market and the 'failure' of a market to be efficient, respectively. Some comments are then offered to indicate other reasons – based in externalities – why markets might fail to allocate resources efficiently. A potential solution to market failure is discussed before we outline the 'peculiar economics of sport'. This is so called because a form of market failure – captured in the uncertainty of outcome hypothesis – is deemed necessary to the evolution and successful operation of sporting leagues. Attention is then turned to outlining this hypothesis in some detail.

Market structures: a brief overview

Perfect competition

Despite there being an array of sophisticated economic models which analyse various issues of a policy or theoretical nature, the central economic policy issue that economics addresses is how to allocate resources efficiently. Since Adam Smith's *Wealth of Nations* was published in 1776, economists have tended to argue that the allocation of resources is best left to free markets. Smith hypothesised that individuals, each acting purely in their own selfish interest, would nevertheless be guided by 'the invisible hand' of (price) competition to take decisions that would simultaneously maximise both individual and general social welfare. Hence, in general, economic activity should be open to competition. While not being responsible for the theory of perfect competition, as described in economics textbooks, nonetheless this theory has come to represent Smith's presumption for economists.

As we noted at the beginning of the book, like all economic theories the theory of perfect competition is highly abstract. The reason for this reflects its main purpose, which is to logically predict the implications of efficiency. The importance of the competitive model thus is that it provides a 'benchmark' from which we can develop models that we suggest capture the main features of reality and hence be able to evaluate alternative institutional arrangements.

In the perfectly competitive model it is assumed that all of the firms in an industry are profit maximisers who sell a homogenous product to perfectly informed utility maximising consumers (utility being the individual's satisfaction). The corresponding sporting industry would be a league of profit maximising clubs each supplying equally competitive sporting 'products' to spectators seeking to maximise their utility or enjoyment of, for example, a fixture. We discuss the issue of utility maximisation and the demand curve for professional team sports more in Chapters 5 and 6. For now we focus on the supply side of the market.

The supply curve in a perfectly competitive market is the sum of the marginal costs of the many, identical small firms that supply the market. Marginal costs are the extra costs incurred from producing an extra item of output. In sporting terms, one might think of this as the costs incurred from producing an extra win. Because firms are small relative to market demand in perfectly competitive markets, they have no power to set prices independently of the market. So, the coincidence of market demand and supply determines the market price and quantity in perfect competition. If demand and supply in the market set the price of the product, individual firms have to supply the product at this price. This implies that the demand curve for the individual firm is horizontal, reflecting the fact that only one price can prevail in the market. The firm is a 'price taker'. In this case the firm's marginal revenue, or revenue received from the sale of the last unit, is equal to market price or average revenue, which is total revenue divided by total sales volume.

Figures 2.1(a) and 2.1(b) illustrate the relationship between the firm's decisions and the constraints it faces from the market. In Figure 2.1(b), the intersection of the demand and supply curves establishes the market price and quantity. Note that in Figure 2.1(b), the market demand curve is downward sloping. This reflects the limits to market demand dependent on the price that prevails. It is assumed that as prices fall, other things equal, demand rises.

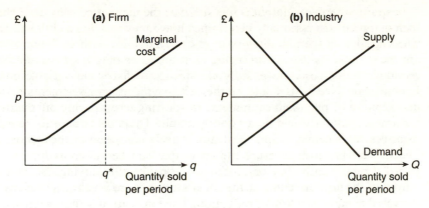

Figure 2.1 The firm and market under perfect competition

Chapter 5 discusses the justification for this relationship in more detail. Note also that in the case of demand and supply analysis the dependent variable 'quantity' appears on the horizontal axis. In general, in mathematics, the dependent variable appears on the vertical axis. This is the case with other economic analysis. The peculiarity of demand and supply stems from an historical 'anomaly' when Alfred Marshall – a famous British economist writing at the turn of the twentieth century – originally conceived that price was the dependent variable in markets. The output of the industry Q is, moreover, equal to the sum of outputs of each of the small firms. If the output of one firm is q and the output of i firms is Σq_i , then the output of the industry is $Q = \Sigma q_i$.

It is clear from Figure 2.1(a) that, facing the prevailing market price, the maximum contribution to the firm's profit occurs where marginal costs are equal to price or marginal revenue.[1] If the firm were to increase its output beyond q^*, then the added cost, as indicated by the marginal cost curve, exceeds the revenue received from the additional sale at market price p. Likewise if the firm reduced its output below q^* then contribution to profit is missed, which implies that profits are not maximised. Because the demand curve is given to the firm by the market, it is clear that the marginal cost curve is essential to understanding how much output firms and hence the market supplies.

---

[1] This is a necessary condition for profit maximisation. It is not a sufficient condition because the diagram does not consider fixed costs. Fixed costs are not part of marginal costs. However, in as much as minimising losses also requires firms to supply where $MC = P$, then the diagram is adequate for our purposes. Because we implicitly allow for the presence of fixed costs, the diagram is indicative of the economic short run in which firms cannot adjust all of their inputs. Nonetheless as the adjustment of all of the firms' inputs is essentially a planning or hypothetical context then, once again, the diagram is adequate for our purposes.

In sporting terms, if output is measured as the number of wins for a club, then marginal cost essentially determines how many matches a club will win when faced with the prevailing price it can charge for fixtures. What, then, are the extra costs that a firm incurs as it increases output by one unit? In economic terms costs are broadly classified into fixed and variable costs. Examples of fixed costs would be the debt payments on investments or the maintenance of plant and equipment. In sporting terms paying off the debt for a new stadium would be a good example. These debts have to be paid regardless of whether or not the team actively competed in their sport or folded. Variable costs measure the costs that can be varied as inputs are varied. Consequently they only need to be paid when varying the level of output of the firm. In economic theory labour costs are usually assumed to be the variable input to a firm's production. The implication is that the firm can more easily adjust labour than capital. In sporting terms we often see players being transfer listed when clubs face financial problems. English rugby union clubs, such as Sale and Gloucester, are currently releasing a lot of their squads to try to cover debts as they adjust to become professional. In the past Widnes and Hull Kingston Rovers rugby league clubs have faced similar problems. In contrast, clubs tend to relinquish their stadium only under extreme financial pressure – when they effectively close.[2]

Accepting the economic classification of costs implies that we can define marginal costs as

Wage rate/marginal product of labour.   (2.1)

In other words marginal cost measures the money cost of an extra employee, or extra work provided by an additional employee, divided by the output produced by the extra worker or work done. Thus if the hourly wage rate was £10 per hour and two extra units of output were produced in an hour by extra working time or an extra employee then marginal costs would be £5. It should be noted that in perfect competition the market for labour as a whole sets the money-wage rate. Like the market for the firm's output prices are set outside the firm. If this is the case, then the only reason marginal costs can rise for a given money wage rate is because the marginal product of labour falls. In the theory of competitive markets, this is assumed to be the case and is known as the assumption of 'diminishing marginal productivity'. It is clear that this assumption is needed in the model because without it there would not be a guarantee that marginal cost would equal price and hence the profit maximising level of output for the firm identified. The efficiency of the perfectly competitive case for the labour market is discussed in Chapter 9.

---

[2] In many cases teams often re-launch themselves and share grounds with other teams. In the UK, the emergent professional rugby union clubs often share grounds with established association football clubs.

Suffice it to say that the product and labour markets are clearly closely related. With this in mind we now illustrate the efficiency of the perfectly competitive market by contrasting it with the case of monopoly.

Monopoly

As discussed later in the chapter, it has been argued in the past that sporting leagues are examples of monopolies. Consequently it is instructive to assess the differences between monopoly and the economists' ideal market system of perfect competition. To analyse a monopoly, economists make all of the assumptions employed in the case of perfect competition with one major exception – as a movement towards examining the real world; this is that the monopoly is assumed to be the sole supplier of a product. In as much that professional sports are often provided by one league, it is clear why they are often described as monopolies by economists.

As the sole supplier of a product, or sport, monopolies can set the price in the market subject to the constraint of the total market demand curve. Thus, the demand curve for the monopoly firm is equivalent to that of the perfectly competitive *industry*. However, because a monopoly is the 'price maker' this suggests that the marginal revenue curve for the monopolist will not be equal to the price of their products or sport. While the demand curve measures the price or *average* revenue of the product or sport in the market, the marginal revenue of the product or sport represents the price of the product or sport sold to the last or marginal consumer. To induce this consumer to buy the product or sport, it follows that the price they paid must be less than the price previously charged in the market (otherwise logically speaking the consumer would already be buying the good or sport). Consequently the marginal revenue curve for the monopolist must lie below the average revenue or demand curve.

Figure 2.2(a) illustrates this proposition with the same cost curves as the perfectly competitive firm drawn on the diagram. This diagram corresponds to a monopoly industry facing the same technology and the same market demand as the perfectly competitive industry. Notice that profit maximising prices in the monopoly case are now *not* equal to marginal costs. This is because the marginal revenue curve is separate from the average revenue or demand curve. The monopolist earns a 'mark-up' or 'profit margin' on its marginal costs.

The inefficiency of the monopoly case relative to the perfectly competitive case is illustrated in Figure 2.2(b). This superimposes the price and output decisions of the perfectly competitive and monopoly markets onto the same diagram. P_c and Q_c are the prices and outputs of the perfectly competitive industry. P_m and Q_m are those for the monopoly. It is clear that prices are higher and quantities of the product or sport supplied lower in the latter case.

Triangles *A* and *B* represent the inefficiency of the monopoly case. Triangle A represents lost consumer surplus or welfare. To understand this concept,

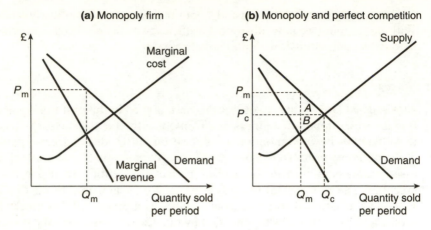

Figure 2.2 Monopoly and perfect competition compared

one needs to note that the demand curve represents *planned* purchases. At any given price, say P_c, Q_c amount of the product or sport would *actually* be demanded. Note that for less of the product or sport consumers would, in principle, pay a higher price than the current market price. This implies that given the price P_c, consumers receive benefits that they have not effectively paid for – consumer surplus.

Triangle *B* represents lost producer surplus. By analogy this is revenue above marginal costs that could have been earned and distributed to competitive firms. Thus by not supplying at the competitive price and quantity a monopoly market fails in the sense that society loses benefits. Prices of products or sports are at their lowest and quantities their highest under perfect competition.[3] It is this result that defines economic efficiency. Having defined efficiency, we can now begin to explore other forms of market failure – or inefficiency – prior to examining the peculiar economics of sport.

Externalities

Market failure may occur for a variety of reasons other than monopoly, but in professional team sports it is generally attributed to externalities and particularly externalities in production. The discussion of efficiency above proceeds on the assumption that all resources are purchased in perfect markets. A consequence of this is an implied assumption that the benefits or costs of buying or selling resources such as players, or products such as

---

[3] Pay-per-view television can be understood as an attempt to extract consumer surplus by sports media. This is discussed in Chapter 8.

matches, measure their true value to society. Technically this implies that only the welfare of the parties carrying out an economic transaction should be affected by the transaction. Should the benefits or costs to a transaction carry over to a third party, then externalities are present. This implies that the 'private' costs and benefits of a transaction are not equivalent to the 'social' costs and benefits of a transaction. A consequence is that markets fail because prices might only measure the private costs and benefits and not social costs and benefits. As a result markets may over or under produce because a proportion of resources or products are deemed either free or are overvalued.

An everyday example of a negative (undesirable) consumption externality is our daily car journey to work; we use the local atmosphere as a sink into which to dump the noise and the waste heat (some embodied in toxic emissions) that inevitably attend the use of heat engines. To the individual motorist the cost of the journey is measured in fuel, wear and tear, and time. To society the cost includes the noise and atmospheric pollution. Since the motorist does not pay the 'market price' for disposal of their waste products, they are liable to consume more car journeys to work than are socially optimal.

It remains, however, that externalities can arise in both production and consumption and involve benefits or costs. In professional team sports a major positive externality is the benefit that leagues confer on the media via the 'league standing effect'. The history and success of many tabloid newspapers is inextricably tied to sports. Interest in the league standings of teams, which Neale (1964) argues is jointly produced with games, is not confined to active spectators. While games could occur without the media input, the media cannot benefit from interest in league standings if the league does not exist. Thus sports leagues have an externality that creates incomes for the media. Team revenues could measure the team owner's private benefit from production, but the social benefit includes the revenue generated in the media as a by-product of the team's activities. This suggests that team sports may under-produce from the social welfare perspective, since the private benefit of their activity is substantially less than the social benefit.

It is important to note that market failure does not necessarily imply that the market actually fails to operate sensibly. Likewise, it does not automatically imply that state intervention is required whenever a market failure is observed. For example, as Coase (1960) stressed, if property rights can be established for the hitherto 'free' or undervalued resource – that is, the recipients or perpetrators of the benefits or costs can be identified – and if a market can be organised to price that resource correctly, optimal allocation of resources, or something akin to it, should follow. As discussed in Chapters 4 and 7, for example, it can be argued that the market itself sometimes acts to establish and to price property rights. Respectively, sports management policies have been undermined and sports leagues have acted collectively to sell the rights to broadcast live matches and highlights. This process is referred to as 'internalising' a portion of the external benefits.

Elsewhere in professional team sports, we can argue that public interest also generates a major externality for the gaming industry. In the UK, association football clubs have long sought to internalise some of the external benefit by running their own 'football pools'. In 1959 (see Szymanski and Kuypers, 1999), the Football League established copyright in its fixture lists and thereby became entitled to a share of the revenues of commercial pools companies whose operations are totally dependent on having access to fixture lists. The Football Trust, another example of the internalisation of an external benefit, was set up in 1979 by the main pools firms to provide funding for ground improvements and other schemes.

Governments occasionally intervene to assist internalisation of external benefits conferred by professional sports – in the UK, a tax is levied on horse-race betting and the proceeds distributed to the blood-stock industry. Nevertheless, there may be situations in which 'the market' needs assistance. Establishing property rights in Football League fixture lists is one thing, doing the same for the air in your city is quite another.

The peculiar economics of sport

Arguably the main source of externality in team sports arises from the simple fact that no team can produce saleable output by itself. It can be argued that teams prefer to beat their rivals, but they cannot aim at a monopoly of sporting success, as they need to play successful teams if the public is to be persuaded to pay to watch professional sports.

The main characteristics of this externality are outlined in an elegantly written paper that also displays a keen sense of humour. Neale (1964) argued that professional sports had general characteristics that not only differentiated them from other industries but also produced some peculiar or paradoxical conclusions from the economic perspective. For Neale, the team, unlike the textbook theory of the firm described above, cannot determine its own output level (as measured by the number of games). That depends on how many teams the league admits and on how many times the league decrees teams play each other during the season. Even more unlike the textbook firm, the team (or the individual sports player) cannot by itself produce saleable output. Every engagement requires the presence of an opponent. Neale thus coined the phrase 'the Louis–Schmeling paradox' to describe this phenomenon. This was so called by the author in reference to the World Heavyweight Boxing Championship contests during the 1930s – which in many respects assumed a significance beyond mere boxing given the political positions in the US and Germany before the outbreak of World War II.

Such considerations led Neale to regard the league as the 'firm' and the team as equivalent to the 'plant' in microeconomic theory, despite the fact that the (real world) team is, in the legal sense, a firm. This creates a further paradox of 'the multi-firm plant' – the inverse to the multi-plant firm of textbooks. The playing field appears, Neale argued, to be the sports team's plant, i.e. the place where production is carried out. Yet the plant cannot be used without the co-operation of many firms, not just the immediate opponents (the Louis–Schmeling paradox) but, thinking of the league standing product, the league, all its constituent teams and the media which transmit league standings. To Neale this suggested that the league itself is not only a firm but that it constitutes a 'natural' monopoly in the sense that a single league can deliver the product at lower cost than a multiplicity of leagues.

In this view the equivalent natural monopoly in an individual sport would be all professional boxers (Neale's example), or in women's professional golf, all professional women golfers. As well as the differences highlighted in the introduction, moreover, there is one important difference between team and individual sports. In team sports the team usually owns or at any rate manages the venues. Tennis players, boxers and golfers supply the labour; production requires co-operation with tournament organisers and owners of facilities. The 'firm' in these other sports must include these other bodies.

Neale (1964) notes that the most valued product is the world or national championship contest, which only a monopoly can supply.[4] In this respect monopoly supply must be the sensible policy option for sport. This stands, of course, in stark contrast to the usual recommendations of economists as discussed earlier. The main reason for this lies in a logical extension of the Louis–Schmeling paradox, that was first noted by Rottenberg (1956), which has become a central organising principle in the economic analysis of professional team sports.

The uncertainty of outcome hypothesis as an organising principle

Rottenberg (1956) argued that, other things being equal, the closer the competition between teams, the greater the interest in the sport and therefore total attendance and revenue. This 'uncertainty of outcome' hypothesis argues that close competition between, for example, team A and team B confers benefits on the league not only via increased attendance at teams' own games but also at games involving teams C and D, hence the externality. Domination of a league by a single club would reduce public interest in the sport, lowering attendance at games not involving the dominant team, even if the dominant team itself continues to enjoy strong support. In the long run even the dominant team suffers.

Taking this thesis forward, Neale (1964) argues that there will be a tendency for sports to gravitate towards monopolies providing there is a feasible economic or sporting basis for competition in the sport. The history (he gives several examples) of sporting leagues is broadly consistent with the

---

[4] Being somewhat tongue-in-cheek, one can argue that these are interpreted as equivalent in the US.

predictions of the natural monopoly thesis. For example, women and men do not often compete in the same sports. Physiological reasons can plausibly dictate why this is legitimate and unlikely to be economic as a spectacle. In contrast many sports have developed along with, for example, the constraints of travel costs. Thus, in Europe and the rest of the world, international competition in association football, rugby and cricket have historically been organised around infrequent contests because of the financial risks in undertaking lengthy overseas tours. More recently, indications of likely sports league evolution have been felt in more immediate environs first. As discussed in Chapter 8, for example, pressures to create a European super league in association football are currently being felt. Likewise in the Southern hemisphere, the Tri-Nations and Super 12's rugby competitions have been established. In Northern hemisphere rugby, Italy have augmented the traditional Five Nations.

In the US, Fort and Quirk (1995) point out that at the end of 1994 monopoly leagues characterised all four major US team sports (football, baseball, basketball and ice hockey). Importantly, it is argued by Neale (1964) that while monopoly profits attract competing leagues, these will usually be short lived since existing leagues resist new entry as it tends to put up labour costs and (dependent on location) reduce ticket revenue and income from TV. A counterexample is the American League (AL) in major league baseball, set up in 1901 and still going strong. But many of today's teams began in rival leagues. Of the 28 teams in the major baseball leagues and the 28 teams in the National Football League (NFL), 12 of the former and 14 of the latter had their origins in other leagues. To late 1994 there had been (since 1876) six rival leagues in professional baseball and (since 1920) seven in professional American football. These figures exclude the black American professional football and baseball leagues that thrived before racial integration saw them absorbed into the major leagues. In 1999 Ted Turner's CNN TV network threatened to run a rival football league to obtain better terms for televising NFL games. The threat was withdrawn in December, when Turner's attention turned to motor racing (NASCAR) instead. Nonetheless, in an increasingly turbulent environment, the new Spring Football League (SFL) has been launched. In addition, a further league, the XFL, is planned and is being promoted by the owner of the World Wrestling Foundation, Vince McMahon. Both of these developments rely on media/entertainment financing. In the former case the plan is to promote football as part of a wider entertainment package including music and is specifically aimed at the family through competitive pricing. In the latter case an individual's media backing is central to developments. The long-term prospects for such rival leagues remains to be demonstrated (*San Francisco Examiner*, 4 February 2000). Such interplay between sports league provision and media financing is discussed further in Chapter 8.

Thus, historically, rival leagues tend to amalgamate as, for example, in English association football the Football League absorbed the weakened rump of the Southern League in 1920, having earlier admitted its most successful clubs. Or they co-exist as separate entities whose members do not compete on the field but come together to produce world champions, the best example being in baseball where the American League and the National League co-operate to produce the annual and extremely lucrative World Series. Or one of them disappears into bankruptcy, the fate that befell the World Football Association (American football that is) which lasted one season, 1974/75. Though not a team sport, professional boxing is rather exceptional in that there are at least four bodies that claim the right to organise world championship contests and recognise world champions, with the effect of undermining the credibility of anybody who happens to hold one of the titles. Nonetheless, it remains that the unifying bout remains the fight that captures most public interest.

While Neale's (1964) predictions appear to be consistent with many *outcomes* of the development of sporting leagues, the rationale for, and description of, the mechanisms by which leagues operate and have developed is perhaps lacking. Neale's thesis essentially implies overall co-operation in matters of league management. As discussed in Chapters 3, 4 and 7, this is often not the case. League evolution can be linked to the pursuit of particular interests rather than a perceived common good. Among these and other reasons, therefore, Sloane (1971) argued that a sporting league and its constituent teams may be more accurately viewed as a cartel than as a multi-plant firm. This is because teams have more freedom to take decisions than Neale acknowledges and yet co-operate to pursue the collective objective of supplying sports. Crucially, this co-operation implies less rigidity and conformity of behaviour than implied in a monopoly *per se*, in which power must, by definition, reside with the league. In a cartel, mutual behaviour is by agreement only and these agreements need to be enforced. If they are not, or better opportunities for members of the cartel appear elsewhere, then they can break down.

Consistent with Sloane's (op. cit.) view that it is the club that comprises the economic firm, it is worth noting that teams in most sports take decisions about investment, about whether to produce at all, and they usually have some control over ticket price. They also control merchandising, which is now a major source of revenue. As discussed in Chapter 8, the evolution of the market selling the rights to televise league matches – to internalise some of Neale's (1964) fourth estate benefit from the league standing effect – has been motivated and driven by pressure from certain teams in the UK. Indeed, the court case brought in England by the Office of Fair Trading (OFT) against the Premier League's selling of exclusive televising rights to BSkyB, discussed in Chapter 8, is predicated upon interpreting the League as a cartel. The OFT did not object to the selling of TV rights but to the Premier League acting as a cartel rather than clubs selling on their own account in mutual competition. They argued that the viewer would face higher prices and less choice than if clubs sold their TV rights in competition.

Neale's (1964) thesis is also linked specifically to US sports. In the US, sports grant a local monopoly to incumbents. The granting of local monopoly is managed differently in the US and in Europe; one needs to remember this when reading Neale. The US major league baseball teams have a franchise covering an area big enough to exclude same-league teams from the city and its immediate region. In New York, Los Angeles and other cities capable of maintaining two major league baseball teams, one is in the National and the other in the American League. They meet on the field – if at all – only at the World Series. Both teams are in economic competition with each other and with other leisure providers, although not in direct sporting competition.

In Europe, professional sporting teams are associated with a single league, implying that in the larger cities (Milan, London) two or more teams may be in both sporting and economic competition. Some degree of monopoly power is granted by ensuring that both teams' home games are not played on the same days. This is more difficult to accomplish in London with (usually) at least five football clubs in the highest league. There is the further complication that in European association football (unlike baseball) promotion to and demotion from the top leagues 'churns' their populations. Occasionally a small city side (Stoke City, Ipswich Town are English examples) joins the top league, or a small city (Sheffield, Nottingham in England) temporarily boasts two top league clubs. Neale's (1964) contrast between monopoly off the field and competition on it may owe more to circumstances peculiar to the US than to the nature of sports leagues in general.

Accepting these problems with Neale's analysis, therefore, conventional wisdom presents the sporting league as a cartel. Despite this change in conception of the sporting league, however, it remains that the uncertainty of outcome hypothesis underpins advice given (not only by economists) to governments and league management bodies about the governance of sport and about the relations to be permitted between team sports and broadcasting. This naturally begs the question, does the evolution of sporting leagues described above provide evidence to support the uncertainty of outcome hypothesis? We would argue for a more qualified conclusion. In particular in this book we maintain that the above sort of developments are indicative of leagues' evolving to produce traditional, historical notions of acceptable competition rather than moving towards a hypothetical maximum level of uncertainty of outcome. Moreover, the chasing of revenues by particular interests in sports also cannot be discounted.

The remainder of the book analyses these issues further to provide justification for these claims. Thus, Chapter 4 argues that the uncertainty of outcome hypothesis has been used to defend many league management policies that have sought to redistribute resources – such as revenues or players directly – between strong and weak teams. The evidence regarding the effectiveness of these policies is discussed there. Clearly, one of the central tenets of the uncertainty of outcome hypothesis is that competition produces extra support. Section B of this book assesses in some detail the effects of uncertainty of outcome, among other factors, on support at professional team sports events and the growth of media related support. Section C of the book examines in some detail the impact of the league management policies that have been targeted at the labour market.

To preempt the discussion to come, we argue that despite its centrality to discussion in the economics of professional team sports, the hypothesis has been somewhat overworked. We argue that the evidence on the hypothesis is scarcely compelling, though there has been a shortage of research in some areas and some mixed results and dubious methods of measuring uncertainty are in evidence. However, we would argue that policies aimed at promoting uncertainty of outcome have had more clear cut effects on the labour market, and that the hypothesis is likely to become more important with the changing structure of demand likely from the growth of TV coverage of sports. Before broaching these subjects, however, we move to an analysis of cartels and some examples of league evolution highlighting the role of clubs in this process.

Conclusions

In this chapter we have outlined some of the key economic theories and concepts that are referred to throughout the book. The chapter also presents a tension that exists between the economic characterisation of professional team sports and usual economic policy recommendations. It has been argued that the uncertainty of outcome hypothesis – based on a market failure known as an externality – has been presented as central to the success of sporting leagues. In turn, this has generated a preoccupation with institutional arrangements in professional team sports that lie outside economists' usual emphasis on free markets. The remainder of this book is given over to critically exploring these themes.

Discussion questions

1. A team owner estimates that if they spend an additional £1m annually on player salaries, other things equal the team will finish the season in fifth rather than sixth place.

   What is the marginal cost of improving league performance by one place? What vital 'other things' are most unlikely to remain equal in a sporting league when one team raises its labour costs? Assuming that there are diminishing marginal returns and that 'other things' remain equal, would it be logical for the owner to believe that for an extra £5 million a year their team could become the champions?

2. Suppose the team owner is a profit maximiser and further that they believe moving from sixth to fifth place would only affect ticket revenues.

   If there are only 15 home games a year, if there are on average only 800 empty seats at home games and if the ticket price is £25, which is set by the league and cannot be altered by the club, will they spend the extra

   £1 million yearly on improving their playing squad? What other factors might they consider?

3.   Suppose the league resembles a perfect market; all teams pay fixed prices for inputs and all teams likewise charge the same price for output. If one team's marginal cost is £x, what is the marginal cost of the team it is due to play next week?

4.   Some teams are able to sell their stadiums out week after week. If they are profit maximisers what ought they to do about the situation? Suppose the owners thought they could get away with extracting their spectators' consumer surplus. Design a method of ticket selling that would extract most of consumers' surplus. Compare and contrast this with what is actually done.

5.   In European association football there are frequent clashes between clubs and national football associations about releasing playing talent for 'international' duty. What does this suggest about Neale's (1964) view of the league as the (monopoly) firm and the club as a plant?

6.   Mostly, economists regard individuals as greedy but 'risk averse'. Offered 5% a year on safe US government bonds and the same on riskier common stocks or on Russian government bonds, we would buy the US bonds. To persuade us to hold riskier assets, a positive 'risk premium' is required. For example, shortly before Russia defaulted on its debt interest in 1998, its bonds were offered at 82% annual yield, compared to 5% for US bonds; a risk premium of 75% a year. Can we reconcile this assumption with Rottenberg's hypothesis?

7.   Sports leagues have operated gate-sharing schemes, some of which survive in the US. How might one use the uncertainty of outcome hypothesis in justification of gate sharing?

8.   How might you assess the uncertainty attaching to a team's next home game? (Hint: dipping into Chapter 7 may help.)

3 The market structure of professional team sports leagues

The firm in professional team sports

Introduction

In the last chapter it was argued that conventional wisdom holds that sports leagues are a cartel. In this chapter we attempt to provide a fuller justification for this argument. It is important to note, however, that this does not imply that Neale's (1964) natural monopoly thesis is redundant. We argue that one of the main reasons why Neale's predictions are consistent with the development of sporting leagues is that likely cartel behaviour will echo that of a monopoly. However, we argue that by adopting the cartel definition of sporting leagues the rationale for, and description of, the mechanisms by which leagues operate and develop is enhanced. To illustrate these arguments some broad empirical developments in sporting leagues are sketched. These are discussed in more detail in subsequent chapters.

In the next section we outline the economic discussion of club objectives. We then explore in more detail the economic rationale for a cartel. Finally, we outline some key themes involved in the evolution and management of sporting leagues from the perspective of a cartel.

Club objectives: profit maximisation versus utility maximisation

Coupled with the debate over the nature of the firm in professional team sports, there has been a lively debate over firms' assumed objectives. By and large American writers take profit maximisation to be the goal of the professional team sports firm (for example El Hodiri and Quirk, 1971; Neale, 1964; Quirk and Fort, 1992; Rottenberg, 1956; Vrooman, 1997). Fort and Quirk (1995) recognise that profit maximisation is a controversial assumption and that team owners also pursue other objectives. However, they argue that profit maximisation simplifies analysis and seems appropriate in long-term competitive equilibrium models, discussed further in Chapter 4. Moreover, it is probably fair to say that US sports have taken place in a highly commercial context. Thus players' salaries have been higher than, for example, in Europe and team franchises have been bought and sold more freely and so on.

According to Quirk and Fort (1992, p. 279) Sloane and others '. . . have presented convincing evidence that in English, Scottish, and Australian football and cricket, the profit maximisation model is inappropriate, and certainly some of their comments can be taken to apply to American sports as well'. They cite Tom Yawkey as an owner who sank a fortune into the creation of a winning side. Nevertheless, they argue that, 'There is no question but that owners are typically highly competitive individuals who enjoy winning intensely. There also is no question but that owners prefer to make more profits than less . . . professional team sports has become such an expensive business to enter that even wealthy owners must take the bottom line seriously' (p. 279).

Sloane (op. cit.) recognised the possibility that divorce between ownership and control in association football might permit managers to pursue non-profit goals, for instance utility maximisation (subject to minimum profit). As indicated in the last chapter, the concept of utility is discussed further in Chapter 5; it is linked with consumer theory and demand. The implication of this assumption for professional team sports owners is that they organise or 'consume' their resources to give them satisfaction and not necessarily profit *per se*. Association football clubs typically then (and now) lose money over long periods despite the fact that owners could stop their losses by leaving the industry. British Rugby League has historically been characterised the same way too (Thomas, 1997). This suggests that such clubs are not profit maximisers.

While in joint-stock or public limited liability companies the shareholders' expectations exercise a powerful influence over management. Historically most British professional clubs, in any sport, were private limited companies, so even the stock market could not impose an external constraint upon management.[1] On grounds such as these, Sloane rejected the profit maximising motive in favour of utility maximising, which he regarded as (op. cit. p. 133) 'intuitively to be the most appealing in the football case'. Although 'utility' could be viewed as a vague objective, Sloane argued that association football has relatively clear objective criteria (playing success) for judging performance. Directors, managers, players and supporters all desire playing success, so the football club 'approaches a unitary system', whose main objective is to produce playing success, subject to financial constraints. It is

---

[1] 'Close' or private limited liability company shares are not traded on stock exchanges, hence they are relatively illiquid. Disgruntled shareholders cannot so readily dispose of them as they can shares in public limited liability companies. There, shareholders who cannot remove the existing management may 'vote with their feet'. Their disposal of shares may drive down the share price and thereby attract a take-over resulting in the sacking of the existing management and the pursuit of shareholder value. The stock exchange can act as an external discipline on management.

clear that this objective function could carry over to other professional team sports. His proposed utility function for the club is illustrated in (3.1).

$$U = U\{A, P, X, (\pi_R - \pi_0 - T)\} \tag{3.1}$$

Functions are discussed in some detail in Chapter 5. For now it is worth noting that they are shorthand vehicles for describing how economic variables interact. Thus, this utility function suggests that average home attendance (A), performance on the field (P), the health of the league, i.e. 'competitive balance' (X) and 'surplus' after-tax profit ($\pi_R - \pi_0 - T$), where π_R is recorded profit, π_0 is minimum acceptable profit (both pre-tax) and T is tax, as arguments determine utility. The club seeks to maximise utility subject to the condition that 'surplus' profit is at least zero as implied in (3.2).

$$(\pi_R - \pi_0 - T) \geqslant 0 \tag{3.2}$$

Or failing that, subject to its having sufficient external finance to ensure survival, even if recorded profit is negative. Playing performance is taken to be the most important argument where objectives conflict, although they may be positively associated.

These differences of opinion on the appropriate objective of sporting teams could present some problems in generalising about sporting leagues. Thus predictions about clubs' behaviour may differ depending on the objective assumed. Pursuing utility (playing success and attendance) at the expense of profits may, Sloane argued (loc. cit. p. 138), produce greater concentration of playing talent than would occur under joint maximisation of club and league profit. This is because teams may attempt to maximise their playing success and retain star players irrespective of their size in relation to other clubs, particularly in view of the fact that even if a club is very successful in its own national league it may have to face a sterner challenge in international competitions.[2,3] The only limit to increased concentration – club profitability apart – lies, Sloane argued, in the league being permitted

---

[2] Due to their relatively unique forms, US professional team sports, with the exception of ice hockey, lack credible foreign opponents. Baseball's 'World Series' involves teams from the American and National Leagues only. Probably no foreign team (Toronto Blue Jays play in the American League) can compete on equal terms, although Mexico and Cuba may soon provide credible challengers. In ice hockey the usually successful Canadians play in the National Hockey League. Thus US sport teams currently have less incentive than their European and Latin American counterparts to over-invest in talent.

[3] By way of light relief we note that Robert Benchley (the father of the creator of *Jaws*) once remarked that if Britain and the US wished to reproduce their political and military co-operation on the sports field they had better abandon both baseball and cricket and take up a sport both countries could play – preferably baseball!

to override clubs' short-run interests in the pursuit of its own long-term interest. This depends on preventing the emergence of a blocking coalition of clubs that would overrule the league or on preventing the formation of a breakaway league comprising the wealthier clubs. In the presence of a blocking coalition, outside intervention may be required to restructure the industry.

It is also clear, however, that profit maximising and utility maximising models might yield similar predictions, making it difficult to distinguish between them. The pursuit of managerial utility could not occur without satisfying some minimum profit constraint. As indicated above, Fort and Quirk (1995) point out that utility maximisers who run loss-making clubs must limit their cumulative liabilities and thus are compelled to look at 'the bottom line'. Thus, while some empirical evidence has been provided by Szymanski and Smith (1997) and Szymanski and Kuypers (1999) that there is no significant trade-off between playing success and profits in association football, it remains that within the industry some acceptable level of profits is required. Sloane argues that profit maximisation and utility maximisation may come to pretty much the same thing if entry to lucrative European competition depends on attaining domestic league success. The partial substitution of the loyal fan base by TV companies seeking to attract large audiences may serve further to blur the distinction between profit and utility. Finally, the growth of commercialisation and financial resources available to European sports from, for example, the emergence of BSkyB and the PLC status of many premiership association football clubs suggests that the profit maximising assumption may not be inappropriate in a European context in the future. For example, the changed ownership of football clubs could imply external pressure on clubs to maximise profits. However, TV coverage, an increasingly vital revenue source, is as Baimbridge *et al.* (1996) maintain, likely to be more sensitive to playing success than the traditional spectator. (This issue is discussed further in Chapter 8.)

It is worth remembering that, on a methodological level as discussed in the introduction, assumptions in economic theory are primarily employed as devices to produce testable predictions. Thus in practice it may not matter greatly which assumption one makes about club motivations at a general level, either analysing relations across teams or substantial time periods. In contrast the assumption and associated predictions might matter much more so when analysing particular clubs. In this respect, ultimately, the adequacy of assumptions stands or falls as part of a package in an analysis. With these caveats in mind, we simply note that the issue of clubs' objectives has not been resolved and is unlikely to be so as league and clubs evolve. However, this has not prevented some interesting theoretical and empirical insights from being generated, which are primarily discussed in the next chapter. For now we turn our attention to examining the problems of conceiving leagues as cartels. Importantly, this analysis runs independently of the assumed objective of clubs and leagues.

Sporting leagues as cartels

As discussed earlier, sporting leagues have been viewed as either cartels or monopolies. We now explore these competing definitions of the market structure of professional team sports in more detail, suggesting why the fomer characterisation is preferred.

To begin with, it is worth remembering that a monopoly is a single firm that supplies a market. A cartel is a collective of firms who, by agreement, act as a single supplier to a market. Thus in sporting terms while leagues comprise groups of clubs who compete on the sporting field by arrangement through a fixture list and according to rules of the sport that are set by them, in themselves these are not activities that really deserve the title monopoly or cartel. As discussed in the Introduction, the appropriate economic title applies once money changes hands as resources are allocated between alternative uses. Clearly professionalism in sport is an integral aspect of this development.

Buying and selling players, or paying for players to perform, for example, requires financing decisions. Thus, gate revenues need to be earned to pay players' salaries. A minimum number of home games is required to let a club cover its labour and other costs. Further, clubs must co-ordinate match schedules since they cannot produce in isolation, and potential spectators must be informed where and when matches are to occur. In turn spectators need accommodation and a means by which payment can be extracted from them while restricting access to the sport to non-payers. Thus, an enclosed stadium is a necessary feature of sporting supply.

For example, in contrast to rugby league and association football in the UK, rugby union has, until recently, been an amateur game. Clubs historically played traditional 'fixtures' and there was an inter-county competition. The absence of a league reflected this amateur status. Indeed the formation of a league for the top rugby union clubs was a precursor to the game becoming professional. Moreover, prior to the inception of the Football League, the only major soccer competition in England had been the FA Cup, which being a knock-out competition did not require the existence of leagues. Most soccer games were non-competitive. Prior to the formation of the Premier League the Football League had no rival after its merger with the rump of the Southern League. At the moment of merger the two leagues had obtained representation in most of the large conurbations of England, leaving few opportunities for successful entry.

Continuing southward drift of population suggests that some northern clubs might be forced to relocate if they are to survive; but relocation is virtually unknown. In spite of that, Waylen and Snook (1990) show that the location of the average club in the Football League has moved steadily southeast. Southern clubs have grown faster in relative numbers and performance, while the promotion of non-League teams, mostly southern, into the lowest division has provided new blood. Thus association football leagues in England have responded, if somewhat hesitantly and haphazardly compared to their US cousins, to the vagaries of the market. American practices like selling franchises, moving franchises to more attractive markets, founding expansion franchises to fill 'gaps', and permitting direct entry to *elite* leagues are unknown in Britain, although this may be about to change in a more profit-oriented environment. Wimbledon Football Club, one of five or six Premier League clubs in the London area, recently sought permission to relocate in Dublin as a local monopoly supplier of Premier League football.

Despite these differences and the general impression one can get that early sporting leagues may have 'growed like Topsy', it is clear that as time passed leagues have understood the need to grapple with threats to their survival through regulation policies. Indeed it is because leagues have regulated, that is organised, both sporting and economic activities in various team sports that they have earned either the title monopoly or cartel. But why these market structures? One can show that these forms of market structure are logically necessary as possible organising vehicles for professional team sports. This is because of both general economic but also sporting reasons such as the uncertainty of outcome hypothesis.

Coping with interdependence: cartel or monopoly?

In the absence of many sellers – that is, for example, perfectly competitive markets – economists since Adam Smith have argued that suppliers might collude to seek profits. The central reason for this is that with fewer sellers, firms become interdependent. They each produce a sizeable proportion of the market. Such market structures are described as imperfectly competitive or oligopolistic. They lie between the extremes of competition and monopoly described in the last chapter. It follows that no firm can ignore the actions of other firms as their respective behaviours can significantly impinge on one another's success in achieving objectives – whatever they may be (for example profits or utility). While in the case of monopoly or perfect competition it is relatively straightforward to predict the likely behaviour of key economic variables such as prices and quantities, as discussed in Chapter 2, this is not the case in imperfect competition and oligopoly. There is indeterminacy in the market.

To appreciate why indeterminacy occurs, consider the pure monopolist (see Figure 2.2(a)) who faces stable average revenue (demand) and marginal revenue curves and thus can compute the price at which marginal cost and revenue are equal and profit is maximised. In contrast, the oligopoly firm has no demand curve since it cannot change its price without the expectation of triggering a reaction by its rivals. All the oligopolist can know about its 'demand curve' is that at the current price it is able to sell the current quantity. Even if it imagines itself to be at a given point on a given demand curve, it cannot 'move along' that curve. It cannot predict marginal revenue thus profit maximising output is indeterminate.

To analyse the likely consequences of such situations, economists have sought to remedy this deficiency in the theory of the firm by proposing models that specifically focus on the interdependence of firms. Cournot (1838) was one pioneer who essentially formalised some of the possibilities. His model does not seem immediately applicable to the professional team sports scenario; however, it yields insights into the competitive process that are relevant to understanding why monopolies or cartels seem integral to the provision of professional team sports.

Cournot stressed that firms competed via variations in the quantity of produce they each supplied – thus accepting the resultant price available. Essentially, each firm maximised its profit on the assumption that other firms did not change their output. Consider a two-firm industry in which Cournot's model describes firm behaviour. Each firm is assumed to set its own output level so as to maximise its own profit subject to the rival's output. The firm is essentially myopic (short-sighted), in making its response to a rival's move its only concern is to maximise its immediate profit. Unlike a chess player, it does not look two or three moves ahead to see where the process might lead. Ultimately, of course, the price of the product depends on the output of both firms and it is assumed that sales will be inversely related to price overall in the market as in the case of perfect competition and monopoly.

Starting from an initial position, firm 1 (say) chooses a level of output that it thinks will give maximum profit consistent with the output level it *expects* firm 2 to produce. Should firm 2 validate firm 1's expectation by producing exactly that level of output, *by implication it is maximising its own profit subject to the actual output of firm 1*, the latter has no reason to change its output. Given no change in firm 1's output, firm 2's expectation will also be validated by experience, leaving it no incentive to alter its own output. The industry will be in equilibrium in the Nash sense.[4] That is to say, because each firm's expectation is borne out by experience, there is no reason for either to change its output. It will appear that the market is shared by the two firms in an 'imperfectly competitive equilibrium'.

In contrast, other possibilities could occur. Starting from a position of disequilibrium, firm 1 will find firm 2 produces an output level different from what it had expected. Since its expectation about firm 2's output is in error, firm 1 then adjusts its own output taking into account the actual amount firm 2 produces, again with the intention to maximise its profit subject to firm 2's (output) response. Firm 1's adjustment now throws firm 2's plans into disarray as it had not expected firm 1 to revise its output. Firm 2 revises its production once more. This in turn elicits further response from firm 1. The process of adjustment may be dynamically stable in the sense that it leads both firms to an equilibrium distribution of production and profit that, because it

---

[4] The Nash equilibrium is one of the most influential notions in the theory of games. Cournot's equilibrium is almost certainly the earliest known Nash equilibrium, having pre-dated Nash's discovery by about 110 years. We refer to some aspects of game theory again in Chapter 10.

always validates both firms' expectations, leaves neither with an incentive to change its production. In this case the above scenario applies. However, this process of competition may also be destabilising and lead to the demise or elimination of one firm and the establishment of monopoly.

Whether the process leads to or away from equilibrium depends on the structure of firm 2's costs. Suppose for instance that firm 1's initial output level *exceeds* its equilibrium value, in which event by implication the output level that firm 1 expects from firm 2 must be *below* firm 2's equilibrium output. If firm 2's cost curves dictate that its (short run) profit maximising response is to *raise* its own output above the level firm 1 had anticipated (i.e. towards equilibrium), this will lower the price below firm 1's marginal cost. To maximise its own (short run) profit subject to firm 2's unexpectedly high output, firm 1 must now reduce its output (i.e. move toward its equilibrium level). The reduction in quantity now raises the price above firm 2's marginal cost, leading to another increase in its output. The adjustment process sees firm 1 gradually cutting back output, matched at every step by increases from firm 2, until equilibrium is attained. No collusion whatever is involved.

Suppose on the other hand that firm 2's costs dictate that initially the best (profit maximising) response is to *lower* its own output. Now adjustment starts with firm 2 moving *away* from equilibrium. This 'sends the wrong signal' to firm 1, since firm 2's cut in production raises the price above firm 1's marginal cost. To maximise its own short run profit, firm 1 naturally *increases* its own output, also moving away from its equilibrium. Firm 2 cuts production once more, yet again encouraging expansion by firm 1. This process, if continued, cannot end otherwise than with firm 1 as a pure monopolist, at least until there is new entry into the industry.

Which of these possibilities seems likely for sporting leagues? The unique features of sports supply suggest neither *per se*. Pure monopoly is out of the question for team sports owners require the continued existence of rivals. Under such circumstances it follows that there will always be incentives to prevent the elimination of competing teams. Consequently, there are incentives for the teams to act as a monopoly, as a teams sports league, as a counterbalance against the likely adverse consequences of the pursuit of a 'genuine' economic competition equilibrium.

This result in theory depends crucially upon the firms' assumed myopia. A long-sighted firm 2 would realise at the outset that carrying out its short run maximising response (reduce output at each successive step) leads to annihilation. To survive it must temporarily abandon (short run) profit maximisation, by *increasing* its own production at every step, forcing firm 1 to reduce output. But in Cournot's model the firms did not understand the process, that complication remained for later writers to model. Note the valuable insight from Cournot's model, however, that to pursue a given goal it may be necessary on occasion to move away from it or, in other words, that acting in one's own best interest may imply deliberately choosing what appear to be sub-optimal moves. The implication is that sports teams and leagues recognise this problem, as clearly implied in Neale's (1964) characterisation of sports as joint products and the need to manage the Louis–Schmeling paradox discussed last chapter.

A further impetus to this process is that the Cournot (imperfectly competitive) equilibrium, wherein both firms survive, leaves each one maximising its own profit subject to the exactly predicted output of its rival. It does not guarantee that maximum industry profit under competition will be at least as large as under pure monopoly.

On the contrary, given that each firm's behaviour is constrained by the existence of a rival, the whole industry is liable to be less profitable under implied oligopolistic competition than pure monopoly. One might as well expect a sprinter constrained to run in Wellington boots to achieve times comparable to their best performances in running shoes. Nonetheless, if the firms colluded to reduce total output they could force up the price, permitting one or both to make at least as much profit as under monopoly. Thus, the legal environment permitting, one would expect them to collude, by the formation of a cartel. A cartel not only provides the key to greater profitability, it also offers the prospect of stability by reducing the threat of all-out price competition, which (like arms races) can prove unstable. In short, Cournot's model predicts that competition may be destabilising, in which case a cartel is inevitable. Even where competition *à la* Cournot is stable, the model suggests that a cartel will produce higher profits *equivalent to those from a monopoly*. Coupled with the need to manage the Louis–Schmeling paradox, it follows that there is very great pressure for sporting leagues to conform to cartel markets. Under such circumstances it is not surprising that in practice professional team sports seem to have structures that are consistent with monopolies or cartels from the outset.

Cournot's analysis thus gives us some economic reasons why we might expect to find evidence consistent with cartel or monopoly behaviour in sporting leagues. Crucially, however, by focusing on the behaviour of individual firms within the market, the analysis also draws attention to the process by which markets might be expected to evolve. It is this that gives the cartel description of sporting leagues some impetus. Apparent monopoly characteristics such as the planned allocation of resources by sporting leagues are not necessarily rather benign reflections of monopoly planning. In contrast, subject to the need to co-operate to produce fixtures, viewing the team as the firm allows for the explicit analysis of teams' interdependence.

For example, the above discussion implies that in the absence of co-operation interdependence would follow due to the (usually) small number of clubs that form a league and to the differentiated nature of the product they offer. Every club supplies a significant proportion of total league output and no team can ignore the possibility that rivals will seek to react to any change in a team's quantity of wins. While one can accept that quantity is not predetermined absolutely by league size, unless one insists on using the number of games as the index of output, there are limits to the ability of the sports team to control its own output. It follows that there is a need for collusion. Moreover, given that a cartel is only as strong as its members permit, this leaves some scope for addressing league evolution from the point of view of attempts to reconcile the frequently conflicting interests of the interdependent membership. Thus, while teams must co-operate to create a saleable commodity, leagues may thrive even in the presence of markedly unequal playing success, as Fort and Quirk (1995) report and which is discussed in the next chapter.

Interestingly, too, the Cournot model throws light upon competition between leagues, which (unlike teams) can produce unaided and may use output as a competitive device. Fort and Quirk (1992, Ch. 8) tell how in 1882 the National League found itself in the embarrassing position of having no baseball franchises in seven of America's biggest ten cities. The three (then) largest, New York, Philadelphia and St Louis, had had no franchise since 1877. The American Association was formed to fill the gap, opening franchises in Philadelphia and St Louis in 1882 and in New York in 1883. The National League responded with new franchises in New York and Philadelphia in 1883. Sports leagues, like nature, seem to abhor vacuums. It follows that exploring developments at both club and league level as indicative of cartel behaviour can thus feed into an analysis of the evolution of sports leagues. A further more detailed example of this follows.

Cartel-based explanations of sporting league developments

As discussed in Chapter 2 and above, the co-operation between teams required in cartels can echo monopoly behaviour. However, it also implies less rigidity and conformity of behaviour than implied in a monopoly *per se*, in which power must, by definition, reside with the league. In a cartel mutual behaviour is by agreement only and these agreements need to be enforced. If they are not, or better opportunities for members of the cartel appear elsewhere, then they can break down. Paramount to the success of a cartel, thus, is the ability to reconcile potential conflicts of interest within the group. While aspects of a cartel's activities can resemble a monopoly, it is shown below that the concept of a cartel is a better conceptual description of a sporting league. It is a more general concept that helps to capture both the monopoly characteristics of leagues while at the same time allowing the analyst to explore the actions of and pressure exerted by particular interests or clubs.

An important aspect of the management of sporting leagues is the distribution of proceeds among members. The motivation for such policies, and their effectiveness, are discussed further in the next chapter. For now we simply concentrate on sketching some developments to illustrate the role of the firms in producing league or cartel evolution. Historically, the main sources to sports leagues have been gate receipts, merchandising, sponsorship, the sale of TV rights, transfer fees (largely redistribution between clubs) and the sale of match schedules to the gaming industry (as exemplified by the UK football pools). Occasionally governments with an eye on spectator safety have subsidised ground improvements (via the Football Trust in the UK). Of these, TV revenues have probably been the most evenly distributed among teams. The main changes during the past two decades have been first, explosive growth in total revenues and second, a marked increase in the relative importance of TV revenues. Regarding overall revenue growth in English association football, Szymanski and Kuypers (1999, pp. 37–38) estimate that total real revenue rose by about 3% a year from 1946 to 1988, but that since 1988 the annual increase has been about 18%. The authors (op. cit., pp. 40–41) also show that for some clubs the importance of gate receipts has shrunk markedly since the middle 1970s. Baimbridge *et al.* (1996) estimate that since 'live' TV broadcasting of English soccer began the earnings from televising matches has risen by over 3000%. They show that the annual rights fee had risen from £2.6m in 1983 when the two terrestrial broadcasters operated as duopoly buyers, to £42.8m in 1992 after BSkyB came on the scene. The *Financial Times* of 29 October 1999 reported that BSkyB had made an informal offer of £1b for a three-year contract for Premier League football, although the current (four-year) contract for £743m still has some months to run. The move looks like an attempt to influence clubs to press the Premier League to a rapid settlement – it was made direct to the chairpeople of two leading clubs. Shortening the contract period by one year may be intended to deflect the attention of European Union competition authorities.

BSkyB controversially holds shares in two Premier League clubs, Manchester United and Leeds United, which may interest the European competition authorities and has already attracted the attention of the Football Association, the organising body in England. Owning clubs or shares in clubs implies the ownership of players' contracts, which would give BSkyB some leverage if another media business were to win an exclusive contract for Premier League football. Likewise BSkyB as owner or part owner of leading clubs could benefit if the competition authorities insisted on clubs negotiating on their own behalf, rather than the Premier League negotiating as a cartel.

The huge influx of television money is not unique to the UK. Fort and Quirk (1995) estimate that major league baseball's real earnings from national and from local TV respectively increased from $13m and $42m in 1962 to $183m and $259m in 1993, using 1982–84 as base. The NFL's total real TV revenues increased from $16m in 1962 to $779m in 1993.

One of a league's primary tasks (acting as a cartel) is to decide how to divide revenues between members. The need to maintain uncertainty of outcome, by preventing domination from successful teams, has been, of course, a central factor affecting such decisions. The full implications of such decisions are discussed in the next chapter. For now we note that at one extreme is the system whereby each club keeps whatever it earns. This is unlikely to have the support of 'weak-drawing' clubs – those teams whose gates are relatively small. At the other extreme is the equal division of revenue between members. This is unlikely to be supported by 'strong-drawing' clubs – those teams whose gates are relatively large. Moreover, equal sharing might remove incentives to perform well either as a team or as a business. Consequently there is likely to be a conflict of interest between individual clubs and a conflict of interest between clubs and the league overall.

In practice leagues have adopted changing attitudes to cross-subsidisation as the balance of power has changed between 'haves' and 'have nots'. Charting such effects thus indicates how leagues can evolve as cartels. In England, leading association football clubs, which provided most of the matches televised, not unnaturally wanted a larger share of TV earnings which had always been equally shared. The voting system in the Football League temporarily prevented redistribution, although through the 1980s the more successful clubs' repeated threats to form a breakaway 'elite league' eventually wore down its resistance. The breakaway took place and the Premier League was formed. Similar developments occurred in rugby league (the Super League was formed). Though, discussed in detail in Chapter 8, it is clear that such developments would be difficult to understand from the point of view of monopoly behaviour. In essence, one cartel broke up and another was formed. This is because a fundamental weakness in all cartels is that in the right circumstances members may take decisions that, while best for themselves, are not optimal for the existing cartel as a whole. The cartel needs disciplinary tools – and must be seen to be willing to use them. All members must be willing to suffer pain occasionally to punish 'cheating' and this creates a credibility problem. The 'prisoners' dilemma' model is often applied by economists to the problem of behaviour in a cartel and helps to explain why they often break down. It is an example of game theory, which is a set of analytical tools used to examine the interdependence of decision makers. Consequently, it is widely used in the analysis of oligopoly in economics. Further discussion of game theory is offered in a discussion of sporting labour markets in Chapter 10.

The prisoners' dilemma is a game that assumes that the police have arrested two suspects (A and B) in connection with a major crime. A and B are held in separate cells and communication between them is prevented. The police lack the evidence to convict either man for the major crime. They explain to each man that if neither confesses to the major offence, both will receive a sentence of one month for a minor offence. If both confess to the major crime, they will receive 12-month sentences. However, if one confesses, implicating the other, who remains silent, the former will be released while the latter receives 12 months for the major crime plus an extra three months for obstructing a police inquiry.

Both men face a choice between confession and silence and each knows that the other faces exactly the same choice. Should A (for example) confess, then B would also prefer to confess and serve 12 months instead of 15, which is what will happen if he does not confess. Should A remain silent, B will prefer to confess and be released instead of keeping silent and serving one month for the minor offence. Each man understands that the returns to him and to the other from confession dominate (are superior to) those obtained by silence, *irrespective* of the other's behaviour. Therefore both men confess and both serve 12 months. This is despite that fact that had they both remained silent, they would have served only one month each. The prisoners' dilemma in this simple form always leads to sub-optimal behaviour as the game is played only once. If A and B can expect to replay and if each can perceive that there may be rewards in the future for 'good' behaviour and that punishment will follow 'bad' behaviour, both have an incentive to acquire a reputation for co-operation with the other. Thus under normal circumstances one can understand, once again, why teams would collude. However, given the relatively unique circumstances in which *new* forms of TV coverage of sports, and their associated revenues, were presented to clubs, it was not surprising that collusion was not the outcome and that the new elite leagues developed.

In general when a league is faced with harsh decisions the temptation for teams to pursue their own interests (not always to their ultimate advantage) is likely to strengthen. It is important to note that the background to the above developments was that, for example, association football league annual attendance in England and Wales was on a declining trajectory from the late 1940s until well into the 1980s. A similar pattern characterised rugby league attendances. In association football, the decline was most marked in the two lower divisions. This suggests that reduced capacity in those divisions might have produced greater league-wide profit, but only the survivors would have benefited. In such times strugglers may stay in production too long, hoping that the departure of even weaker teams will enable them to survive. Or they may reason that once the bulk of excess capacity has been eradicated, at the expense of its owners, the few remaining weak teams will receive compensation for closing down. Fort and Quirk (op. cit. Chs. 8 and 9) cite instances in US team sport where survivors have indeed compensated losers in periods when capacity was being cut, for example when the Federal League (baseball) was wound up in 1915 and at the settlement between the NFL and AAFC in 1949.

In the circumstances facing English association football in the 1990s, perhaps no single league could have reconciled the conflicting interests of 90 clubs. The leading clubs' substantial investments in players generated most of the market for televised football. The advent of multi-channel satellite and cable broadcasting promised a great increase in the flow of TV money, which under existing arrangements would be divided equally. For some time the Football Association had favoured reforming English professional soccer to promote more international success at club and at representative levels and was anxious that the funds from TV should be applied to this end. Consequently, the FA effectively encouraged Football League Division One teams to defect to its own newly formed Premier League, which would negotiate terms for live TV broadcasting separately. A similar development occurred with the English Rugby League.

As well as these developments, associated primarily with TV revenues in the UK, similar trends have occurred in the US. Top-level US professional team sport leagues seem to have been less stable than their European counterparts. Fort and Quirk (1995) (op. cit. Chs. 8 and 9) recount that leagues have come and leagues have gone – some conceived solely as bargaining counters to extract concessions from existing leagues and be immediately wound up. To the already tortuous twentieth century history of gridiron football leagues was added AFL IV in 1960, an exception to the rule in being so successful that it eventually merged with the established league. The immediate reason for its emergence was Lamar Hunt's desire to obtain an expansion franchise in Dallas, which had been blocked by NFL owners. At the time expansion proposals required unanimity. Initially the founders of AFL IV did not envisage franchises in New York and Los Angeles, but were soon persuaded of the necessity of opening there to attract TV. Thus TV was also influential in setting up AFL IV, and the revenue from TV helped ensure its success. In 1966, AFL IV negotiated a merger with NFL, which occurred in 1970 at the expiry of current TV contracts.

Conclusions

In this chapter we have argued that the precise motivation of professional team sports club owners remains unsettled for economists; do they maximise profit or utility? We have also argued that it probably does not matter too much so long as economists are able to derive useful predictions about the markets in which they operate based on certain assumptions. Of perhaps more importance we have also argued that a cartel is probably a fair representation of the sports league. We do not imply that Neale's (1964) natural monopoly thesis is entirely redundant. We argue that one of the main reasons why Neale's predictions are consistent with the development of sporting leagues is that cartel behaviour may echo that of monopoly. However, we argue that by adopting the cartel definition of sporting leagues the rationale for, and description of, the mechanisms by which leagues operate and develop is enhanced. To illustrate this some broad empirical developments in leagues are sketched. These developments are particularly associated with the rise of TV revenues in sport and are further discussed in Chapter 8.

Discussion questions

1. Consider why one might in theory choose between the profit maximising and utility maximising models of the professional sports team. To what extent is it possible to distinguish them from one another?
2. As we write, a higher proportion of association football clubs are public liability companies, the FA no longer restricts dividends to 7.5% a year

and (in the Premier League especially) there are clubs making large profits regularly. Do you think that if Peter Sloane were to address the profit/utility goal question again he would come to the same conclusion? Explain.

3. Sloane asserted that the majority of football league clubs were in the business of survival. Does that proposition still apply?

4. Explain why cartels such as for example sports leagues have potential credibility problems.

5. Compare and contrast the ways in which (a) Szymanski and Smith and (b) Fort and Quirk measure 'success' and explain why the latter approach is not directly applicable to European sport.

6. Consider whether (and why) sports leagues in Europe are less likely or more likely to experience stability in the future.

Suppose a sports league is considering granting an expansion franchise and that the decision is by a vote of all members. Is the intending entrant's chance of acceptance affected by whether league profits are equally divided or every team keeps whatever profit it earns?

4   Cross-subsidisation in professional team sports leagues

Introduction

In this chapter we discuss the issue of cross-subsidisation in professional team sports leagues. This has always been one of the central economic policy issues for professional team sports for a number of reasons. Firstly, it is intrinsically linked to the uncertainty of outcome hypothesis discussed at length in Chapter 2. As we noted there, since Neale's exposition of 'the peculiar economics of sports', the uncertainty of outcome hypothesis has been a central and distinguishing feature of the literature. It follows that cross-subsidisation of weaker teams by stronger teams has been argued to be a vehicle for maximising league benefits through promoting uncertainty of outcome.

Secondly, the recent rise of TV revenues in UK and to an extent world team sports as discussed in Chapter 3, changes in competition regulations for professional sports leagues and the emergence of elite leagues have increased claims that revenues are being directed towards a few large clubs at the expense of other clubs. In this respect, calls for the reversal of this financial trend are being made.

In this chapter we re-examine the economic rationale for cross-subsidisation in team sports leagues. A widely cited model of team sports leagues is presented, as well as key empirical results associated with the model. Together with a discussion of the limitations of the model and analysis it is suggested that, despite the theoretically assumed centrality of the uncertainty of outcome hypothesis to the team sports literature, various policies of cross-subsidisation do not appear to have had the desired effects. Policies aimed at increasing overall league profits and revenues by maximising uncertainty of outcome do not appear to affect uncertainty of outcome. An economic explanation of this result is discussed. Importantly, it is argued that the resultant impact of these policies is primarily in the players' labour market. As a result these policies produce conflicts of interest between clubs and players over the distribution of profits, which is further discussed in Chapters 9 and 10. While cross-subsidisation policies may affect the costs and revenues of clubs, therefore, the relative dominance of certain clubs within leagues may not be affected.

The rationale for cross-subsidisation

The economic rationale for cross-subsidisation in professional team sports lies in the market structure of sporting leagues. In Chapter 3 it was argued that sporting leagues can be understood as cartels of competing producers of sports. Within these cartel arrangements, clubs need to compete in sporting terms but, at the same time, they also need to co-operate to ensure that the sports are managed effectively, which can give the impression that they are monopolies. Thus, governing bodies of sporting leagues have traditionally set the sporting terms upon which clubs meet in competition as well as directly influenced the economic aspects of sporting competition. For example, league authorities have shaped admission price structures, negotiated television deals and sponsorship arrangements. This is in addition to controlling the terms upon which sports players move between clubs. In economic terms, sporting leagues' actions have produced the cross-subsidisation of clubs.

This is an unusual phenomenon in economic terms. In any other industry the direct regulation of the terms under which separate firms meet in markets has been ruled as acting against the public interest. As discussed in Chapter 2, on welfare grounds, it has been argued that monopoly practices lead to higher prices and less output than is socially desirable. These general ideas have become enshrined in industrial policy. For example, as far back as 1890 in the US, the Sherman Act made it illegal for firms to act in restraint of trade, i.e. to collude, or intentionally work towards producing monopoly power. The Sherman Act is the central plank of US competition policy. Other aspects of US competition policy stem from the Clayton Act and the Federal Trade Commission Act. Both of these pieces of legislation were enacted in 1914. The former Act rules against commercial activities that seek to price discriminate in a non-competitive context. Likewise it rules against merger activity which produces the same effects. The latter Act rules against deceptive practices or unfair methods of competition. Similar emphases appear in other countries. In the UK, somewhat later, the Monopolies and Restrictive Practices Act 1948 is the landmark of competition policy. In 1956, the Restrictive Trade Practices Act separated out the legislation concerning monopoly policy and restrictive practices. The former was intrinsically concerned with potential legal sanctions for industries charged with acting as a monopoly. The latter was concerned with legislating against particular practices such as sharing out markets.

Moreover, since 1997, the framework of competition policy adopted in the UK has been to embrace the terms and conditions implied in the Treaty of Rome. This lays down terms and conditions that are analogous to the Sherman Act and previous UK legislation. Thus Article 85 prohibits the restriction of competition between firms and Article 86 the abuse of dominant or monopoly power by firms.

Despite these legal frameworks for competition policy, in general government intervention in sporting markets has been low. Indeed, in the case of baseball, in 1922 the Supreme Court in the US ruled that it was exempted from the Sherman Act because it did not represent interstate commerce. While this decision has been criticised it has never been overturned. Moreover, 'While other US sports have not enjoyed the full exemptions granted to baseball, the competition authorities have still tended to look favourably on restrictive agreements. In particular the 1961 Sports Broadcasting Act exempted the collective selling of TV rights for sports leagues' (Szymanski and Kuypers, 1999, p. 249).

As discussed further in Chapter 10, moreover, similar examples apply to the labour market which, as discussed below, has been a central target for league management policies. As far as UK sports are concerned, patterns have largely followed the US lead. It is fair to say, however, that in the UK for example in the traditional professional team sports such as association football and rugby league there has been little general interest shown by the regulatory authorities until fairly recent developments in these games. The recent rise of 'elite leagues' in the provision of professional team sports linked to the growth of TV revenues in league finances is one factor. This is discussed in more detail in Chapter 8. Linked to these developments, recent changes in the labour market are discussed further in Chapter 10.

One of the central defences that has been used by sporting leagues to defend their policies of cross-subsidisation has undoubtedly been the uncertainty of outcome hypothesis outlined in Chapter 2. This has been expressed in the desire to create 'competitive balance' in leagues. To recap the logic behind this idea, the following passage is succinct:

> One of the key ingredients of the demand by fans for team sports is the excitement generated because of the uncertainty of outcome of league games. For every fan who is a purist who simply enjoys watching athletes with outstanding ability perform regardless of the outcome, there are many more who go to watch their team win, and particularly to watch their team win a close game over a challenging opponent. In order to maintain fan interest, a sports league has to ensure that teams do not get too strong or too weak relative to one another so that uncertainty of outcome is preserved. If a league becomes too unbalanced, with too much playing talent concentrated in one or two teams, fan interest at the weaker franchises dries up and ultimately fan interest at the strong franchises dries up as well.
>
> (Quirk and Fort, 1992, p. 243)

The implication of this thesis for league management is clear. Based on the hypothesis that competition between equally matched opponents will raise overall interest in sports – as a positive externality to a particular fixture – this, in turn, will increase demand to watch sports which will consequently raise attendance and revenues in leagues. It follows that leagues should attempt to transfer resources from stronger, more successful teams, to smaller less successful teams. This will enable smaller teams to have the resources necessary to attract some of the best sporting talent to them and consequently raise their competitive capabilities on the field because, '. . . The more evenly receipts are divided, the greater is the prospect of equalised playing performance' (Cairns *et al.*, 1986, p. 62). In short, the uncertainty of outcome hypothesis outlines a virtuous circle of overall benefit to the league that can be actively promoted and sustained by cross-subsidisation policies.

Clearly, however, one consequence of this policy may be that the originally stronger team will lose out in both relative and absolute terms because of the redistribution of resources. It is not surprising, therefore, that leagues and clubs have recently come into conflict in European sports such as football and both codes of rugby. The developments in the financing of leagues noted in the last chapter have produced some instability in the traditional cartel arrangements of sports. With, for example, the extra sources of revenue open to clubs from TV contracts and, in particular, BSkyB, incentives exist for the top clubs to pursue their own objectives rather than those of the league as a whole. As discussed in Chapter 3 and further in Chapter 8, the rise of the English Premier League in association football and the Super League in rugby league can be understood in these terms. Similarly the top Scottish football clubs and the top rugby union clubs are also in an uneasy relationship with their previous 'managers' because of these pressures. The English Professional Rugby Union clubs have been in many publicised conflicts with the Rugby Football Union both over the distribution of the finances from the newly formed professional game as well as the administration of the professional game.

Notwithstanding these recent developments, however, leagues have actively promoted policies of cross-subsidisation. Thus, in baseball since '. . . the 1870s, owners have used the need for competitive balance among teams to justify restrictions on the rights of players to sell their services in a freely competitive labour market' (Quirk and Fort, 1992, p. 243).

Similarly, the accepted need for competitive balance in sporting leagues figured prominently in the deliberations over the Bosman ruling, which is further discussed in Chapter 10. More recently in the UK context the financial analysis of association football has included reference to this issue. Thus:

> The economics of sport is tied to a guaranteed competitive balance within a league, as uncertainty over the outcome feeds the fans' support and interest. However, the increasing polarisation among premier league teams both in terms of results and revenue base, endangers this principle.
>
> (Salomon Brothers, 1997, p. 3)

Not surprisingly, therefore, a wide variety of policies aimed at redistributing revenues within leagues have been employed and defended at various times in the history of most professional sports. The next section outlines these main policies.

Cross-subsidisation polices

There have been a large number of ways in which league authorities have intervened in the management of clubs' finances in order to promote cross-subsidisation between clubs. While the particular administrative details may vary, however, they have had two major targets: the sporting labour market and revenue distribution.

Sporting labour markets

Targeting sporting labour markets as a means of cross-subsidising clubs may, at first hand, appear to be a rather indirect method of implementing a policy that ultimately affects a team's results. Policies that are primarily aimed at promoting different outcomes in terms of *output*, that is results, are being aimed at *inputs*, that is players. However, when one examines the nature of the sporting production process, it is clear that such a policy target is not as indirect as first thought. First of all players' salaries and wages comprise a large proportion of sporting clubs' costs in both the US and Europe (see, for example, Scully, 1989; Szymanski and Kuypers, 1999). Policies that affect players will thus have a large direct financial effect on clubs. Second, and directly concerned with the uncertainty of outcome hypothesis, it is the players who ultimately affect a club's success or failure in matches. Consequently, both the resources of clubs as well as their results can in principle be affected through policies aimed at the labour market.

Leagues have attempted to influence club financing and results through implementing three major types of labour market policy: drafting systems, salary caps and reserve option arrangements. The most well known example of a drafting system is the 'rookie draft' in American football. Indeed the National Football League (NFL) was the first league to institute a drafting system in 1936. The National Basketball Association (NBA) had a similar system in the 1950s and Major League Baseball (MLB) in 1965. The National Hockey League (NHL) followed this pattern a few years later.

Basically, a drafting system rations the order in which professional teams can sign new talent – rookies. In the reverse-order-of-finish draft of the NFL, teams that finish the lowest in the league get the first option to sign the best new talent. The source of recruitment to the NFL is college football. It comprises amateur players and lends itself to this system nicely. There is an established widely observed window in which new talent can advertise its capability from which lists of players can be identified by ability and targeted to sign professional contracts. In contrast, in MLB and the NHL players are typically signed from minor leagues. Consequently, the emphasis of labour market policy has been different as discussed below. Indeed these leagues mirror those of rugby league and association football in the UK and association football in Europe where similar restrictions have applied. Draft policies are thus aimed at proactively reallocating the best talent so that, in principle, poorer teams over time will be more able to compete with the currently strong teams in a league. There is effectively a transfer of resources to weaker teams. Players who clearly could command lucrative contracts from a free market arrangement can be signed on more favourable terms to the club than would otherwise be the case.

While drafting systems, being targeted at the physical reallocation of sporting talent, have an indirect financial implication for clubs, salary caps are targeted at the financial cost of players directly. Salary caps imply a maximum amount that clubs can spend on players. One of the first examples in US sports was the NBA in 1980. The NFL adopted a cap in 1993 and baseball in the mid-1990s. In these cases teams' salary bills have been restricted to a certain proportion of clubs' turnover. A similar policy is currently in force in rugby league and is being currently discussed for rugby union (in 1999). In contrast, maximum wages for individual players were in force in association football in the UK between 1900 and 1961. The intended implication and justification for these policies is that, in principle, they make the best talent affordable to all teams.

The final form of labour market policy employed by sporting leagues has been reserve option clauses. The most famous example of this is in baseball where a form of this contract has been in force since 1880 and currently still exists in a much weaker form for rookie players. Chapter 10 discusses the impact of these clauses, of which the 'retain and transfer' system in football has been a European counterpart, in more detail. For now it is worth noting that they essentially tied players to clubs for their lifetime. When a club signed a player, clauses gave the club the option to renew the player's contract when it expired. In the early days of this contract, the player had little choice but to accept the new contract if the club would not release him. Otherwise he could not continue to be employed in the sport. Not surprisingly, as discussed in Chapter 10, these contracts have formed the basis of much conflict between players and clubs over the years. Nonetheless, the justification put forward for the reserve option clause was that it prevented financially powerful teams from buying up all of the talent available in leagues. Combined, therefore, policies such as these have targeted the physical availability of players to other clubs as well as their costs.

Revenue distribution

The other main form of cross-subsidisation policy adopted in sporting leagues has been to force clubs to redistribute some of their revenues. Traditionally, this has focused on gate revenues – monies earned by spectators coming through the turnstiles. More recently, discussion has focused on TV revenues. This has particularly been the case in Europe with the growth of TV funding of sport.

As far as gate-sharing arrangements are concerned, from its inception baseball operated a 50 : 50 split on gate revenues. Half of gate receipts went to the home team and half to the away team. However, away team shares have fallen steadily over the years and, currently, a variety of arrangements exist ensuring that the home team receives the largest share of revenues. Likewise, the NFL operates under a 60:40 split in favour of the home club, while the NBA and NHL have no gate sharing. In Europe, similar arrangements have applied. In association football for example, in England between the 1920s and the 1980s an 80:20 split on gate revenues existed in favour of the home club. Moreover, the football league imposed a 4% levy on all receipts that were then redistributed in equal absolute shares. Similar arrangements existed in rugby league but currently no gate-sharing arrangements exist.

As far as TV revenues are concerned, currently in the US local TV coverage provides no revenue for visiting teams (Fort and Quirk, 1995, p. 1291). In contrast there are egalitarian arrangements for redistributing national TV revenues:

> National TV contracts in all sports uniformly involve equal sharing of such revenues by all league teams (with some negotiated, temporary exclusions for expansion franchises). In a one-team-one-vote environment, equal sharing is more or less guaranteed because the national contract can be approved only if there is a virtual consensus among league teams.

This said, however, as implied in Chapter 3, this system evolved in the US in a complicated way. For example, the merger of the American Football League (AFL) with the NFL was in large part promoted by the national TV contracts obtained by the AFL but not the NFL. The NFL had contracts with local and regional TV stations (see also, Mason, 1997).

The most radical changes in TV financing of sports have evolved outside the US, with the growth of BSkyB and satellite TV coverage of sports in Europe and Australia. The nature and implications of these developments are discussed more fully in the UK context in Chapter 8; however, it is clear that the growth of BskyB's funding of association football and rugby league, for example, has substantially reduced the extent of cross-subsidies. A huge financial gulf now exists between clubs within and outside of the Premier League or Superleague. Moreover, the funding arrangements within these leagues further reinforce the financial gap between the successful and unsuccessful clubs. It is developments such as these that have led to the recent increased interest in cross-subsidisation policies in the UK noted above.[1]

---

[1] It is in this environment, thus, that rugby league have unveiled plans to tighten the salary cap for the 1999/2000 season and the Premiership One rugby union clubs agreed to a salary cap.

An economic framework for understanding cross-subsidisation

Having discussed the main issues associated with cross-subsidisation, it is instructive to present an economic model of team sports leagues. Crucially, it is with reference to such an economic model that the empirical findings on the effects of cross-subsidisation can be understood. The model presented here has its origins in El Hodiri and Quirk (1971). It has been subsequently developed and used in Scully (1989), Quirk and Fort (1992), Fort and Quirk (1995), Vrooman (1997) and Campbell and Sloane (1997).

For ease of exposition and understanding, a diagrammatic representation of the model is presented, in Figure 4.1 below, as made popular by Quirk and Fort (1992). As they note:

> It will be easier to follow the economic argument if it is presented graphically. In order to do this, we will look at the special case of a two-team league in which one team, team A, is located in a strong drawing area, and the second team, team B, is located in a weak drawing area. *We should emphasise that the essence of the basic economic argument we will make extends to the case of a league with an arbitrary number of teams; it is only the graphics that restrict us to the two-team case.*
>
> (p. 270, emphasis added)

Thus, the basic assumptions underlying the model are as follows.

(a) Teams aim to maximise profits.
(b) Players aim to maximise incomes.
(c) Market equilibrium prevails such that the demand and supply of professional team sports are equal.
(d) There are two teams of unequal size in the league.
(e) Spectators exhibit diminishing marginal utility from seeing their team increasingly win matches.
(f) Admission prices are fixed in a competitive market.
(g) The money cost of extra talent is fixed in a competitive labour market.
(h) The productivity of extra talent is constant.
(i) League output is equivalent to teams' win percent ratios.

The first two of these assumptions are aimed at capturing the behaviour of teams and players. As discussed in Chapter 3, the first of these assumptions is perhaps controversial in a European context where, as Sloane (1971) has argued, utility maximising behaviour might best have characterised football clubs historically. Recognising that, for example, a minimum profit constraint needs to be earned even with utility maximisation, over the long run it is perhaps acceptable to argue that profit maximisation is an appropriate behavioural assumption to make for sporting leagues. Moreover, assumption (c), which is a methodological assumption, implies that the model is concerned with the long run, when all adjustments have been made in the market place. It follows that similar arguments could be made to justify assumption (b). However, as discussed in Chapters 9 and 10, it is clear that any relaxation in restrictions on players' salaries lead to salary increases. The implication of this result is that players genuinely pursue the highest salary possible.

The remaining assumptions in the model are of a more technical nature. They specify key characteristics of the sporting market. Assumption (d) implies that there is a large, financially resourced team and a small, less well financed team in the league. This assumption reproduces, albeit in skeletal outline, the (purported) problem of dominance in sporting leagues. It is assumed that the demand or support for each of the teams represents some fundamental features that promote the imbalance in resources. Thus, in the US context the model is specified to refer to a team that has a large catchment area for support and a team that has a small catchment area for support. Consequently, for any given set of results the 'large' team will always attract more spectators than the 'small' team. As these spectators pay a fixed admission fee set in the market, as implied by assumption (f), then revenues will always be higher for the large team.

Clearly this essentially geographical source of the imbalance in resources between teams is not that important to the model. What matters is the existence of the resource imbalance and there may be many reasons for this. Chapters 5 and 6, for example, review the literature on the demand for professional team sports and chart the reasons why it is that demand and revenues might be expected to vary between teams. Any of these factors could be invoked in the model. Likewise, Chapter 8 explores the recent rise of BSkyB revenue in UK sports. This could also be applicable to analysis by the model.

The behaviour of the teams' revenues is underpinned by assumption (e) – the diminishing marginal utility of spectators. It is worth simply noting that this implies that extra wins by each team will attract extra support and hence revenue. However, the increments of extra support and revenue will eventually fall in size. Consequently, while teams face increasing total support and total revenue for winning their fixtures, the increases will take place at a declining rate. The *marginal revenue* of teams will thus *fall* as they become more successful. This is a standard assumption made by economists about consumer preferences and it is discussed further in Chapter 5.

Teams' costs are also linked directly to their employment of playing talent. Justification for this assumption lies in similar arguments given above when discussing the reason why sporting leagues have targeted the players' labour market with cross-subsidisation policies. This assumption, together with the fact that player wages are assumed to be set in a competitive market and that each unit of talent has the same potential effect on results, i.e. that players do not differ in abilities, implies that in order to win extra fixtures, teams will have to buy extra talent at a fixed *marginal cost*. As discussed in Chapter 2, this is defined as the additional cost required to produce one more unit of output. The validity of this assumption is discussed further below in connection with the effects that policies have had on competitive balance. The labour market in sports is discussed more fully in Chapters 9 and 10.

The final assumption in the model, as indicated in the above discussion of marginal revenue and marginal cost, is that the output of clubs and hence the league can be measured as a 'win percent'. This is a potentially problematic assumption because it implies that there can be no draws in the sporting leagues. This may seem a plausible assumption in US sports such as baseball where draws are almost impossible. Moreover, in many US sports arrangements exist to produce a result if a tie occurs. Thus in US association football 'shoot outs' have been introduced. However, this does not seem so plausible as an assumption in European professional sports such as association football and both rugby codes. Draws are not an exceptional result in association football, which is by far the most economically important professional sport. Indeed gambling arrangements like the 'pools' are testimony to this. The football pools, prior to the introduction of the National Lottery, were the largest single form of gambling in the UK. Essentially they rely on scarce distributions of draws to produce high payouts. It follows that the defence of this assumption must lie in less literal grounds.

A convincing argument that can be put forward to this effect lies in the empirical adequacy of the model. It can be argued that the model is merely a simplifying device for understanding complex issues. In fact, one can defend all of the assumptions in this way. As discussed in the Introduction, it is a key tenet of economic methodology that the adequacy of assumptions ultimately stands or falls according to the usefulness of the model in making empirically sustainable predictions rather than their literal descriptive relevance. Consequently, it is in assessing the model's predictions about the *impact* of cross-subsidisation policies that judgements must be made about the model's adequacy.

In order to understand the predictions of the model, the above assumptions can be combined to produce a representation of sporting leagues indicated in Figure 4.1. In this diagram the vertical axis on the left measures the costs and revenues of the large team. Moving from left to right on the horizontal axis measures the win percent of the large team, A. It begins at 0% where the axes intersect and increases towards 100%. The vertical axis on the right-hand side, in contrast, measures the costs and revenues of the smaller team, B. Moving from right to left on the horizontal axis indicates an increasing win percent of the small team. Thus, the intersection of these axes indicates a zero win percent for the small team, which increases to 100% as one moves leftwards. Clearly, by construction, this diagram indicates that in a two-team league an increase in one team's win percent must imply a fall in the other team's win percent. The teams are in a 'zero-sum game' as the sum of gains and losses is zero.

Following the assumptions (d), (e) and (f), the marginal revenues of the two

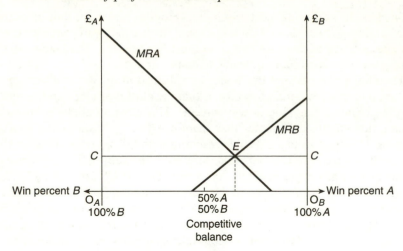

Figure 4.1 Competitive imbalance in sporting leagues

teams can be drawn as indicated by *MRA* and *MRB*. Note that both marginal revenues decrease as the individual teams' win percent increases. The only difference is that *MRA* > *MRB* because it has the power to attract more revenue regardless of ticket prices. As far as the costs of teams are concerned, the assumptions (f), (g) and (h) imply that marginal costs of players are constant at *C*. Given this information, therefore, one can predict that team *A* will have a greater win percent than team *B*. In other words, one can show that the larger team will 'dominate' the league.

To produce this result, assumptions (a) and (c) need to be employed in the analysis. Assumption (a) implies that teams maximise their profits. Assumption (c) implies that the league will be in equilibrium. In a manner analogous to the discussion of profit maximisation under a market structure of perfect competition or monopoly, and discussed in Chapter 2, the model predicts that profit maximising equilibrium will be where *MRA* = *MRB* = *C*. In this situation the revenue earned by employing the last unit of talent for each team just covers the costs of hiring the talent. This is indicated at point *E* on Figure 4.1 and clearly corresponds to a higher win percent for team *A* than team *B*. Point *E* can be identified as a profit maximising equilibrium because any movement from this point will reduce profits to both clubs. For example, if we move leftward horizontally from point *E*, *MRA* > *C* and *MRB* < *C*. This suggests that team *A* could increase its profits by buying extra talent at cost *c* that would increase wins and generate revenue from spectatorship greater than this cost. In contrast, team *B* could increase its profits by selling players at 'price' *c* and reducing its win percent. While this will reduce overall attendance, marginal revenue will rise and contribute to the team's profits. Given the assumption that teams profit maximise, therefore, it can be shown

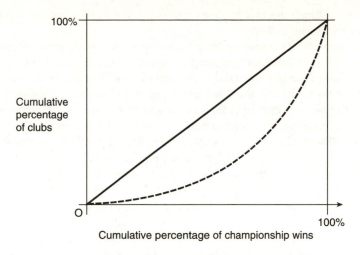

Figure 4.2 Hypothetical Lorenz curve for a sporting league

that an unequal competitive balance will be the outcome. The model thus appears to present a logical justification for cross-subsidisation policies.

It follows that extensions of the model can be used to explore the impact of cross-subsidisation policies in sporting leagues. Prior to engaging in this activity, however, attention is turned to the empirical evidence on sporting balance in leagues.

Empirical evidence on competitive balance

Having just described the theoretical representation of unequal competitive balance, the first empirical evidence worth discussing is measurements of competitive balance in sporting leagues. To measure competitive balance economists make use of various measurements of market concentration that have been developed as part of industrial organisation analysis, which examines the market structure of industries. Concentration measures the dominance of suppliers in a market – in essence the monopoly power in markets. Consequently sporting economists are assessing the domination of sporting leagues by particular sets of clubs.

Various measures of concentration exist. One way of measuring concentration is by 'Lorenz' curves. These devices were originally used to describe income distribution within an economy. In a sporting economics context Lorenz curves plot the cumulative percentage of clubs against the cumulative percentage of championship wins. They indicate the concentration or otherwise of sporting output – that is wins – amongst sporting suppliers – that is teams. In a competitively balanced league, a 45° line should emerge. This implies that clubs win an equal proportion of championships. The unbroken line on Figure 4.2 illustrates this. It is clear that deviations from this line would indicate competitive imbalance.

To plot the actual distribution of championship wins researchers take each team in turn and calculate their percentage 'share' of the league. Thus, with ten teams in a league each team would represent 10% of the league, i.e. set of teams. Starting then with the most successful team, researchers calculate the percentage of championship wins for this team out of the total championships they are examining. If this team had won, say, 20 titles over 50 seasons, this would be 40% of championships. They then plot a point corresponding to 10% of teams and 40% of wins. They then take the next successful team. If this team had won, say, 12 titles out of 50 seasons, that is 24% of wins, this implies that 20% of clubs had won 64% of the championships. This point is thus plotted and the process continued until all championships and clubs have been accounted for. A likely representation of the data is also illustrated in Figure 4.2 by the dotted line. The fact that the curve bulges to the right of the 45° line indicates that the league exhibits competitive imbalance. If follows that the competitiveness of leagues can be ranked by comparing Lorenz curves.[2]

In US sports, Fort and Quirk (1995) provide a useful summary of competitive balance in sporting leagues using the Lorenz curve method, among others. Comparing the main US professional sports from their inception until the 1990/1991 season, they argue that the NBA is the least competitive, followed by the NHL and the NFL. Historically, in baseball the AL (American League) lies above the NFL but below the NHL. The National League (NL) is the most competitively balanced. It remains that all of the sports exhibit a lack of competitive balance.

One problem with using Lorenz curves is that, as a general relative measure of concentration, they do not take into account that teams have been in leagues for different periods and that each league has different schedules: 'In particular, the longer is the league schedule, and the more years a team has been in a league, the more significant is a high lifetime . . . [win percent ratio] . . . for a team' (Fort and Quirk, 1995, p. 263).

It also follows that while the Lorenz curve gives an indication of long-run domination – as indicated by the cumulative share of win percents – it does not capture the possibility that particular seasons may have been closely fought. Consequently, Fort and Quirk also calculate the standard deviation of the win percents for each league each season. This is obtained by subtracting the league average win percent from each club's win percent, squaring the differences then summing them across all teams before dividing them by the total number of teams in the league.[3] Standard deviations are informative

---

[2] The degree of 'bulge' below the 45° line can be measured by a Gini coefficient. It measures the area between the Lorenz curve and the 45° line.

[3] This is clearly problematic in the case of sports in which draws are prevalent.

because, if win percents were distributed according to the normal distribution, approximately 68% of the win percents would lie within one standard deviation above or below the mean, 95% between two standard deviations from the mean and 99% three standard deviations from the mean and so on. As such it follows that low standard deviations suggest that results cluster around the average for the league. Consequently, this would imply competitive balance.

In order to compare each league's competitive balance allowing for differences in league composition, however, they also calculate the mean and standard deviation of a hypothetical league in which the probability of each team winning a match is 0.5. Appendix 4.1 indicates that it is possible to show that the mean of such a 'competitively balanced league' is the same as that for an unbalanced league. It also shows that the standard deviation in the former case is equal to $0.5/\sqrt{n}$ when n is the number of matches played by a team in a league schedule. Clearly, therefore, league schedules are accounted for in such measures of dispersion as well as the spread of potential win percents per season.

By comparing the ratio of the actual standard deviation of win percents to those in an idealised balanced league, Fort and Quirk (1995) are able to provide a relative comparison of the competitive balance in leagues that allows for different schedules of fixtures, etc. Based on these comparisons the NFL appears as the most competitively balanced league, while the NBA is the least competitively balanced. While the NL is less competitively balanced than the AL in baseball, the difference is not statistically significant. Moreover, the NHL is less competitively balanced than the NFL but more so than the NBA. While the rank order changes a little, it remains that US sports are characterised by relative competitive imbalance.

Using a similar approach, in Europe, Szymanski and Kuypers (1999) analyse association football. Using the Lorenz curve approach, they identify the English football league as the most competitively balanced. This is followed by the football leagues in Scotland, Italy, Spain and the Netherlands. However, they acknowledge the limitations of the Lorenz curve analysis. Consequently they also make use of standard deviations to assess competitive balance. They have to modify their approach, however, because draws are common in football. Consequently they descriptively analyse the standard deviations of *points* earned by teams each season rather than win percents.[4] In such a case, in a competitive league one would expect individual club's points to be close to the mean of the points earned in the league. Thus, standard deviations would be lower than in the case in which points were spread more widely between dominant winning teams and persistent losers. Under this type of analysis, English association football remains more competitively

---

[4] Having three possible outcomes to a match precludes modelling league results in terms of the binomial distribution discussed in Appendix 4.1.

balanced than in the Netherlands, but is less balanced than in Italy and Spain. The implication is that English association football leagues are bifurcated. A small group of clubs may contest the championship, but many stand no chance of winning. It is worth noting in this regard that English association football has larger divisions than elsewhere. An implication is that a reduction in the size of the divisions may be called for.

Taken collectively, the upshot of this analysis is neatly captured by Fort and Quirk, as they argue:

> One obvious conclusion from our . . . look at historical data on competitive balance in the five major team sports leagues is that none of the leagues comes close to achieving the ideal of equal playing strengths. There is ample evidence of long-term competitive imbalance in each league . . . [yet] . . . the leagues have not only survived but have flourished, with growth in number of teams, in geographic coverage, in attendance and public interest, and in profitability.
>
> Owners of sports teams, league commissioners, and most sports writers argue that an important reason for this success is that the leagues have achieved an acceptable level of competitive balance. They further argue that this acceptable level of competitive balance is due in no small part to the restrictions that have been imposed on the player market in sports.
>
> (pp. 269–270)

It follows that other league policies of cross-subsidisation could be defended on these terms as well. Thus it also follows that a key hypotheses that needs to be tested empirically is the effects of cross-subsidisation policies on competitive balance. The most comprehensive attempt at this is presented in the later work of Fort and Quirk (1995), and it is to this issue that attention is turned. While the evidence is based on US sports, it is clear that lessons for European sports can be learned.

Empirical evidence on the effects of cross-subsidisation policies

An interesting feature of the cross-subsidisation polices associated with the players' labour market is, as discussed in Chapters 9 and 10, that leagues have been forced to radically reduce their intervention since the 1970s and, on occasions, respond to the changes this has produced. In empirical terms, sporting leagues have produced historical analogies to 'experiments'. Researchers are able to examine the distribution of win percents in leagues before and after a policy change. For example, if sporting cross-subsidisation polices relaxed since the 1970s then, following the uncertainty of outcome hypothesis, one would expect to see, on average, an increase in the standard deviation of win percents. This would indicate a fall in competitive balance. This is because the means of win percent distributions are always equal to 0.5.

The empirical method adopted by Fort and Quirk (1995) thus involves testing for significant differences in the average value of standard deviations of win percents, calculated for the league, both before and after changes in cross-subsidisation policy.

The procedure adopted by Fort and Quirk was to employ regression analysis to establish if there was any statistical change between calculated standard deviations of win percents over the period in which cross-subsidisation policies applied and the period in which they were removed. Technically this implies 'regressing' the calculated standard deviation of win percents for the total sample period on a constant and dummy variables to represent the periods before and after the policy change and which also control for changes in league composition. Regression analysis and the use of dummy variables are discussed more fully in Chapter 6, when discussing the demand for professional team sports. Suffice it is to say at the moment that the regression analysis calculates the conditional average value of the standard deviations. With no effect of the cross-subsidisation policy, this would be estimated as the value of the constant. Statistically significant dummy variables would indicate that the change in league policy statistically affected this constant value implying a systematic effect on competitive balance. A positive estimated effect or negative estimated effect would imply that standard deviations increased or decreased on average over the two time periods. Finally, the variables measuring changes in league composition identify the effects this might have had on the standard deviation of win percents independently of the policy changes.[5]

In the case of MLB, Fort and Quirk (1995) argue that there was no change in the standard deviation or variance of win percents over the period 1966–85, which embraced the breakdown of the reserve option clause with the move to free agency in 1975. In the case of the NBA, a salary cap became operational in 1984–85 to help to control players' salaries following the move to free agency. However, the results of their tests indicated that there was no change in the distribution of win percents. As far as the NFL is concerned, along with MLB, a rookie draft has been in operation. In the former case, examining the period between 1930–41, because the draft was introduced in 1936, no significant difference in distributions was detected. In the case of MLB,

---

[5] One difference worth noting is that the test statistic employed to assess the significance of the estimates is known as the Studentised Range Test. The calculation and interpretation of this test is similar in approach to the *t*-ratios discussed in Chapter 5 when examining the literature on the demand for professional team sports. However, it allows for the potential adjustment of the distribution from being normal to non-normal as the policy effects take place. Standard *t*-ratios would only be approximate under such circumstances. One potential problem with this approach, however, is the extent to which it implies that the standard deviations of each season are independent. More recently, cointegration analysis has developed to account for the time-varying nature of distributions. This is further discussed in the appendix to Chapter 6. The cointegration analysis of these relationships would thus be a fruitful line of future inquiry.

covering the 12 years before and after 1964 when the draft was introduced, and hence not being affected by free agency in 1975, once again no change in the distribution of win percents was detected. In short, Fort and Quirk find no evidence to support the case that cross-subsidisation polices have affected competitive balance in leagues.

Moreover, as well as the inferences obtained from tests of significance, they also report that the descriptive trends associated with an analysis of Gini coefficients calculated from Lorenz curves also supports this case (see footnote 2). This is important because there was no possibility of statistically testing the effects of changes in revenue sharing policies between teams in particular leagues. Thus as far as changes in gate-sharing or local TV revenue sharing arrangements are concerned, comparing the NFL, which has favourable sharing arrangements, to the other sports indicates that the Gini coefficient is lower in the NFL than elsewhere. Moreover, there is evidence that revenues are more equal in the NFL. This could suggest that revenue sharing arrangements might be important instruments of league policy. However, theoretical arguments suggest that this might be implausible as a basis for policy as discussed below. Finally, as far as national TV revenues are concerned, there is little formal evidence available. In the US, payments of national TV revenues are independent of results and are typically negotiated at a league level under a one-team-one-vote system. This is for good reason. When the NFL began to negotiate TV revenues on a league rather than a team-by-team basis in 1962, Fort and Quirk (1995) note that revenues rose by 33%. Consequently, there appear to be demonstrable benefits to this policy and there should be no effect on win percents. However, in as much as the league may be able to negotiate greater TV revenues by encouraging strong teams to compete, this could produce incentives to promote policies that work against competitive balance. An example of this is in European sport, as discussed in Chapter 8, where TV revenues and results are connected. In short, the empirical evidence seems to suggest to date that cross-subsidisation polices have been ineffective and that this is particularly the case for polices aimed at the labour market.

The Coase theorem and professional team sports leagues

Understanding why these policies have had little effect on competitive balance can be revealed by tracing through the effects of each of the policies in the model of sporting leagues identified earlier. An example of this is the case of the reserve-option clause. Figure 4.3 reproduces the equilibrium of sporting leagues discussed earlier. There, C_1 represents a lower cost of a unit of talent resulting from the reserve option clause. While it is clear that a policy that equalises spending on talent across the league must imply competitive balance, Figure 4.3 reveals a problem in sustaining or achieving this outcome. At the new salary level C_1, both team A and team B would look to buy talent because at the old equilibrium point E, $MRA = MRB > C_1$. Profits could be

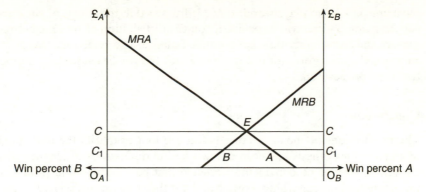

Figure 4.3 The reserve-option clause and competitive imbalance

obtained by buying talent and winning more matches. Team *A* would like to move to point *A* and team *B* to point *B* where their marginal revenues equal the new marginal cost of playing talent. This is clearly impossible because both teams cannot increase their win percents. The implication is that both teams could make greater profits, if team *A* bought players and team *B* sold them. This suggests that the league could be forced back to its initial equilibrium position of competitive imbalance. The intended restriction upon player's mobility will have no effect on the actual allocation of players. There is an underlying economic process based on financial incentives that creates an 'enforcement' problem for the policy.

It follows that a similar analysis would apply in the case of a salary cap, which explicitly reduces the cost of talent. The implication is that the rookie draft would be subject to the same pressures in as much that weak teams would pay high quality new talent less than they could get elsewhere. Finally, Fort and Quirk (1995) show that revenue sharing will likewise not affect competitive balance. The reasons for this are more complicated and are discussed in Appendix 4.2.

There is a sensible economic explanation for these results. It is an example of the 'Coase theorem' discussed in Chapter 2. In a sporting context, the profit maximising choice for both teams will emerge as the 'efficient' solution to the 'externality problem' in sporting leagues. Thus regardless of the initial distribution of property rights, that is the legal rules describing what economic agents can do with their property, established by the policy attempting to achieve competitive balance, players and clubs will 'internalise' the externality and seek a solution that maximises their welfare. Thus players will look to increase their salaries and clubs their profits. A market will come to exist regardless of the regulations. Even under, say, the reserve option clause or retain and transfer system, thus, players are bought and sold by clubs despite clubs' rights to hold onto them. It is profitable for clubs to do so. There are, of course, also incentives to cheat the legal system with payments in kind to players and so on. It follows that the effects of the cross-subsidisation policies will be primarily on the distribution of revenue between players and clubs rather than competitive balance. The evidence above firmly supports the first proposition. Chapters 9 and 10 provide evidence to support the latter proposition.

Conclusions

The implications of the above discussion are that primarily the uncertainty of outcome hypothesis has been overworked in discussions of league policy. Currently, there is no convincing evidence that policies aimed at promoting uncertainty of outcome have worked and yet they remain strongly advocated. Of course, this is not to say that uncertainty of outcome generally, or the targeting of it by league authorities, has no effect on sporting leagues. In the latter case it is clear that such policies will have financial consequences for the distribution of financial returns within the game. In the former case it is likely that uncertainty of outcome will have some affect on team and league revenues.

The major conclusion that should be drawn from this discussion is that the effects of policies aimed at affecting competitive balance are unlikely to be captured in models and manipulated in policies in a simple way. Following the discussions of Chapter 2, for example, we need to be aware that sporting leagues evolve and adjust institutionally through time. What may matter more than the hypothetically complete competitive balance implied in the literature is the perception or relative state of competitive balance. This implies that analysis should begin to focus more on the time profiles of competitive balance and league results and finances. In this respect the Coase theorem results could be interpreted as reflecting leagues evolving to retain acceptable competitive balances. Moreover, the Coase theorem is a theoretical result that is constructed upon comparisons of the same market and profit maximising behaviour. It follows that as alternative profit making opportunities arise or alternative 'markets' get defined, then uncertainty of outcome as a planned concept, if not an actual state of leagues, may be an important prompt for these changes. This may be the case for example, if the nature of demand for sports is thought to change and, perhaps, becomes more 'event' oriented than reflecting deep-seated spectator interests and allegiances that are unlikely to switch to other teams. This may well be the case as the commercial context of sports develops. In contrast, alternative objectives for clubs may persist. This may affect the course of development of leagues.

From a practical point of view therefore a number of themes emerge for future research. The first theme is conceptualising the nature of uncertainty of outcome and competitive balance adequately. One first step here would be to extend the models discussed above to capture some of the institutional characteristics of professional team sports. Thus, as Chapter 10 notes that bargaining issues have become central to the sporting labour market, it follows that bargaining models of the league need to be developed. A second step would be empirical. As discussed in Chapter 8, efforts to achieve an adequate measure of competitive balance have been mixed. It follows that further work needs to be done here and particularly in producing time-dependent measures of uncertainty of outcome. These might be amenable for inclusion in empirical work of a more long-term nature.

A second step, and probably a prerequisite for the first step, would be to increase our understanding of both the demand and supply of professional team sports. It is clear that the above model involves simplifications on both of these counts. The demand curve and the supply of talent are treated simplistically. While, as Chapter 1 notes, there is nothing intrinsically wrong with simple models, it follows that the depth of our understanding of what is happening in professional team sports can only increase with more sophisticated models. The remaining chapters of the book thus begin to explore the current state of our knowledge in both of these cases.

Appendix 4.1: Measuring competitive balance in sporting leagues

Calculating the dispersion of sporting success in leagues

If a team plays n matches in its set of league fixtures, and it wins w of them, then its win percent will be equal to

$$w/n. \tag{4.1.1}$$

Likewise, if it loses l of them, its loss percent will be

$$l/n. \tag{4.1.2}$$

This implies that

$$w/n + l/n = 1, \tag{4.1.3}$$

because in US sports, fixtures are either won or lost. This implies that each w has a corresponding l. It also follows that for the league as a whole, summing across all teams,

$$\Sigma(w/n) = \Sigma(l/n). \tag{4.1.4}$$

If there are T teams in a league, the mean value of $\Sigma w/n$ for the league as a whole will be

$$\Sigma(w/n)/T. \tag{4.1.5}$$

It follows that the mean value of the loss percent will be

$$\Sigma(l/n)/T. \tag{4.1.6}$$

As both n and T are equal in the league and, at the league level,

$$\Sigma(w/n) = \Sigma(l/n), \tag{4.1.7}$$

it follows that

$$\Sigma(w/n)/T = \Sigma(l/n)/T. \tag{4.1.8}$$

Moreover, it follows that

$$\Sigma(w/n)/T + \Sigma(l/n)/T = 1, \tag{4.1.9}$$

because for each team $(w/n + l/n) = 1$. So aggregating over the league implies

$$\Sigma(w/n) + l/n) = T, \tag{4.1.10}$$

thus,

$$\Sigma(w/n) + \Sigma(l/n) = T. \tag{4.1.11}$$

As

$$\Sigma(w/n)/T + \Sigma(l/n)/T = 1, \tag{4.1.12}$$

implies

$$\Sigma(w/n)/T + \Sigma(w/n)/T = 1 \tag{4.1.13}$$

or

$$\Sigma(l/n)/T + \Sigma(l/n)/T = 1, \tag{4.1.14}$$

then

$$2\Sigma(w/n)/T = 1, \tag{4.1.15}$$

or

$$2\Sigma(l/n)/T = 1. \tag{4.1.16}$$

Consequently,

$$\Sigma(w/n)/T = \frac{1}{2} \text{ or } \Sigma(l/n)/T = \frac{1}{2}. \tag{4.1.17}$$

Crucially, this implies that the mean value of win (or for that matter loss) percents for teams in a league in which teams win or lose their fixtures will be $\frac{1}{2}$ or 0.5. It follows that the standard deviation will be the square root of the variance of win percents, that is equal to $\sqrt{(\Sigma(w/n) - \Sigma(w/n)/T)^2/T - 1}$ or $\sqrt{(\Sigma(w/n) - 0.5)^2/T - 1}$.

Calculating the dispersion of sporting success in a competitively balanced league

The key to understanding the mean and standard deviations of win percents in a competitively balanced league lies in noting that sporting leagues in the US can be understood in terms of the binomial probability distribution. This distribution provides a means of answering binomial probability questions that are common in many aspects of business and economics. Typically, binomial problems have the following characteristics:

(a) There are n independent trials.
(b) There are two possible outcomes to each trial, 'success' or 'failure'.
(c) The probability p of a particular outcome occurring is the same in each trial.

Under these conditions, the binomial random variable is the number of successes that occur in the n trials.

This distribution describes US sporting leagues that are balanced. For example, taking the league just described

(a) There are n fixtures.
(b) Fixtures have to be won or lost.
(c) Crucially, the probability of a win for a team is the same in each fixture and must equal 0.5 in a *balanced set of fixtures*.

This means that one can define win percents as a binomial random variable. The mean of a binomial distribution is np, which in a sporting context must be equal to $0.5n$. The standard deviation of a binomial distribution is $\sqrt{np(1-p)}$, which in a sporting context is $\sqrt{0.25n}$. As the win percent for any team is w/n, the mean win percent will be given by $n(w/n) = w = 0.5$. The variance of the win percent will be equal to $\text{Var}(w/n) = \text{Var}(w)/n^2$. As $\text{Var}(w) = np(1-p) = 0.25n$, $\text{Var}(w/n) = 0.25n/n^2 = 0.25/n$. The standard deviation of a balanced league win percent will be equal to $0.5/\sqrt{n}$.

Appendix 4.2: Competitive balance in sporting leagues under revenue sharing

Team A and team B both have revenues R that are a function of their win percents, here defined as w rather than w/n for brevity. Thus, respectively,

$$RA(w) \text{ and } RB(w). \tag{4.2.1}$$

Marginal revenues will be

$$\delta RA/\delta w \text{ and } \delta RB/\delta w, \tag{4.2.2}$$

where δ refers to a derivative. Under gate sharing a proportion a of revenues will be retained and a proportion $(1-a)$ will be given to the opposing team. Thus 'home' team revenues become

$$RA(w)^* = aRA(w) + (1-a)RB(w) \text{ and } RB(w)^* = aRB(w) + (1-a)RA(w). \tag{4.2.3}$$

Marginal revenues of winning (rather than losing) are now

$$\delta RA/\delta w^* = a\delta RA/\delta w - (1-a)\delta RB/\delta w \tag{4.2.4}$$

and

$$\delta RB/\delta w^* = a\delta RB/\delta w - (1-a)\delta RA/\delta w. \tag{4.2.5}$$

Thus a win for team A (or team B) will increase its own support and revenue but decrease the support of the losing team, B (or team A) and hence contribution of revenue from the gates of that team. As $0 < a < 1$, and marginal products are positive, so that the second term in (4.2.4) and (4.2.5) must be positive, this implies

$$\delta RA/\delta w > \delta RA/\delta w^* \tag{4.2.6}$$

and

$$\delta RB/\delta w > \delta RB/\delta w^*. \tag{4.2.7}$$

Under gate sharing, both teams experience a fall in marginal revenues associated with winning more matches. Furthermore, equating (4.2.4) and (4.2.5), as implied in an equilibrium in the league, suggests that

$$a\delta RA/\delta w - (1-a)\delta RB/\delta w = a\delta RB/\delta w - (1-a)\delta RA/\delta w \tag{4.2.8}$$

or

$$a\delta RA/\delta w - \delta RB/\delta w + a\delta RB/\delta w = a\delta RB/\delta w - \delta RA/\delta w + a\delta RA/\delta w.$$

(4.2.9)

Thus,

$$\delta RB/\delta w = \delta RA/\delta w,$$

(4.2.10)

which are the marginal revenues implied without gate sharing. The implication of these results is that both marginal revenues fall for any given win percent as a result of revenue sharing. However, the output that corresponds to profit maximising behaviour remains the same because the first-order conditions for both cases are identical. Consequently, equilibrium 'output' is unchanged.

Discussion questions

1. At first glance the introduction of a 'rookie draft' appears to imply the subsidisation of weaker teams by stronger ones. Is this the whole story?
2. Which part is played by the assumption of profit maximising teams in Fort and Quirk's (1995) model of a league? Which part by the assumed interchangeability of 'output' and 'win percent'? Which part is played by the assumption that teams differ in their 'drawing power'? What is the implication of the fact that the determination of 'drawing power' is not a part of their model?
3. Fort and Quirk find that the distribution of win percents, both within a given year and over long periods, is significantly different from that which one would expect to find in an evenly balanced league. They also find that the distribution of win percents seems to be unaffected by changes in league policies, such as the abandonment of the reserve clause in baseball. To what do they attribute this 'invariance'?
4. Win percents cannot be sensibly applied to the analysis of performance in European team sports. Why? What alternatives are available? Try to define one that (like win percent) imposes the constraint that it is not possible for team *A* to improve its performance unless team *B*'s is impaired. Explain why the constraint is important in the model.
5. Fort and Quirk are careful to qualify their findings by noting that none of their pieces of empirical work is comparable to a properly designed experiment. Explain to a moderately intelligent layperson why, for example, their finding that the abandonment of the reserve clause did not appear to affect competitive balance in baseball was not the outcome of a properly conducted experiment. (Hint: think about the possible non-equality of 'other things'.)

Section B

The demand for professional team sports

5 Theoretical and empirical issues

Introduction

In this chapter we begin a more detailed exploration of the demand for professional team sports. The basic underlying economic theory of demand is outlined first of all. We then outline the central features of the statistical method employed by economists to measure the demand for professional team sports and, for that matter, most economic relationships. We outline the results of an investigation into the demand for Scottish association football to exemplify this material. This example is chosen because of its sophisticated measure of the effects of uncertainty of outcome on the demand for professional team sports. Finally some conceptual issues associated with the modelling and measurement of the demand for professional team sports are then discussed.

The next chapter surveys the literature of empirical studies on the demand for professional team sports and produces a commentary on the main results. Because of the centrality of the uncertainty of outcome hypothesis to the economics of professional team sports, the subsequent chapter then explores in more detail the attempts that have been made to measure this variable.

The theory of demand

As implied in Chapter 2, the theory of demand, in conjunction with that of supply, is in part intended to explain or predict how the prices and the quantities bought and sold in markets vary in response to changes in the economic environment. Demand theory begins with the behaviour of an individual. It then extends the analysis to the market on the assumption that the 'market' demand curve is simply the sum of the individual demand curves. Understanding the individual's demand curve is thus tantamount to understanding market demand in a qualitative if not quantitative sense.

At the core of the theory of demand is the utility maximising, rational, income constrained individual consumer. Following the methodological precepts discussed in the Introduction, while this individual does not actually exist, their usefulness derives from the fact that based on certain assumptions the economist can derive clear testable predictions about their, and hence market, demand (see Friedman, 1953).

The key assumptions are that:

(a) The consumer receives satisfaction, welfare or utility from consuming goods and services.
(b) The consumer has a complete set of preferences or tastes associated with the consumption of goods or services. Thus, the consumer can rank combinations of goods or services consistently, prefers more goods or services to less, etc. It is important to note that preferences are assumed to be *ordinal* rather than *cardinal*. This implies that while the consumer can be said to prefer one set of consumption alternatives over another, there is no meaningful measure of *how much* this preference might be. Consequently, preferences are not comparable between individuals.
(c) The consumer has perfect information about products, their prices and the effects of their consumption on their personal welfare or utility.
(d) The consumer only considers their own welfare or utility (preferences are assumed to be independent of other persons').
(e) The consumer's preferences are 'given' (they never change with respect to their consumption behaviour).
(f) The consumer is limited by expenditure constraints which make it impossible to spend more than their current income, which is 'fixed' in the short run.
(g) The consumer is an individual so small in relation to the whole market that their individual decisions (whether or not to buy) do not affect the prices of goods.

Understanding analytically how consumption affects the consumer's welfare or utility and consequently shapes the consumer's demand depends on two main analytical tools for the economist.

The utility function

The first is the utility function. This maps the relative preferences for goods and services into a measure of utility. As preferences are ordinally defined, the utility function is too. Basically any mathematical function that preserves the rankings implied by the preferences of the consumer will do. There is usually only one restriction placed on the utility function. This was referred to in the last chapter and is known as the assumption of diminishing marginal utility. This implies that the marginal utility of any commodity – the addition to total utility arising from the last unit consumed – is always positive, but declines as consumption of the good in question rises. Hence the greater the amount of any good or service consumed, the greater the total utility obtained from it, although total utility increases at a decreasing rate.

The budget constraint

The other analytical tool used to model the demand decisions of consumers is the budget constraint. Given unlimited resources the consumer would simply consume commodities up until their marginal utility was zero. Such a limiting case would be specific to individuals and leave us with very little to say about how the consumer might make (marginal) adjustments to consumption patterns as their environment changed. Thus, in effect we could say nothing at all about how their consumption might alter in response to variations in prices or income and thus say nothing about how prices and quantities in the market would behave.

The budget constraint – a reality for all consumers – solves this analytical problem. In its simplest form this states that the amount of their money income (assumed given) equals their total expenditure – the sum of prices (also assumed given) times the quantities they consume per period. Prices and incomes are assumed as given to the consumer who is seen as small relative to the (perfectly competitive) economic system. Given their preferences, their money income and the prices of goods, their job is to determine how much of each good to buy. If their object is simply to maximise their own utility, they must arrange their consumption so that the 'marginal utility' derived from the last penny spent on good *A* equals that from the last penny spent on good *B*. ('Penny' is used here in the sense of a small amount of money in any currency.)

To see why this is so, suppose for a moment the last penny spent on *A* produces more utility than the last penny spent on *B* (e.g. if *A* has just become cheaper). The consumer can obtain higher total utility from the same total expenditure simply by substituting some *A* for some *B* until the utility of the marginal penny spent on both goods is equalised once more. The budget constraint gives them a determinate demand for *A* and *B* (and other goods). In other words, we should in principle be able to discover which combinations of goods and services they would consume as their money income and/or the prices of goods vary.

Hence, we think of the individual's demand for a good as being determined by their preferences (not directly observable), their income, the price of the good itself and the prices of all other goods. In the latter case this is especially those of close substitutes (e.g. return flights to the US by Virgin and by British Airways) and complements (motor cars and petrol). The economist proceeds to analyse the consumer's response to small variations in these stimuli *ceteris paribus* – 'other things equal' – that is to say, on the assumption that the other stimuli are unchanged. This exemplifies the ideal experimental design: vary your 'controls' one at a time and measure the effects on the system. Thus you separately identify the effects of the control variables. We now follow this procedure in a theoretical sense deriving the predictions about demand following changes in prices, incomes and preferences or tastes.

The consumer's response to price change

Assume the price of A increases. This affects the consumer in two ways. First, the purchasing power of their fixed money income is reduced (the 'income effect'). Second, commodity A is now dearer in relation to other goods and the rational consumer will therefore substitute (the 'substitution effect') away from it. The substitution effect is always negative in sign (a *higher* price induces *lower* consumption, other things equal) – this is the origin of the 'law' of demand that prices and quantities demanded vary inversely employed in the discussion in Chapter 2. However, the total effect of the price change on the quantity demanded depends on the above two sub-effects. If they work in the same direction, the sign of the combined effect is always negative. If they work in opposite directions, the sign of the overall effect is potentially unpredictable.

The income effect could be either negative (an 'inferior' good) or positive (a 'superior' good). If A is a superior good like skiing holidays, then (other things equal) after an increase in its price the substitution and the income effects reinforce one another to reduce consumption and the 'law' of demand holds. If A is an inferior good such as bus travel, the rise in price which induces substitution away from it also lowers the consumer's income which (other things equal) tends to make them buy more of it. The effects work counter to one another. The effect cannot be predicted unambiguously, though it is supposed that it is only in unusual cases that the income effect will be so great as to overwhelm the substitution effect so that the 'law' of demand is contravened.

Measuring the effects of changes in price, and for that matter other variables, on demand is discussed later in the next chapter. It is worth noting however, that the economist and the supplier might (for different reasons) be interested in estimating the 'elasticity' of demand for a good with respect to its price rather than simply establishing how much demand changes as, say, price changes. While the economist's interest is intellectual the supplier's is earthier; other things equal, the lower the price elasticity the greater the potential profit margin. Price elasticity measures the percentage rate at which quantity purchased changes (other things equal) in response to a 1% change in price. An elasticity of zero means the industry can raise its price with no effect on sales; elasticity between zero and -1, allowing for the law of demand, implies that changes in price outweigh changes in demand. Thus, total revenue increases in response to the price rise despite demand falling. Petroleum, alcohol and tobacco products are well known products with inelastic demands. This is why sales tax increases on these products are prevalent as they raise revenue for governments. As indicated in the next chapter it appears that professional team sports have an inelastic demand. This explains why certain English premier league association football clubs can afford to increase their gate prices in the manner in which they have recently (Dobson and Goddard, 1995; Szymanski and Kuypers, 1999).

A price elasticity of exactly -1.0 means a 1% price rise (*ceteris paribus*) reduces sales volume by 1%, so total sales revenue remains constant. Price elasticities of less than -1, for example -1.5, would reduce sales by 1.5% in response to a 1% price rise, hence sales revenue falls. The more easily the consumer can find a substitute for good A, the greater, in absolute terms, its price elasticity.

Cross-price elasticities of demand can also be calculated. These measure the relative effects that changes in the price of one good or service have on another good or service. Suppose the price of a substitute for A falls (as an exercise replicate the analysis that follows for a fall in the price of a complementary good). This has an income effect (purchasing power increases) and a negative substitution effect on demand for A. Should (say) Virgin Atlantic raise its transatlantic fares by a certain percentage while other carriers do not, Virgin customers will switch to other airlines. The greater the percentage who switch to American Airlines in response to, say, a 1% increase in Virgin's price, the greater the cross-price elasticity of demand for American Airlines with respect to the price of Virgin Atlantic. It is likely that the cross-price elasticity of demand for tickets to professional sporting encounters is much lower than that for seats on airplanes.

One can suggest to the average Tottenham Hotspur (Spurs) supporter that watching an association football encounter at north London rivals Arsenal is not (unless Spurs are the visitors) a substitute for watching Spurs at home. Even if Spurs raised their prices and Arsenal did not, few if, any, supporters who deserted Spurs would go to Arsenal.[1] They would take their pleasure in activities other than watching live association football.

As an aside it is worth noting that such British attachment of the supporter to the club and of the club to its local area may strike US readers as odd. The Brooklyn Dodgers relocated successfully 3,000 miles to Los Angeles – sensibly taking the product from a static or declining market to a growing one – without provoking a national outcry. Here the attempt by owner Robert Maxwell to merge soccer clubs Reading and Oxford United and move them both 20 miles to a new stadium enraged both teams' supporters and engaged the interest of the national media. As noted in Chapter 2, the geographical distribution, see Waylen and Snook (1990), of English association football clubs has (like population and economic activity in general) shifted south-easterly and from inner cities to suburbs, but many clubs remain in towns whose population and industry have declined this century. Such 'movement' has occurred in large part as a result of the accession of Southern League clubs to the Football League and to the demise of northern clubs rather than to actual relocation. Anecdote aside, however, it remains that the precise

---

[1] Discussion with our friend, colleague and Spurs fan Joe Riordan confirms that this is not simply a hypothetical result – though we accept that this only a sample of one!

nature of the determinants of demand needs exploring in a more sophisticated way.

The consumer's response to income change

Now assume our consumer's money income has fallen, while prices are
constant. Clearly there will be an income effect (their purchasing power is
lower) and equally clearly there can be no substitution effect (prices are in the
same relationship to each other). The outcome for demand depends only on
the income effect; if A is superior/inferior they buy less/more in response to
their lower real income. Analogous to the discussion above, the economist and
the supplier may be interested in measuring the income elasticity of demand
for A, which is simply the percentage by which units sold changes as a result
(other things equal) of a given percentage change in real income. For inferior
goods the income elasticity is negative; e.g. if the income elasticity of demand
for bus travel is -2.8%, a 1% rise in consumer incomes will lead (other things
equal) to a 2.8% decline in bus travel. If the income elasticity of demand for
A is positive and lies between zero and 1, this implies that despite increasing
demand, consumers spends less of their budget on the good, service or sport.
If the income elasticity of demand exceeds 1, consumers not only buy more of
A as their incomes rise. They spend a larger proportion of their incomes on A.
There is evidence that demand for some recreational sports (yachting and
horse riding to name but two) may have this characteristic. Such goods are
termed 'luxury' goods.

The consumer's change in tastes

The remaining control in the simple demand model is the consumer's own
preferences or tastes. These are, of course, not directly observable. It is clear,
moreover, that it would be unreasonable to assume that a given consumer's
tastes remain constant over any length of time, and that there are not systematic variations in tastes between occupations, age groups or the sexes at any
given moment. This is almost certainly going to be the case with supporters
of professional sports teams. Hence in studies aiming to estimate the price,
cross-price and income elasticities of demand the possibility of systematic
variations in taste must be allowed for. Lacking direct observations, the
researcher looks for 'proxy' variables for tastes, these being variables which
are observed and which there is reason to expect are correlated with the
unobservable tastes. Hence, the researcher might obtain information about
the amount of TV coverage of the sport, the nature of the team or particular
players participating in a fixture, the competitive balance of the fixture or
weather conditions during the season (outdoor sports) in the expectation that
these will shift the demand for attendance. The variety of measures that have
been used in demand studies of professional team sports are discussed in
Chapter 6. As will become apparent, a notable exception is that in the UK

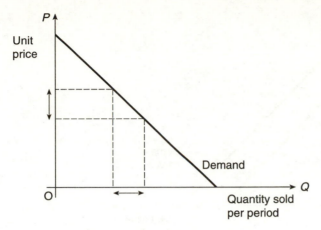

Figure 5.1 Movements along the demand curve

General Household Survey's triennial survey of recreational sport participation the researchers are able to discover the respondents' occupational
groups, sexes and ages. These personal characteristics seem to be systematically related to participation and might help to proxy tastes. No study of
attendance at professional team sports known to the writers embodies this
level of knowledge about the characteristics of individual consumers. Data
are typically of a much more aggregate level.

Having reviewed the basic model of the consumer we are able to postulate
that (the quantity of) consumer demand will depend on price, other prices,
income and tastes. The latter are not observable but we can find proxies for
tastes to incorporate into our analysis.

Modelling demand: regression analysis

When economists try to quantify and test an economic model through
statistical analysis they employ econometric analysis. The core statistical tool
at the centre of econometric analysis is linear regression analysis. This section
outlines the basic elements of regression analysis in the context of the demand
for professional team sports and suggests key points that one should look for
in reading journal articles in the professional team sport literature.

As noted earlier, when explaining demand for a product, economists
usually argue that demand depends on prices, incomes, the price of other
goods etc. Typically economists argue that *ceteris paribus* – other things
equal – an increase/decrease in price will lead to a decrease/increase in
demand. On this basis economists often draw a demand curve sloping downwards from left to right on axes labelled price and quantity, as illustrated in
Figure 5.1. An increase/decrease in income would then usually shift demand

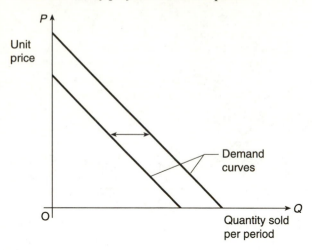

Figure 5.2 Shifts in the demand curve

to the right/left indicating that demand has risen/fallen for any price that could be charged, as illustrated in Figure 5.2.

In contrast to this qualitative analysis, regression analysis is useful to the economist for three main reasons:

(1) Regression analysis helps the economist to quantify the demand relationship. For example, we can find out how steep the demand curve is, and how much it shifts with changes to other factors affecting demand.
(2) It enables the economist to explore the role of many factors affecting demand *simultaneously* in a pseudo-experimental setting. Economists cannot typically construct experiments in the manner of, say, laboratory work. Consequently, the economist has to be careful not to reach spurious conclusions. For example, if we naively observed that sporting fixture prices were going up at the same time as attendance at sports fixtures, we might conclude that the economic 'law' of demand, that demand and price normally vary inversely, did not apply to sports. However, it may be the case, for example, that the increased success of the home club is promoting the increased demand. Demand is therefore shifting outwards and hence causing prices to rise. Regression analysis helps us to disentangle the various elements affecting demand by approximating their effects *ceteris paribus*.
(3) Finally, in drawing upon statistical theory, regression analysis allows economists to make inferences beyond their particular sample of data. This is important because economists never have access to populations of data but can typically only work from samples.

Causal models

Regression analysis is often referred to as the estimation of a causal model. In other words, in the case of demand for professional team sports, the underlying causes of demand are identified. Following earlier discussion, such a model might be represented as (5.1):

$$A_t = \beta_1 + \beta_2 P_t + \beta_3 Y_t + \beta_4 UO_t + \varepsilon_t, \tag{5.1}$$

where A represents the dependent variable. This could be measured as the numbers of spectators, for example in 000s, at games for a club. In accordance with economic theory this variable is assumed to depend on the following causal or independent variables. P represents admission price. This could be measured in a particular currency, for example pounds sterling. Y represents the income of supporters. This could be measured in, for example, thousands of pounds sterling. UO represents uncertainty of outcome as a proxy of tastes for the sport and could be measured by the relative league standings of teams in a fixture. ε represents other factors that randomly cause attendance to vary. t represents an index of observation. This refers to the data or observation on each variable.

Observations may be collected cross-sectionally, in a time-series or by 'pooling' cross-section and time-series data. An example of cross-section data would be observations based on fixtures for a number of clubs in a particular week or season. An example of time-series data would be observations on a particular club or league over a period of time. Pooled data would involve, for example, observations on fixtures for a number of clubs over a period of time. If precisely the same clubs were observed over time this is referred to as a panel-data set. As you will see discussed in the next chapter, researchers have employed all of these data types in their investigations into the demand for professional team sports.

The beta letters in front of the variables are called coefficients. They represent the conjectured influence of the variables in the model. Regression analysis can be used to estimate the sign and magnitude of these coefficients from the observations on the variables – the data set. Knowledge of the values of the coefficients then enables the researcher to appraise the importance of the assumed causes of attendance. For example, the first coefficient is a constant. Its value, when estimated, represents average attendance *regardless* of the influence of prices and incomes on attendance. The second and third coefficients are referred to as partial slope coefficients. When estimated they measure the average unit impact on attendance following a unit change in the independent variable – *ceteris paribus*. The changes in the variables here refer to the variation in the observations in the data set. Thus with cross-section data one might be referring to the differences, i.e. changes, in attendance, admission price and spectator income across a set of clubs. With time-series data one might be referring to changes in attendance, price and income for a particular club, over time. With pooled data one might be referring to changes in attendance, prices and income between clubs and over time.

More precisely, assuming a time-series data set of a club's attendance, admission price and spectator income, the second coefficient would measure the slope of the demand curve over the time period concerned. The coefficient might be estimated as -2.5. This would suggest that if price goes up/down by £1, then, on average over the time period concerned, attendance would go down/up by 2500 *ceteris paribus*. The third coefficient measures the impact of income on attendance. A value of 0.001 would suggest that as spectator incomes rise/fall by £1000, on average over the time period concerned, attendance would rise/fall by 1000 spectators.

One word of caution needs to be noted at this point. Regression analysis only identifies an association or correlation between the variables of interest. It does not *prove* causality between the variables in the direction postulated by your equation. Tests of (a particular notion of) causality are available to economists, but they are beyond the scope of this book.

As noted earlier, an advantage of causal models is that they enable the researcher to make inferences beyond their particular sample of observations. As a statistical model, regression analysis readily allows the economist to both test the reliability of their results as well as to make claims of more generality than the particular data-set employed. The basis of these claims, as well as other desirable properties of the regression model, is now outlined.

Estimating a regression equation

Linear regression analysis applies the principle of 'least squares' to estimate the coefficients of the demand function. This can be shown to have some desirable implications if certain assumptions about the specification of the causal model are satisfied. The assumptions are:

(1) The equation is linear in coefficients (that is, that the coefficients are separated by a + or −.)
(2) The independent variables are non-random. In this respect the random influences ε only affect the dependent variable.
(3) The mean value of ε is zero.
(4) The variance of ε is the same for all observations.
(5) Each ε is independent of the others (i.e. their probability distributions are independent).
(6) Each ε has a normal distribution.

If the assumptions are not satisfied then the economist has to modify the regression model. Some of the main reasons for these cases are noted below. The corrections to the model are usually fairly standard but beyond the scope of this book, so the details are not discussed here. They are referred to below.

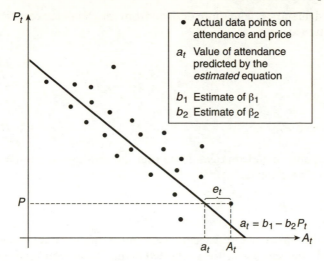

Figure 5.3 Ordinary least-squares residuals

In the next two chapters some critical assessment of the econometric procedures adopted by researchers are offered.

If the assumptions do hold, the desirable implications that stem from them pertain to the nature of the estimated coefficients. They are:

(1) On average the estimated values of the beta coefficients equal the true or population coefficients – which we can never know. In other words, the estimates are unbiased.
(2) The estimated coefficients have the smallest variance – 'our potential set of estimates are the closest to the truth as possible'.

These properties mean that the ordinary least-squares estimators of the coefficients are 'best linear unbiased'.

Of course they imply that the estimators have a probability distribution. It is a normal distribution that derives from the random disturbance. This is important as it reminds us that we are only estimating the demand function. We can never say that we can obtain the actual demand function. The most we can do is to make probability statements about demand on the basis of our estimates. The next section explains this issue further.

The least-squares principle

Because of the random variation that affects sports demand, a straight line through the data based on estimated demand coefficients will not pass through all of the points. There will be residual differences, as is indicated in Figure 5.3. These 'residuals' represent the horizontal differences between the actual values of demand, A_t, and those derived from the estimated equation.[2] They can be written as:

$$e_t = A_t - a_t, \tag{5.2}$$

or:

$$e_t = A_t - b_1 - b_2 P_t, \tag{5.3}$$

if, say, our model only included prices. Note that the residuals e_t are not the random terms ε_t. These are:

$$\varepsilon_t = A_t - \beta_1 - \beta_2 P_t. \tag{5.4}$$

It is clear that the values of e_t will depend very much on the values taken by the slope, b_2, and intercept, b_1, of the estimated demand function. The least-squares principle chooses the estimated coefficients for the function as those that minimise the sum of squared residuals (i.e. chooses b_1, b_2 by minimising Σe_t^2). Intuitively this ensures that as much of the variation in attendance that is possibly associated with price is identified. This is achieved by use of calculus. Formulae or estimators for b_1 and b_2 are derived involving both A and P variables that satisfy the minimisation of Σe_t^2. Significantly because A is involved then the random variation attributable to ε is transferred to the demand function's coefficients. This gives the formulae or estimators of b_1 and b_2 the desirable statistical properties covered above.

The interpretation of regression results

As noted earlier, in general a coefficient tells you how much, on average, attendance will change following a unit change in the independent variable associated with the coefficient assuming other things are equal. There are two important qualifications to this that are worth noting when reading the professional team sports literature:

(1) If the variables are measured in their original form or units, the value of the coefficient has to be interpreted with the units of measurement used in mind.
(2) To avoid this, economists sometimes measure their variables by using the logarithm of their value. Basically this implies that the economist thinks

---

[2] As discussed in Chapter 2, in economics demand and supply quantities, though dependent variables, appear on the horizontal axis. Consequently in more general discussions of OLS residuals, the reader will probably see references to the 'vertical differences'.

the model is non-linear. Importantly this means that the estimated coefficients will be elasticities of demand as discussed above. Recall that this is advantageous because elasticities are unit-free measurements. For any given % change in the independent variables, the elasticities tell you the average percentage change in quantity demanded *ceteris paribus* that will follow. Thus if $b_2 = -2$, prices are measured in log(£s) and attendance in log (000s) of spectators, this means that a 1% increase/decrease in price will lead, on average, to a 2% decrease/increase in spectators.

Dummy variables

In much of the sporting literature reference is made to the use of dummy variables. These are so called because they attempt to measure qualitative characteristics quantitatively. They are naturally employed in attempts to proxy tastes. Thus, while we can measure attendance in terms on the number of spectators, and prices in £s, how can we measure the influence of, say, a local derby on attendance?

A dummy variable can do this for us. To measure the fact that a match is, say, a local derby, we could specify a variable which adopts a value of 1 if a match is a derby or 0 otherwise. In this case if the dummy variable is statistically significant it implies that local derby games do affect attendance independently of other factors such as price, etc. The coefficient on the dummy variable measures the average difference between attendance at normal and derby games (independent of the influence of other variables). Graphically, you can think of the dummy variable as shifting the intercept of the demand function. An example of dummy variable analysis is given in Chapter 8 in discussing the effects of TV coverage on the demand for professional team sports (see also, Figure 8.2).

Standard items of regression output

Regression analysis is always conducted by dedicated computer packages. Some standard items of output are given by most packages that are usually referred to in the literature and can be used to check how good an estimate of, for example, the demand equation is. They derive from the probabilistic nature of regression analysis (embodied in the assumptions given above). While one need not know all of their detail, one will see them referred to in reading the literature.

T-ratios

These are ratios obtained by dividing the estimate of the coefficient by the standard error of the coefficient ($se(b_n)$). For each coefficient, these ratios test the null hypothesis

$H_0: \beta_n = 0,$ (5.5)

against the alternative hypothesis:

$H_1: \beta_n \neq 0,$ (5.6)

using the t-distribution:

$$\frac{b_n - \beta_n}{se(b_n)}.$$ (5.7)

The t-distribution is derived from the normal distribution – the assumed distribution of the random disturbances – but is used in practice rather than the latter because in economics one only has sample data. Consequently one has to estimate the standard deviation of ε_t (sometimes referred to as the standard error of the equation). In turn, this is instrumental in deriving the standard error of the estimated coefficients. The standard error of the coefficient is the square root of the variance of the coefficient. It is an indication of the dispersion of possible estimated values of the coefficient around its true value. Intuitively one would like to have a 'small' value for this so that our estimate is 'close' to the true value that we can never know.

More specifically, one can assess the statistical adequacy of the estimated coefficients. For example one can be *approximately* 95% confident that β_n is contained in the range, or confidence interval $b_n +/- 2\ se(b_n)$. (Remember the coefficient estimators are normally distributed random variables with a mean of the true value of the coefficient and a variance.) Moreover, if the absolute value of the t-ratio is greater than 2, i.e. $|t|, > 2$, then one can reject H_0 at approximately a 5% significance level. This implies that a non-zero estimated coefficient has not really been a chance occurrence. Technically it implies that there is a 5% chance that one rejects the null hypothesis in error. This latter approach to assessing the statistical adequacy of coefficient estimates is the approach to testing hypotheses most often employed in econometric work.

The value of 2 referred to in these formulae is known as the critical value and is obtained from the t-distribution. The procedure employed is to identify a 'significance level', i.e. degree of acceptable statistical error, and then based on the number of degrees of freedom one has, one can identify the appropriate critical value from the statistical tables that calibrate the t-distribution (such statistical tables exist for widely used probability distributions). Intuitively degrees of freedom measure the independent information available in a data set. Ideally this would be equal to the number of observations one has in a sample. However, as the data is employed to calculate a number of statistics, such as the estimated coefficients, then some of the information becomes 'lost'. In t-tests, there are $n - k$ degrees of freedom where n is the number of observations in the sample and k the number of estimated

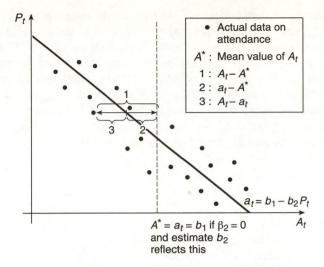

Figure 5.4 Residual and explained differences from the mean

coefficients. It follows that such confidence intervals or tests of significance can be conducted for a variety of levels of confidence or significance, respectively. For those unfamiliar with hypothesis testing and, in particular, the normal and t-distributions, we refer the reader to any elementary statistics text.

R^2

This is called the 'coefficient of determination' and addresses the equation as a whole. It is derived as follows. If all of the 'genuine' independent, explanatory, variables in the demand equation were set to zero, then the estimated demand function would be:

$$a_t = b_1, \tag{5.8}$$

or the constant. In fact, b_1 would be the arithmetic mean value of A_t. The difference between the values of the actual data on demand A_t and b_1 in this case would be attributable to residual variation. In essence the model explains nothing. Figure 5.4 illustrates this, as indicated by the horizontal distance 1 for a particular data point.

If one found that β_2, for example, was significantly different from zero, and this was reflected in the estimated coefficient b_2, then, as can be seen from Figure 5.4, the amount of this residual variation is reduced. The equation 'explains' a proportion of the variation in the data on the dependent variable from its mean, as indicated in the horizontal distance 2. The residual variation is now reduced to an amount indicated by the horizontal distance 3. This is because on some data points the regression variation is negative. In order to evaluate the overall impact of the addition of the explanatory variable, therefore, the explained and residual variations of each point are squared. By summing these squared magnitudes one can derive an indication of the relative amounts of explained and residual variation given by the demand function compared to the mean of the data. We can write that:

$$TSS = ESS + RSS, \tag{5.9}$$

or

$$\text{Total sum of squares} = \text{Explained sum of squares} + \text{Residual sum of squares.} \tag{5.10}$$

That is,

$$\Sigma(A_t - A^*)^2 = \Sigma(a_t - A^*)^2 - \Sigma(A_t - a_t)^2, \tag{5.11}$$

and hence that,

$$R^2 = \frac{ESS}{TSS} \quad \text{or} \quad 1 - \frac{RSS}{TSS} \tag{5.12}$$

A value of 1 implies that the demand equation fits the data perfectly, i.e. $ESS = TSS$ or $RSS = 0$. A value of 0 implies that the demand equation does not fit the data at all, i.e. $RSS = TSS$ or $ESS = 0$. Note that this measure follows from an identity. It does not test how good the fit is. Indeed in many practical contexts the limiting values of R^2 are unlikely to occur. One problem that might arise because of this is that simply adding more and more explanatory variables to the equation will probably increase the value of R^2 by reducing the residual sum of squares by some amount. To overcome this a corrected value, $\bar{R}^2$, is often quoted. This penalises the value of R^2 when adding new variables to the equation. Rather than being derived from the ratio of two sums of squares, this measure is derived from the ratio of two variances obtained from the ratio of explained and residual variation. In general, variances are derived by dividing a sum of squares by some number of observations in the study. With the residual sum of squares the number of observations is reduced by the number of coefficients estimated. The variance derived from the residual variation thus increases, other things equal, as more variables are added to the equation. This counters the natural tendency of the residual sum of squares to decrease and hence increase R^2 as variables are added.

F-statistic

This tests whether or not the value of R^2 is a chance occurrence. Effectively it is testing, in one go, whether or not all of the partial-slope coefficients, 'b_n' are equal to zero against the possibility that they are jointly significant. To evaluate this statistic one uses the F-distribution. As with t-tests, F-distribution tables give a critical value of the F-distribution for degrees of freedom (df) $1 = k - 1$ and degrees of freedom (df) $2 = n - k$. If the F-statistic exceeds the critical value obtained from the tables, then one can conclude that R^2 is significant. In effect the coefficients are jointly significantly different from zero. It is clear therefore that this test is useful when the individual effects of variables may not be discernable because of multi-collinearity, as discussed further below. Alternatively, some modifications to this test can be employed when the researcher is interested in testing for the significance of a subset of variables of interest (an example of this occurs in Chapter 10).

The above items of computer output can all be used to evaluate the statistical value of the econometric model estimated. Implicitly it was assumed that the estimates that were obtained were the best. Unfortunately, in practice, *OLS* does not always give best, unbiased estimates. Two important problems that often occur in regression studies are when assumptions concerning the nature of the random term ε_t do not apply.

Serial or auto correlation

Serial or auto correlation is often a problem encountered with time-series data and stems from some systematic relation between the (assumed) random terms over time. It can cause bias if it stems from the omission of a variable, and inefficiency (larger variance than otherwise), at least, if it does not. In this case cyclical factors may be at work as variables are linked through the general pattern of economic activity. Other lagged relations between variables may cause serial correlation as well as manipulation of data by, for example, smoothing techniques. Also if a linear relation is used to estimate a non-linear relation without including the variables in their non-linear form (i.e. using P for P^2, for example), then serial correlation will follow as the cyclical pattern of the relation is picked up as residual variation. In general, it can be detected by examining the pattern of residuals – as proxies for the disturbances.

The Durbin Watson test (*DW*) can be used to test for the presence of 'first-order' serial correlation. This is when the pattern of serial correlation relates to immediately adjacent time periods. It too makes use of the residuals. More sophisticated patterns of serial correlation can be detected, of course, by more sophisticated tests. There are a variety of ways that economists deal with this problem. Typically it involves a more complicated form of estimation known as 'generalised least squares'.

Heteroscedasticity

Heteroscedasticity occurs typically in a cross-section context when different units of analysis are examined at the same point in time as opposed to time-series when the same unit of analysis is examined at different points in time. Heteroscedasticity is present when the variance of the random error is not constant for different observations. Its form and detection require quite sophisticated measures. Ultimately its remedy requires the use of generalised least squares if the heteroscedasticity is not the result, say, of missing key variables out of the model. As will be seen in the next two chapters, some empirical studies in the professional team sports literature simply ignore these two problems, which casts doubt on their reliability.

Multicollinearity

Notwithstanding these points above there is a general problem often encountered with regression analysis involving many explanatory variables. This problem is multicollinearity and stems from a correlation between the independent variables. As will be seen in the next chapter, economists typically assume away this problem which can question the validity of the findings. For now it is worth noting that its presence does not really affect the overall fit of the equation estimated and in this sense it may not pose a problem. However, it does affect the estimation of individual coefficients and in the most extreme cases may prevent estimation being possible. In these cases it is of much importance as misleading inferences can be made on key variables. Ultimately there is little one can do about multicollinearity. It is a problem with the data. One may be forced on this basis to leave variables out at a possible cost of serial correlation or heteroscedasticity and inefficiency and bias, or combine variables in some way that does not give information on the original causal relations hypothesised.

Measuring demand: some key conceptual and data issues

Prior to exploring an actual study of the demand for professional team sports, to exemplify the comments above, it is also worth noting some of the key measurement problems that face researchers in empirical work as a precursor to this discussion. First, we consider the difficulties in obtaining a measure of quantity. Second, we ask whether it is possible to get an accurate measure of the price and by implication incomes in professional team sports. Third, we reconsider the assumption of independent preferences. Fourth, we introduce the notion that the demand for a given game may depend upon the 'quality characteristics' of the game as perceived by the potential spectator. Fifth, we reconsider whether the consumer's tastes are 'given' and in particular whether they are independent of their previous consumption patterns.

Measuring quantity

If demand for a game or a season's games by team X is purely for live attendance the number of tickets sold might be a suitable measure. However this treats as identical the experiences of the standing spectator, the seated season ticket holder and the corporate client entertained in the firm's own 'box'. The researcher may attempt to produce a quality-weighted measure of attendance in response to this problem. Even so, attendance data should not be used uncritically. Events like the Super Bowl or the UEFA Cup Final or games between local rivals can generate so much demand that stadia are sold out. Attendance data for such matches measure supply – not demand. Most of the published studies of live attendance familiar to the authors either ignore or pay lip service to this problem.

A related question is how to treat demand for sport on TV and in the press. One cannot add 45,000 live spectators to 3.4 million viewers to get a match audience of 3.445 million. The two experiences are radically different. A separate treatment is required – but one which recognises the interdependence of the products. Most of the empirical work on live attendance has simply ignored TV – which is clearly the best substitute. Also problematic is how to handle a range of demands for goods, which are complementary to live attendance. Travel, refreshments, consumption of other (e.g. newspaper) media sport news, 'merchandising' by the clubs themselves, which can raise more revenue than ticket sales, are examples. It is not clear that all these forms of demand are purely complements to spectating; in the case of travel for example the journey may itself give utility so that it is more a joint product with attendance than a complement to attendance. Furthermore, the existence of these forms of demand indicates that the consumption of a sport is not limited to periods of play. Professional team sport is, in this respect, a consumer durable.

Measuring price and income

The price of a team shirt or a stadium ticket is readily observed but the price of attendance is not. It includes travel cost, which will vary from match to match for any given spectator and on any given occasion between spectators dependent on modes of travel and distances. More subtly one ought to include the spectator's opportunity cost of time spent in travel and attendance, which even the spectator can hardly compute with accuracy. The researcher might use a measure of average real after-tax hourly earnings times hours spent as a crude index of the 'average' spectator's time cost of attendance at a given game. If however spectators actually enjoy the journey, or if it is made partly for other purposes, e.g. to visit family, this procedure is liable to over-estimate the time cost.

It also indicates that attempts to measure spectators' incomes can also be relatively crude. Some average measure of real wages or real disposable income is invariably used.

Interdependent preferences

The assumption that consumers have independent preferences can be seen as problematic in professional team sports. There is the suggestion of the operation of 'bandwagon' effects (Leibenstein, 1950), whereby the consumer's demand for a given product depends not only upon prices and income, but also on the extent to which it is demanded by other consumers. The consumer gets utility from others' consumption of the product. In the presence of bandwagon effects the demand for the product will always be more price elastic than the income and substitution effects by themselves would suggest.

To see why, assume that the individual consumer's demand for commodity A responds directly to the quantity demanded by other consumers, the implicit assumption being that the consumer is able to detect changes in other consumers' demand. This is not unrealistic; apart from attendance data in newspaper reports, one might observe more filled seats at home games or more cars parked in the neighbourhood on match days. Following a price cut, the representative consumer buys more than previously (this is where the basic model stops). The rise in attendance does not cease at that point; observing the initial growth in attendance, fresh individuals join the bandwagon – assuming supply is available – further stimulating demand. To avoid 'runaway' behaviour it is clearly necessary to assume that the marginal effect of observing others' consumption diminishes as total sales increase.

Quality characteristics

As discussed earlier, attempts to measure consumer tastes have involved the attempt to measure quality characteristics. Attempting to measure the response of spectator demand to prices and income without taking systematic (predictable) quality variations into account (what economists call 'specification error') may lead to biased estimates of the price and income coefficients or elasticities. The literature can be understood as following Court (1939) in treating physically non-homogeneous goods as delivering (in varying combinations) amounts of a fairly homogeneous set of 'quality characteristics' and Lancaster (1966) in asserting that 'utility' derives from the characteristics rather than directly from the goods.

A given league's matches in themselves are arguably too non-homogeneous to let the investigator treat the teams involved as competitors in a single market. Viewed as rival providers (in varying amounts) of a standard set of characteristics, the teams may be seen as operating in the same product market. One would not necessarily assume that a minor league baseball game offers the identical set of characteristics as a World Series game offers, any more than a Ford Escort and a Ferrari do. There are limits to the degree to which it makes sense to aggregate markets. However, it may make more sense to treat all the games in a particular league and season *as if* they represent varying combinations of a common set of quality attributes rather than as if they are perfect substitutes.

The economist seeks to identify the most important quality characteristics and to estimate their effects on demand. The first problem is to define a set of characteristics; as implied earlier most writers identify team or player characteristics, entertainment and uncertainty of outcome as the essential qualities. The second problem is how to obtain measures of these quality attributes; Chapters 6 and 7 survey attempts to do this.

Habit persistence

It is conceivable that the individuals' preferences for professional team sports are embedded in loyalties to the local or national team, or to the team with which one's family and friends are identified. Supporters appear to display habit persistence. Researchers into the product market have attempted (see Chapter 6) to capture habit persistence by the addition of lagged attendance to the demand function. The estimated coefficient on past attendance is interpreted as an indicator of habit persistence; Borland (1987), Dobson and Goddard (1995) and Simmons (1996) exemplify this approach.

Borland (op. cit.) recognises that there is an 'identification problem' here. The identification problem arises in econometrics when trying to establish the economic relationship presented in the data. A simple example occurs when, say, the researcher has data on the prices and quantities. Using regression analysis to estimate a line of best fit between the data could in principle measure both supply and demand. One cannot simply presume that, say, demand has been 'identified'. In this context, Borland (op. cit.) argues that lagged attendance might also pick up (ticket) price expectations formation and lagged adjustment by spectators rather than habit persistence. He dismisses these possibilities, however, on the bases that ticket prices are set in advance and not subject to short-run change, and that there do not appear to be significant costs in adjusting attendance behaviour respectively. The former argument is more persuasive (although the ticket price is only a portion of the price of attendance) than the latter. First, the relative preponderance of season ticket buying implies significant short-run adjustment cost for today's supporters. Second, the regulars who buy match tickets on the day are effectively buying a consumer durable ('the season') on a game-by-game instalment plan, which suggests that there are significant adjustment costs (not wholly pecuniary) even to the non-season ticket holder. This is hardly a novel concept – Neale's (1964) 'fourth estate benefit' recognises that the consumption of professional team sports as an activity is not limited to attendance. We must not confuse consumption activity with consumption expenditure. As an illustration of the problems associated with this issue the technically minded reader should examine the appendix to this chapter.

Case study: Scottish professional football and the uncertainty of outcome hypothesis

Having discussed some of the theoretical end empirical issues associated with applied economic research in the professional team-sport context, we illustrate the application of econometrics to the economics of professional team sports. This is undertaken by examining Nick Jennett's (1984) paper, 'Attendances, uncertainty of outcome and policy in Scottish league football', published in the *Scottish Journal of Political Economy*.[3] Although the research is now somewhat dated, the paper is well worth reading because it employs a widely cited and discussed measure of short-run uncertainty of outcome, as we discuss in Chapter 7. The paper also illustrates how the standard model of demand in economics is extended to professional team sports. The context of the paper was the declining trend in attendance at Scottish association football fixtures in the post-war period, a phenomenon experienced by association football in general until recent years.

Jennett took data from 1080 Scottish Premier Division games from the 1975/76 to the 1980/81 seasons to produce a pooled data-set.[4] It comprises a cross-section element of each week's fixtures, and time-series elements associated with the progression of a particular season and the progression of each season. Jennett hypothesised the following variables as important causes of attendance at Scottish football fixtures. The abbreviated variable names are in brackets.

As with any economic study, the first two variables we would expect to see are prices and incomes. Jennett includes price (*PRICE*). This is defined as the minimum adult admission price at fixtures. Income, however, is not measured directly. The variables that Jennett uses to proxy income are the population of the city of the home club (*HPOP*), unemployment rates in the home and away areas (*URATEH, URATEA*) and male unemployment in the areas (*MALEUNEM*). This illustrates some of the problems in measuring variables in practice in the absence of experimental conditions. *HPOP* is really a measure of market size regardless of individual sports consumers' incomes. Likewise the unemployment measures, while clearly related to income, could also measure more sociological factors underpinning demand, such as a need for a community identity associated with attendance at fixtures, than simply income. In addition Jennett also includes a variable that measures the propensity of away fans to travel to fixtures (*POPMIL*). This was calculated

---

[3] With due deference to Neale, as Europeans, or at least an Englishman and a Scot, we refer to association football rather than 'soccer'. We are, of course, mindful of Neale's (1964) accusation that '. . . soccer (mistakenly called football by literally minded foreigners) . . .' may be the more appropriate name. Hence we do not simply use the term 'football'.

[4] For the technically minded reader, Jennett did not employ any panel-data techniques such as exploring for the possibility of fixed or random effects. This might undermine the reliability of some of his results. The next chapter discusses some of these issues further.

by dividing the away team's local population by the distance between the cities in which the fixture took place. Because it includes travel costs it is clear that this variable is also likely to be associated with the economic price of attending matches. As noted previously, therefore, it is likely that the study suffers from a degree of multicollinearity, although Jennett, along with researchers generally in the economics of professional team sports as discussed in the next chapter, never refers to this.

The main sporting or taste variables that Jennett includes in his analysis are, as the title of his research indicates, the championship significance of home and away fixtures (*HSIG, ASIG*) and the relegation significance of fixtures (*RELSIG*). These variables are used to try to assess the uncertainty of outcome within seasons. Closer competition both to win the championship and to avoid relegation would imply greater uncertainty of outcome. These variables were calculated by taking each fixture in turn and:

> . . . on an *ex-post* basis the number of points required to win the Premier Division championship was observed for each season. From this the *ex ante* significance of each game was established. For example, in season 1979/80 49 points would have been required to beat Aberdeen to the championship. At the start of the season this implies a common significance score of 0.02. By 1 December, after 16 games, it was no longer possible for Hibernian (subsequently relegated) to obtain 49 points and so the remaining games took a significance score of zero . . . Celtic, Aberdeen's nearest challengers, remained in contention until 23 April when they lost a vital game with a significance score of 0.143 at home to Aberdeen. Aberdeen secured the title in the final game of the season, requiring just one point. This game took a significance score of one.
>
> (Jennett, 1984, p. 185)

And:

> Based on an *ex post* assessment of the number of championship points required to avoid relegation from the Premier Division, this variable . . . takes a positive value based on the reciprocal of the number of games remaining for clubs whenever they are out of contention for the championship title, but are not yet secure from relegation.
>
> (Jennett, 1984, p. 186)

The uncertainty of outcome hypothesis thus suggests that the longer the struggle to win the championship or avoid relegation, the higher attendance will be at fixtures.

Jennett also included dummy variables in his analysis. *CHAMP* was assigned to take a value of 1 in any fixture in which the home side had already won the championship and 0 otherwise. It is designed to capture the 'glory' of success. Likewise, *RELEG* is assigned a value of 1 in any home fixture in which

Table 5.1 A model of attendances at Scottish league football: pooled match data
1975–81

Variable	Estimated coefficient value	Estimated standard error of coefficient
Constant	9889	Not given
PRICE	−141.49	85.026
HSIG	13105.08*	2298.95
ASIG	7595.73*	1786.65
POPMIL	0.2643*	0.0098
HPOP	0.04922*	0.00152
SEASON	646.38	353.09
URATEH	−170.58*	65.75
URATEA	−237.159*	64.16
CHAMP	6741.76*	3127.19
RELSIG	−8262.63	5658.2
RELEG	−3476.65*	844.11
Other statistics	Value	
R^2	0.69	
DW	1.54	

a side has already been relegated and 0 otherwise. It is intended to capture a
despair factor. Finally, because of the underlying declining trend in attendance
at football games, Jennett included a trend variable (*SEASON*). As a modified
dummy variable, this involves assigning a value of 1 to the variable in the first
season, 2 for the second season, 3 for the third season, and so on.

Jennett's regression model can thus be summarised as

$$A_{it} = \beta_1 + \beta_2 PRICE_{it} + \beta_3 HPOP_{it} + \beta_4 URATEH_{it}$$
$$+ \beta_5 URATEA + \beta_6 POPMIL_{it} + \beta_7 HSIG_{it} + \beta_8 ASIG_{it}$$
$$+ \beta_9 CHAMP_{it} + \beta_{10} RELSIG_{it} + \beta_{11} RELEG_{it}$$
$$+ \beta_{12} SEASON_{it}, \tag{5.13}$$

where *A* is attendance and the index of observation implies that the data is
pooled over the *i*th fixture and the *t*th season. Table 5.1 reports Jennett's results.

From a statistical point of view, significant coefficients are marked with an
asterisk. They are significant because their *t*-ratios are greater than 2 in
absolute terms as detailed earlier in the chapter. Note that the *t*-ratio can be
calculated by dividing the coefficient value by the standard error of the
coefficient under the respective null hypothesis. So, in the case of *HSIG*,
the coefficient value of 13105.08 for β_7 divided by the standard error of the
coefficient 2298.95 is equal to 5.7. This value allows Jennett to reject the null
hypothesis that β_7 is equal to zero with approximately a 5% chance of doing
this in error. Rejecting the hypothesis that the coefficient is equal to zero thus
implies that the coefficient value, although different from zero, is not the result
of chance alone. Along with *HSIG, ASIG, POPMIL, HPOP, URATEH,*

URATEA, CHAMP and *RELEG* are shown to be significantly associated with attendance. Under the maintained hypothesis that these factors are determinants of demand, one can argue that these are the significant *causes* of demand for football. Because the theory of demand is a general theory, one can also suggest that one should expect to see similar results apply to the demand for all professional team sports. As will be seen in the next chapter, however, this is not generally speaking the case. The presumption is, therefore that the results are rather more specific than the statistics and theory imply.

In more general terms, the results imply that the significant economic factors determining attendance are associated with income. This is because the result on price is insignificant. However, two factors caution against ruling out the impact of price on attendance. In the first instance, as noted above, there are measurement problems associated with attempting to capture the full economic price. Second, the variable *POPMIL* explicitly controls away the influence of one aspect of the full economic price of attending matches (why?).[5]

Nonetheless, while the results on the other economic variables are statistically significant, their economic effects are small. For example, the coefficient on *HPOP* implies that 1000 extra people in the vicinity of a club would, on average for the club over the time period, and assuming other factors remained constant, produce 49 extra spectators.[6] Similarly 1% rises in the home team and away team's unemployment rates would reduce support by approximately 171 and 237 spectators.

In contrast the *HSIG* and *ASIG* variables show a much more pronounced effect. If home matches remain significant in terms of winning the championship, approximately 13105 spectators are attracted to matches. In away games the support attracted is approximately 7596 spectators. While *RELSIG* is insignificant, these results suggest that sporting competition in pursuit of the championship is economically important in attracting spectators.

As far as the dummy variables are concerned, the insignificance of *SEASON* suggests that the temporal decline in attendance is captured in the behaviour of the other variables. The coefficient on *CHAMP* implies that approximately 6742 spectators are attracted because of the glory of winning the championship. The coefficient on *RELEG* implies that approximately 3477 fans are lost upon relegation.

The R^2 value for Jennett's results is 0.69. This suggests that the variables account for 69% of the variation in attendance around its mean value over the

---

5 Because each observation on away population is divided by the distance between clubs, this captures an element of travel costs and influences the away club's population in deciding to travel to the game.

6 When interpreting a (partial) slope coefficient, one should always remember that they measure average effects assuming other factors are constant. This qualification is not made explicit on the remaining comments to avoid needless repetition.

sample of data. While R^2s can vary between zero and one, in practice they tend not to and are usually low with cross-section data and very high with time-series data. This value would thus be indicative of a 'good fit' with pooled data. In turn, as a simple test for serial correlation a value of the *DW* statistic close to 2 is seen as acceptable. The value reported is some way off 2 but, as Jennett notes:

> It is obviously important to be aware of the potential hazards of serial correlation is time-series work, but here there is in effect a combination of time-series and cross-section data. Given this 'hybrid' nature of the data set, it is not clear that much can be inferred from the DW statistic.
>
> (Jennett, 1984, p. 188)

The results of this study raise a number of interesting empirical issues. They suggest that the standard economic approach to understanding demand has some relevance to the study of professional team sports. Moreover, the results suggest that more unique sporting factors associated with spectators tastes, such as the uncertainty of outcome hypothesis, are particularly significant.

Conclusions

In this chapter we began a more detailed exploration of the demand for professional team sports. Both the underlying economic theory of demand and central features of the statistical methods employed by economists to measure the demand for professional team sports, and other economic relationships, have been outlined. Some conceptual issues associated with the modelling and measurement of the demand for professional team sports are also discussed. This material has been illustrated with reference to an investigation into the demand for Scottish Association Football. In the next chapter this empirical understanding is further refined in an evaluation of the demand literature more generally.

Appendix 5.1: Problems of measuring habit persistence

This appendix, though not necessarily representing precisely how particular authors arrived at their models of demand, illustrates some problems that arise in the interpretation of habit persistence.

Consistent with the discussion of the chapter, in a simple case we might specify a linear demand for attendance as (5.1.1),

$$A_t = a_1 + a_2 P_t + a_3 A_{t-1}. \tag{5.1.1}$$

Here, A is the level of home game attendance (perhaps by club by season), P is a measure (possibly ticket revenue divided by attendance) of price, and the subscripts date observations. The parameters a_1, a_2 ($a_2 < 0$) and a_3 ($0 < a_3 < 1$) are to be estimated by some regression procedure. One might conceive a_1 as the home team's 'base level' support, a_2 as the slope of the demand curve and a_3 as the rate at which current attendance responds to a unit change in the previous home attendance – a loosely defined index of habit persistence. Subscript t denotes the period, hence period $t - 1$ precedes period t immediately. The interval between home matches is the interval between period t and its neighbour. (5.1.1) has been simplified by excluding income and other possible influences in order to highlight the issues involved in modelling habit persistence. At first glance it seems an odd specification of habit persistence to ignore all but one past consumption level.

(5.1.1) is consistent with the partial adjustment and adaptive (backward-looking) expectations models applied by Koyck (1954) and others to modelling investment, consumption, wheat supply and inflation expectations, among other things. While sluggish adjustment to price change might be consistent with habit persistence, we shall demonstrate that it is not so if (5.1.1) is the demand function. At this point, a little mathematics will materially assist the exposition. Suppose that the economic structure underlying (5.1.1) has been and currently remains in force. It follows that by analogy a set of equations associated with previous time periods can be written as indicated in (5.1.2–5.1.4):

$$A_{t-1} = a_1 + a_2 P_{t-1} + a_3 A_{t-2} \tag{5.1.2}$$

$$A_{t-2} = a_1 + a_2 P_{t-2} + a_3 A_{t-3} \tag{5.1.3}$$

$$A_{t-N} = a_1 + a_2 P_{t-N} + a_3 A_{t-N-1}. \tag{5.1.4}$$

Based on these equations one can apply successive backward substitution to remove past attendance levels from the right-hand side (hereinafter RHS) of (5.1.1) in order to discover what actually drives attendance other than the current price. We start by substituting (5.1.2) into (5.1.1) to remove A_{t-1}. This leaves

$$\begin{aligned} A_t &= a_1 + a_2 P_t + a_3 A_{t-1} \\ &= a_1 + a_2 P_t + a_3(a_1 + a_2 P_{t-1} + a_3 A_{t-2}) \\ &= a_1(1 + a_3) + a_2(P_t + a_3 P_{t-1}) + a_3^2 A_{t-2}. \end{aligned} \tag{5.1.5}$$

This transformation introduces A_{t-2} but we can remove this by substituting (5.1.3). Doing this leaves

$$A_t = a_1(1 + a_3) + a_2(P_t + a_3 P_{t-1}) + a_3^2(a_1 + a_2 P_{t-2} + a_3 A_{t-3}). \tag{5.1.6}$$

We gather terms (which helps us see the emerging pattern clearly) and thus come to

$$A_t = a_1(1 + a_3 + a_3{}^2) + a_2(P_t + a_3P_{t-1} + a_3{}^2P_{t-2}) + a_3{}^3A_{t-3}, \qquad (5.1.7)$$

which after further substitutions resolves into

$$\begin{aligned} A_t = {} &a_1(1 + a_3 + a_3{}^2 \ldots + a_3{}^{N-1}) + a_2(P_t + a_3P_{t-1} \\ &+ a_3{}^2P_{t-2} \ldots + a_3{}^{N-1}P_{t-N+1}) + a_3{}^NA_{t-N}. \end{aligned} \qquad (5.1.8)$$

(5.1.8) states that today's attendance is a geometrically weighted distributed lag function of price. In terms of the model represented by (5.1.1), A_t depends not on P_t alone but on the whole history of prices. For a_3 close to zero the current price dominates past prices in determining attendance but if a_3 is close to one, the influence of past prices tends to dominate. The importance of any given price declines geometrically as time passes, the 'weights' being a_2 multiplied successively by 1, a_3, $a_3{}^2$, $a_3{}^3$, $a_3{}^4$, etc.

Unfortunately (5.1.8) is not consistent with habit persistence, and the very last RHS term shows why. Since as N goes to infinity, $a_3{}^N$ goes to zero, past attendance (A_{t-N}) plays no role whatsoever in determining current attendance A_t. In a supposed habit persistence model we find past attendance insignificant. What we actually have is a partial adjustment model with a_3 determining the speed with which attendance responds to price change. Contrary to what one might naively imagine, the long-run decline in attendance following a price rise is actually greater when a_3 is close to 1 than when it is close to 0. To see why, assume the market for home games to be in static (no change) equilibrium. Denote the equilibrium price and quantity as P^e and A^e respectively. Put these values into (5.1.1) and call it (5.1.9),

$$\begin{aligned} A^e &= a_1 + a_2 P^e + a_3A^e \\ \Rightarrow A^e &= [a_1/(1 - a_3)] + [a_2/(1 - a_3)] P^e. \end{aligned} \qquad (5.1.9)$$

The simplification is possible because the static equilibrium value of attendance is the same at time t as at time $t - 1$. Hence the implication that the long-term rate of response of attendance to a unit price change is $a_2/(1 - a_3)$ which is greater the larger is a_3.

The thought underlying (5.1.1) confuses two separate processes: habit formation and adjustment to price change. Parameter a_3 may be naively expected to pick up the first but in fact picks up the second. To make sense of habit persistence we need a model that allows both processes to occur and enables us to estimate their speeds.

We now consider the habit persistence model due to Brown (1952), used by Borland (1987) and by Simmons (1996) to justify the inclusion of the lagged dependent variable in their regressions. Our aim is to investigate the implications of incorporating partial adjustment in this model. Attendance at time t depends linearly (*inter alia*) on the 'stock' of habits (H_t) for the team's home games. The rate of change (ΔH) of the habit stock at time ($t - 1$) is a linear function of current attendance and of the previous level of the stock:

$$\Delta H_t = A_{t-1} + (h - 1)H_{t-1} \ (0 < h < 1), \tag{5.1.10}$$

implying

$$H_t = A_{t-1} + hA_{t-2} + h^2A_{t-3} + \ldots \tag{5.1.11}$$

and further that in 'the long run' H is proportional to A, the proportion being $1/(1 - h)$. (5.1.10) specifies net investment in habits; current gross investment is given by the previous attendance level *minus* depreciation of the stock of habits. Depreciation is simply the negative of the habit decay rate $(1 - h)$ times the lagged stock H_{t-1}.

The demand function becomes

$$A^*_t = a_1 + a_2P_t + a_3H_t, \tag{5.1.12}$$

where A^* denotes the (unobserved) equilibrium attendance level. We assume partial adjustment of actual to equilibrium attendance in any period, the process being defined by:

$$\Delta A_t = g(A^*_t - A_{t-1}), \tag{5.1.13}$$

where $g(0 < g < 1)$ defines the proportion of the adjustment completed in any single period. Substitute (5.1.12) into (5.1.13) to obtain an expression for A_t which does not include the unobserved A^*_t:

$$A_t = ga_1 + ga_2P_t + (1 - g)A_{t-1} + ga_3H_t. \tag{5.1.14}$$

This cannot be estimated as it stands since H is never observed. Substitute (5.1.11) into (5.1.14) to remove H and we arrive at:

$$\begin{aligned} A_t = {} & ga_1 + ga_2P_t + (1 - g)A_{t-1} \\ & + ga_3(A_{t-1} + hA_{t-2} + h^2A_{t-3} + \ldots), \end{aligned} \tag{5.1.15}$$

which has an infinity of RHS terms. To obtain an equation that one might estimate, apply the Koyck transformation to (5.1.15) to get to:

$$\begin{aligned} A_t = {} & (1 - h)ga_1 + ga_2P_t - hga_2P_{t-1} + [(1 - g) + ga_3 + h]A_{t-1} \\ & - h(1 - g)A_{t-2}, \end{aligned} \tag{5.1.16}$$

from which it is clear that two lags in attendance and one in price are required if both habit persistence and partial adjustment are to feature in the model.

(5.1.16) contains five behavioural parameters (the a_i, g and h) and five reduced form parameters, hence identification may be obtained. It is clear that estimates of the reduced form coefficients on A_{t-1} and A_{t-2} carry no significance for the extent of habit persistence. The former compounds the rate of habit formation, the rate of partial adjustment and the short-term (instantaneous) response of attendance to the habit stock. The latter compounds the rates of habit formation and of partial adjustment.

A slightly simpler version of (5.1.16) results if there is complete adjustment within the period ($g = 1$),

$$A_t = (1 - h)a_1 + a_2 P_t - ha_2 P_{t-1} + [a_3 + h]A_{t-1}. \tag{5.1.17}$$

This corresponds to habit persistence without partial adjustment. The double lag in attendance drops out, but unlike (5.1.1) there is one lag in price. The reduced form coefficient on lagged attendance compounds both habit persistence (h) and the instantaneous effect (a_3) on attendance of a unit change in the habit stock. (5.1.17) (habit persistence alone) has four behavioural parameters (the a_i and h) and four reduced form parameters and so may be identified. Both (5.1.1) and (5.1.17) are nested within (5.1.16), so potentially one might hope to reject two of the implied models.

Estimating the structural model may be of more than academic interest. Imagine a team owner who has been advised on the basis of estimates of the reduced form parameters of (5.1.16) that there is strong evidence of long-running 'loyalty' to the team and therefore supporters will not react greatly if the price is raised. The owner needs to be informed how the long-run responsiveness of attendance to prices is determined. Fortunately the answer is easily determined; simply find the equilibrium solution to (5.1.16) by plugging in the equilibrium values (denoted by superscript e) of price and attendance, which we proceed to simplify to find the answer

$$A^e = (1 - h)ga_1 + ga_2 P^e - hga_2 P^e + [(1 - g) + ga_3 + h]A^e - h(1 - g)A^e$$

$$\Rightarrow A^e = ga_1(1 - h) + ga_2(1 - h)P^e + [(1 - g) + ga_3 + h - h(1 - g)]A^e$$

$$\Rightarrow A^e[1 - (1 - g) - ga_3 - h + h - gh] = ga_1(1 - h) + ga_2(1 - h)P^e$$

$$\Rightarrow A_e[g - ga_3 - gh] = ga_1(1 - h) + ga_2(1 - h)P^e, \tag{5.1.18}$$

after more simplification (g factors out) and rearrangement we get the long run solution

$$A^e = a_1(1 - h)/(1 - a_3 - h) + a_2(1 - h)/(1 - a_3 - h)P^e. \tag{5.1.19}$$

It is clear that the long run response of attendance to a unit price increase can be inferred from the reduced form coefficient of lagged attendance in a regression like (5.1.16). However, nothing can be inferred about the process whereby that response is determined unless some underlying structure is hypothesised. To any given long run response $[a_2(1 - h)/(1 - a_3 - h)]$ corresponds (taking a_2 as given) an infinite number of combinations of h and a_3. The more rapidly habits decay (small h, large a_3), the greater will be the long-run sensitivity of attendance to price. Slower habit decay (large h and small a_3) implies less long run sensitivity to price.

The moral is that we cannot presume to pick up the effects of habit persistence by simply adding lagged values of attendance to demand equations. At worst (5.1.1) the investigator is estimating the reduced form of a partial adjustment model with no habit persistence effect. At best (5.1.17), the coefficient of the lagged dependent variable is a reduced form coefficient from which it is still necessary to disentangle the habit decay $(1 - h)$ and habit impact (a_3) parameters. More likely the investigator is looking at a model which should incorporate partial adjustment and habit persistence (5.1.16) and the coefficient on lagged attendance is a combination of three parameters.

Discussion questions

1. How do economists approach the problem of understanding the demand for professional team sports?
2. What factors do economists take into account in estimating the demand for professional team sports?
3. Carefully consider how an economist would define the demand for a soccer game. How would they define the supply? Why would games such as the FA Cup Final pose additional problems to the researcher?
4. How would you define the price of attendance at a professional sporting encounter?
5. Assume you are interested in estimating the cross-price elasticity of demand for a professional spectator sport. How would you observe the price of a close substitute?
6. How would you measure the 'quality' of an encounter? Bear in mind that what you need to know is not what YOU think of it *ex post*, but how the potential spectator views it *ex ante*.
7. Carefully interpret the reported least squares regressions by Jennett. Do they lend support (in terms of coefficients' signs, magnitudes, partial and overall significance) to his maintained hypotheses?
8. What do these results suggest about the view that football spectating is an inferior good?

6 Traditional findings and new developments

Introduction

The last published survey of the demand for professional team sports was undertaken at least a decade ago by Cairns (1990), as an extension of Cairns *et al.* (1986). His survey work is critically extended in this chapter as a means of producing a clearer understanding of the determinants of demand at professional team sport events. In the next section of the chapter, it is argued that the existing literature has suffered from a short run and aggregate emphasis which has tended to overstate the importance of sporting factors in determining attendance. The main results of this literature are critically outlined and extended with reference to some widely cited recent papers. Recent developments in demand estimates for the long run are then discussed.

Conclusions are drawn from an assessment of the diversity of results discussed. It is argued that the findings of more recent long-run studies should be emphasised because of their more appropriate econometric methodology, and because they reflect a changed emphasis from aggregating or averaging results across clubs over short time periods. The chapter argues that a new research agenda is required in demand studies, that allows researchers to explore both the long run and short run determinants of demand simultaneously, of both a sporting and economic character. Moreover, regressions should avoid averaging over clubs. The cost of this approach is the time and expense of the researcher in constructing a data-set. The benefit would be results that are of more use to the sporting commentator and regulator than are currently available.

The traditional emphasis of demand studies

While the underlying nature of the demand for professional team sports is an integral part of analyses of sporting leagues, as discussed in Chapter 4, and indeed sporting labour markets, which are discussed in Chapters 9 and 10, the treatment of the determinants of demand in these areas is of secondary importance. Consequently, the demand studies that are reviewed in this chapter are those that are, '. . . somewhat more valuable . . . [as] . . . fully fledged investigations of the nature of the demand function' (Cairns *et al.*, 1986, p. 13).

As an extension of this work, Cairns (1990), surveys 22 articles covering 7 sports. Cairns' survey raises two issues of importance. The first is econometric and the second concerns the scope of the studies. As far as the first issue is concerned, as implied in Chapter 5, the basic framework of analysis employed in many of the studies is that attendance at sporting fixtures is treated as a proxy for demand and this is then regressed upon various assumed causal factors. These typically include economic factors, such as market size, income and prices and sporting factors, such as uncertainty of outcome, team and player quality, weather conditions, the scheduling of fixtures and TV coverage of fixtures. Primarily, rather elementary applications of OLS are employed. Econometric discussion qualifying the importance of the results is thus required. This is presented below in a discussion of the literature and particularly in the context of some of the more recent studies of demand.

The second issue concerns the scope of the studies. Association football and baseball are the sports most often covered by researchers. Six out of the seven UK studies reviewed by Cairns (1990) refer to association football. Six out of the eleven US studies refer to baseball. The other studies are from elsewhere and cover other sports. The dominance of association football and baseball presumably reflects both intrinsic interest and access to data. In the UK association football is by far the largest spectator team sport. Association football archives are available and more widely accessible than in other sports (one of the author's own interest and experience in collecting data on rugby league stands in marked contrast). In the US, baseball has figured in the earliest work on professional team sports, for example Rottenerg (1956), and is renowned for its statistical data.

Despite these factors, however, of the twenty-two studies surveyed by Cairns, seventeen involve pooled time-series and cross-section data. The vast majority of studies are based on time periods of less than ten seasons. Indeed eight of the studies cover only a single season. While Cairns bases his conclusions upon these studies, it is clear that the longitudinal aspects of demand have not been particularly well researched. It follows that the impact of socio-economic factors influencing demand may be understated. In addition, in essentially cross-section work, results are averaged across clubs. This produces results that are deemed to be typical for leagues. However, heterogeneity between clubs has not been investigated, which could mean the results are misleading. For example, as discussed in Chapter 4, a stylisation of professional sports leagues is their historical domination by a few large clubs in both the US and the UK (Dobson and Goddard, 1995; Fort and Quirk, 1995). In short, therefore, there is a short run and aggregate/average bias to the literature. While these issues have recently begun to be addressed, which will be examined later in the chapter, for now the main results of Cairns' (1990) survey are examined and updated. In reviewing the literature on the impact of the economic and sporting factors on attendance, a disconcerting feature of the literature is that many of the recent studies reinforce the traditional emphases.

Major findings in the literature: sporting versus economic determinants of demand

Market size

Cairns (1990, p. 5) begins by considering the role of market size. He concludes: 'When included market size is invariably an important determinant of demand, despite the problems of multi-team cities and the aggregate nature of the measures adopted'.

A variety of variables have been used to proxy population in the catchment area. For example, Geddert and Semple (1985) used standard metropolitan statistical areas; Hart *et al.* (1975) use total male population; Jennett (1984) makes use of local authority data; while Dobson and Goddard (1995) make use of census data on population for the city in which the club is located. While Cairns does not fully discuss the rationale for the inclusion of this variable, one can identify two reasons. The first reflects trying to measure the catchment area of support *per se*. Market size would be of relevance, for example, in studies that attempt to measure attendance across a cross-section of clubs. It may also be of relevance in a time-series study over a time-scale in which demographics change. It is also clear that in this context this variable may also proxy local income. The second reason for introducing the variable could be allied to issues of policy in sports league management and, particularly, the cross-subsidisation of clubs as discussed earlier.

Of the more recent studies, Wilson and Sim (1995) explore the determinants of attendance at semi-professional soccer in Malaysia. They include a measure of population of the major urban area in the home team states based on housing and census data. They also echo Jennett (1984), in using a variable measuring away team market size. This is calculated by deflating away-team population by the distance in miles between the teams. They suggest that the costs of travel must be taken account of explicitly. Based on a panel-data set of 399 games over three seasons, OLS estimates are derived. In additition, regression models based on OLS, but specifically developed to analyse panel-data such as fixed-effects and error-components estimators are employed. The first of these is discussed in more detail later in the chapter. The results imply that home market size has significant and strong positive impacts on attendance. There are significant but small impacts of away team market size on attendance.

Similarly, Baimbridge *et al.* (1995; 1996) explore the determinants of attendance in the first division of rugby league and the Premier League in association football in the season 1993/1994 using a semi-logarithmic specification. This implies that the log of attendance was regressed on the explanatory variables, with these measured in original units. In the case of rugby league, population divided by average attendance is used to measure market size. In the case of soccer, based on census data, the home team's population is included as well as the away team's average support (based on when they play at home) divided by the distance between the clubs. In both of these cases the market size variables are significant.

Hynds and Smith (1994) explore the demand for test match cricket in Britain between 1984 and 1992. While there is no intrinsic home 'population' for a test match, which is an international contest, nonetheless they include dummy variables associated with the venues. As they argue:

> . . . test match attendance varies greatly by venue and opposition. With regard to location, there are six test-match grounds, *viz.* Edgbaston (Birmingham), Trent Bridge (Nottingham), Old Trafford (Manchester), Headingley (Leeds), the Oval and Lords (both London). Demand variation by venue will reflect both the size of the catchment population, the attractiveness of the Stadium, and local interest in live international cricket . . . Since there are large ethnic populations in Britain's major cities, interaction dummies are also constructed by venue for Pakistan, India and the West Indies. For these opponents it is expected that the existence of large communities with corresponding ethnic origins will augment attendances.
>
> (pp. 2–3)

Baimbridge (1997) provides an interesting extension to this international work. His study explored match attendance at 'Euro '96' – a four-yearly association football tournament for national sides in Europe which took place in the UK in 1996. Functions for both actual match attendance as well as the proportion of stadium capacity filled were estimated. This latter dependent variable was utilised' . . . as the tournament only revolved around eight football grounds including the national stadium in London' (p. 555).

To measure the size of 'home' and 'away' team support in this instance, in which essentially all matches took place in a different country, Baimbridge models the former by taking a measure of foreign nationals in the UK. In the latter case support is measured by taking the away team's national population and dividing it by the distance from the capital to London. This measure is then averaged for each match. In general the results for market size are insignificant with the exception of the coefficient on home support in the capacity equation. This, however, has the wrong (negative) sign. These results would seem to suggest that either the proxies are wrong or there is a degree of uniqueness to such a tournament. In contrast, in one of the most sophisticated studies of match attendance, further discussed below, Dobson and Goddard (1995) find that population is a significant determinant of attendance. In summary, it appears that local population remains a ubiquitous influence on attendance, though the reasons advanced as to why this is the case remain varied.

Econometric issues

One of the primary concerns for Cairns (1990) in discussing market size is econometric. Market size could well be a source of heteroscedasticity in cross-section work, the presence of which, as discussed in Chapter 5, could lead to inconsistent estimates of OLS coefficients. Moreover, Cairns is concerned about the interaction between the variables on the right-hand side of regressions, for example between market size and, say, the effect of performance on attracting support. This breaks one of the assumptions of the classical linear regression, that the causal variables are independent of one another. Multicollinearity can occur. Likewise if some of the independent variables are themselves determined in part by attendance, then simultaneous equation bias may result (an issue that is of significance in our discussion of the sporting labour market in Chapter 9). These concerns, which are to an extent related, are now discussed in turn.

Cairn's concern about heteroscedasticity, as stated, is much too specifically focused. Heteroscedasticity should be a general concern to those working with cross-section data. Indeed a general form of adjusting the standard errors of estimates to produce more robust, i.e. consistent, *t*-ratios on which to base statistical inferences, White's adjusted standard errors, have now become a standard feature in econometric work elsewhere. With regard to the demand for professional team sports, the recent work of Hynds and Smith (1994), Dobson and Goddard (1995), Wilson and Sim (1995), Baimbridge *et al.* (1996), Baimbridge (1997) and Peel and Thomas (1997) allow for heteroscedasticity.

A sophisticated example of this is Kuypers (1996), who allows for the possibility of groupwise heteroscedasticity/autocorrelation in estimates of a pooled data set of twenty-two Premier League association football clubs over twenty-one home games. Moreover, his analysis explicitly accounts for the fact that 10% of matches were sell-out fixtures in a 'tobit' model. This is a model which explicitly allows for the fact that observations on the dependent variable, attendance in this case, may not follow a normal distribution but in contrast reflect a truncated distribution. This issue is one that remains a subject for further, less superficial, treatment. Wilson and Sim (1995) note the potential problem, but offer that the matter cannot be easily dealt with in their panel-data set. Even in the sophisticated studies of, for example, Dobson and Goddard (1995) and Simmons (1996), the standard attempt to control for this problem remains one of noting that capacity constraints in stadia are reached in the minority of cases. To the extent that capacity is reached, this is treated as a possible source of heteroscedasticity and dealt with accordingly. The traditional argument is that below capacity, attendance measures effective demand.

Of the older studies that explicitly refer to the problems created by capacity constraints, Noll (1974) concludes that a significant capacity constraint variable indicates that excess demand applies. Schollaert and Smith

(1987) and Kahn and Sherer (1988) also find that a capacity constraint variable is significant in attendance functions and imply that a reduced form of an attendance equation is estimated. Of attempts to circumvent the problem, Geddert and Semple (1985) attempt to adjust their attendance data of hockey teams that regularly sell out by multiplying the attendance data by the excess of the average price charged by teams over the average price for the league. As Cairns (1990) notes, this approach 'is of dubious merit' (p. 8). Finally, Seigfried and Eisenberg (1980), in their study of minor league baseball, explicitly leave out a capacity constraint on the grounds that it will induce simultaneity by including a supply side variable on the right-hand side of a regression equation measuring demand.

Borland (1987), in a study of Australian rules football, argues that the availability of substitute events implies that the problem is overstated. This seems implausible in the light of the recent work, discussed below, which highlights the roles of cultural ties in attendance. It follows that a broader recognition of the potential impacts of heteroscedasticity on the traditional predominantly cross-sectional literature is needed.

The second issue that needs more general comment concerns multicollinearity. Cairns (1990) implies that a double-logarithmic specification of the demand model solves problems of independent variable interaction. This is also implied in the semi-logarithmic specifications of Baimbridge (1997) and Baimbridge *et al.* (1995; 1996). Of course, in a theoretical sense this is correct.[1] However, and despite the predominantly cross-sectional emphasis of the literature, little attempt is made to allow for, or comment on, the problems of multicollinearity. For example, price and travel cost, income and unemployment are likely to be related variables.

Muticollinearity is a phenomenon that affects econometric work in general. Unlike researchers in other fields, for example sociology, marketing and psychology and implied in such software as SPSS, economists have been

---

[1] If we take the demand model $A_t = B_1 P_t^{B_2} Y_t^{B_3}$ where A refers to attendance, P is price and Y is income, t is the index of observation, i.e. either time period or subject, and B_i are coefficients then the demand model is *non-linear*. This is because the coefficients are powers (this type of model is very common in empirical studies). This model cannot, therefore, be estimated by a linear regression. In contrast, we can estimate a linear regression model relating attendance to price and income if we use the logarithm of the values of the variables. Specifically, this implies that we have changed the model to $\text{Log} A_t = B_1 + B_2 \text{Log} P_t + B_3 \text{Log} Y_t$. As noted in the previous chapter, the coefficient estimates from this model will be elasticities. This is because changes in logarithms are proportionate changes. Moreover, the interaction between the variables is removed. Consequently, for example, B_2 would measure the slope of the logarithmic model $\partial \text{Log } A_t / \partial \text{Log } P_t$ which will be the proportionate change in attendance resulting from the proportionate change in price – the price elasticity of demand. Note that the slope in the original non-linear model will not be $\partial A_t / \partial P_t = B_2$ but a more complicated function based on the interaction of the variables, i.e. $\partial A_t / \partial P_t = B_2 B_1 P_t^{B_2-1} Y_t^{B_3}$.

reluctant to use techniques such as factor analysis for coping with such problems. Factor analysis, for example, identifies the degree and extent of mutual correlation between sets of variables. This may simply be ignorance of these techniques, it may reflect deep-seated methodological bias or simply reflect inertia from economists' training. Of course factor analysis does not in itself give the researcher insights in the ways originally desired, but none-theless taking account of the problems of multicollinearity explicitly is desirable.[2] In addition such an approach would help to formulate useful descriptive insights into which clusters of variables empirically appear to move together. For example, it may help to distinguish more appropriately which influences on attendance may be meaningfully classified as economic variables, cultural variables and so on. Such categorisation is increasingly attempted by researchers, as the subsets of variables in cross-sectional studies increase, but they are essentially categorised on the basis of prior judgement rather than systematic investigation.

Importantly, Davies *et al.* (1995b) offer a pilot study exploring the role of such a technique by exploring the determinants of attendance at rugby league matches.[3] Interestingly, in the light of findings discussed further below, they find that cultural and traditional factors are important determinants in match attendance. For example, while 25% of the sample could be indicative of purely economic motives associated with match attendance; 46% of the sample indicated that cultural and traditional motives such as locality, duration of support and involvement with the club in some other way than attending matches was important.

As Cairns (1990) notes, simultaneity is another econometric issue the literature on economics of professional team sports has essentially avoided. He writes that: 'The standard practice has been to specify a single equation model of demand without explicitly considering whether it is structural or a reduced form equation' (p. 5).

Of the studies that Cairns surveys, only four attempt to address the problem of simultaneity. Demmert (1973) specifies a five-equation model of attendance, prices, number of televised matches, stock of talent and team quality. Demmert postulates a recursive structure to the model. Such a structure is discussed more in Chapter 9, in the context of the players' labour

---

[2] Interestingly this is not the case with time-series econometrics. As DeMarchi and Gilbert's (1989) volume on the development of identification in econometrics notes, concern over the issue of multicollinearity as a form of model specification versus a problem of data, that dates back to the origins of the discipline, has been discussed in the context of the development of cointegration analysis.

[3] As discussed in the text, time-series econometrics has produced a meaningful classification system based on the data. Of course this is in terms of establishing the short run and long run effects of variables. Factor analysis could play a similar role in cross-section studies where the number of independent variables is much larger and getting increasingly so.

market. The structure implies that attendance can be adequately estimated by a single equation. Hart *et al.* (1975) exercise care in noting that the estimated coefficients in their equations modelling attendance at association football matches reflect both away and home team support – and as such are not structural parameters. Jones and Ferguson (1988) attempt to recover the structural parameters associated with market power and team quality in analysing the National Hockey League. Borland (1987) moreover discusses the problems of applying a single-equation approach and attempts instrumental-variable estimation. This approach is similar to a technique referred to as two-stage least squares. It is also discussed in the context of sporting labour markets in Chapter 9.

One remaining problem with this focus in the literature, a central factor that arises in discussion of other results later, is that it is essentially tied to a simplistic – static demand and supply – model of the sports market. Given the standard, albeit intuitively, dynamic reasoning applied to the professional team sports markets, when consideration of subsidisation and uncertainty of outcome is concerned, and the increasing focus on general equilibrium analysis of sporting markets, as discussed in Chapter 4 (see, for example, Fort and Quirk, 1995; and Vrooman, 1997), some more systematic treatment of endogeneity is required.

As Davies *et al.* (1995a) note, based on causality tests in the case of five rugby league clubs, one can argue that attendance drives success – that is relative league position – and not *vice versa*. This would suggest that a supply side force is dominant. Attendance could plausibly produce resources the employment of which produces success on the field. These causality tests involve performing the regression analysis outlined in Chapter 5 to see if success explains attendance and then performing a regression in which attendance is used to explain success.

Adopting the same approach, Dobson and Goddard (1998), on a sample of 77 association football clubs, also argue that revenues are significant factors in determining success. Given that success, or league ranking in one form or another, has been a ubiquitous and significant argument in most (presumed) demand studies, suggests that the inferences drawn may be biased and require re-examination. Simultaneity is not simply a problem associated with capacity constraints but is a fundamental feature of sporting economics. As discussed below, moreover, the results on uncertainty of outcome in the literature appear to hinge on the role of success in demand studies. Consequently, these results cast some doubt on the uncertainty of outcome hypothesis.

Income and price

We now turn attention to the two key economic variables assumed to underpin demand choices – price and income. Taking price first, Cairns notes that 12 studies have included price but only five have a significant and negative relationship: Bird (1982), Borland (1987), Demmert (1973), Seigfried and Eisenberg (1980) and Whitney (1988). The results, in keeping with Jennett's (1984) work, suggest that price is unlikely to be an important component of sporting demand.

In contrast, however, more recent studies such as Borland and Lye (1992), Carmichael *et al.* (1998), Dobson and Goddard (1995), Hynds and Smith (1994), Simmons (1996), Welki and Zlatoper (1994), and Wilson and Sim (1995) generally find significant price effects. However, the results are also broadly indicative of price-inelastic demands.

There are some anomalies. Because of the quadratic, that is 'u-shaped' relationship postulated between price and attendance, Baimbridge *et al.* (1996) find that attendance demand has both normal and inferior good characteristics because the price–demand relationship has a minimum at the bottom of the 'u'. Moreover, Baimbridge *et al.* (1995) identify a positive relationship between price and attendance in rugby league. Despite these statistical results, however, the general emphasis of the literature is that there is a relative lack of response of attendance to price changes.

One should, however, caution against taking these results too literally. As indicated in the previous chapter, there are problems in measuring the real economic price of sporting fixtures. In the past, for example, minimum adult admission prices have been used, for example by Bird (1982) and Jennett (1984). It has always been popular to use an average price based on revenues and attendance. For example Demmert (1973) and Noll (1974) weight ticket prices by their share of the stadium seating. More crudely, Hynds and Smith (1994), Baimbridge *et al.* (1995) and Dobson and Goddard (1995) simply divide receipts by attendance. It follows that as sports increasingly engage in price discrimination then any given supporter is unlikely to pay something that is close to the calculated average price. This may blunt the estimated relationship.

It also follows that the real economic price paid by spectators will involve complementary activities such as travel and so on. This argument has received recent theoretical support by Marburger (1997). He argues that complementary consumption, typical of the consumption of entertainment services, is likely to produce inelastic demands. It is interesting to note that when distance between clubs is included in regressions, there is evidence of a negative relationship recorded with attendance (see, for example, Baimbridge *et al.*, 1995; 1996).[4] Finally, it is worth noting that the long run evidence on price effects of Bird (1982), Dobson and Goddard (1995) and Simmons (1996) always suggests a significant relationship. The latter two studies are of

---

[4] In their 1996 study, the authors included distance in their regressions in a quadratic manner. The results suggest a minima which implies that local derbies are important but that committed fans do not let distance put them off attending fixtures.

particular importance in that they also are the first major attempts to disaggregate longitudinal research by clubs. The heterogeneity of their results between clubs is worth noting in the light of recent trends in demand. Dobson and Goddard (1995) also allude to stable cultural demands too. In these respects these studies are discussed further below.

With respect to income, perusal of Cairns (1990) reveals that of the 14 studies to which he refers, three do not include income variables in their regressions and 6 find no effect of income on attendance. Of the remaining five studies, some suggest that there is a positive relationship between income and attendance and some a negative relationship. The elasticity values provided lie in the range $-1 < 0 < 1$. Rather like price, therefore, this suggests that there are not particularly strong or elastic relationships between attendance and income and, indeed, sports can often be identified as inferior goods. As Cairns writes:

> The evidence suggests that basketball and Australian-rules football are normal goods but hockey is an inferior good. In the case of baseball and soccer the results have been mixed. Investigators often cannot find any significant impact of income on attendance.
>
> (p. 10)

The results for association football (soccer) and baseball are particularly interesting in that they are the sports researched most often.

As with price effects on demand, however, one of the central problems is that the short-run nature of the majority of the studies is unlikely to produce much variation in income data. This is, of course, true for price data too. Unlike sporting variables – which inherently are focused around the current season – economic variables are much more likely to vary over a number of seasons than over a single season or few seasons. Without explicitly discussing this matter, Cairns notes that the findings of three of the longer-term studies, Gartner and Pommerehne (1978), Bird (1982) and Borland (1987), produce significant income effects. The first and last of these studies find positive but inelastic responses in football and Australian rules football. Bird finds a negative income elasticity of demand for association football, suggesting that it is an inferior good. The issue of long-term longitudinal studies is referred to further below.

A second problem with measuring income effects occurs because of the proxy measure used. The theory of demand refers to the individual's disposable income. In practice researchers have to rely on averages of earnings or expenditure. For example, Bird (1982) uses total real consumer expenditure in his examination of aggregate football attendance. To be a meaningful proxy this assumes stable relationships between consumption patterns and income, which did not seem plausible during the 1970s. In contrast, Borland (1987) uses regional average earnings. However, the aggregate nature of this sort of measure of income implies less variation in the data relative to less aggregate data. As such the effects of income on attendance will be masked.

Of the more recent studies of attendance demand, Hynds and Smith (1994) use average wage rates divided by the retail price index as a proxy for income. They find no significant relationship between attendance at test cricket matches and income. Simmons (1996) also uses wage rates in his study of football and finds positive relationships between income and attendance for some football clubs. Synonymously with price effects, therefore, interpreting the full effect of income implies also taking into account variables that might also pick up the influence of income on demand.

As noted earlier, market size is a significant component of most studies and the results are always significant with a positive relationship with attendance implied. While this variable does capture the potential scale of demand in the locality, this is of course, linked to the purchasing power available. Likewise, unemployment is likely to vary with levels of income. While authors such as Jennett (1984) identify that football is a superior good because unemployment and attendance are negatively related, Baimbridge *et al.* (1996) find a significant relationship between unemployment and football attendance which would suggest that football is an inferior good. Dobson and Goddard (1995), moreover, use measures of social class to tease out socio-demographic impacts upon support. It is clear that these will be related to income. In general they find that middle-class support has been most stable relative to other classes in the post-war period.

This is an interesting result in that it implies that working-class support has left association football in the post-war period. As real incomes have risen over this period this might confirm that association football is, in some aggregate sense, an inferior good. This could be because working-class supporters now increasingly choose alternative forms of leisure, as the supply of these activities has increased. It could also reflect the increasing insecurity (of income) of the working classes because of the process of deindustrialisation experienced in most of the western economies since the 1970s. What is without question is the declining trend in football attendance in the UK since 1948. Whatever the cause, the 'male cloth-cap shilling supporter' now no longer dominates the 'terraces'.

This, of course, might help to explain some of the variety of results observed in the literature. The declining trend in association football attendance, a process mirrored in other sports such as rugby league, is ultimately the result of shifts in taste in the light of changing socio-demographic conditions. In conjunction with earlier comments, this raises econometric issues ignored in the literature. If the underlying structure of demand is changing, then individual studies conducted at different time periods may well produce conflicting results unless account is taken of the structural changes. This could take place, for example, by using dummy variables to control for the periods before and after the change took place. This procedure would mirror that used by Fort and Quirk (1995) in another context and discussed in Chapter 4.

Uncertainty of outcome and sporting determinants of demand

Having discussed some of the main economic determinants of demand, attention now turns to sporting determinants of demand. A central feature of the economics of professional team sports that has been stressed in the literature is the 'uncertainty of outcome' hypothesis. This suggests that spectator interest is maximised when sporting competition is at its most intense, for example between equally strong opponents. This hypothesis has four forms. These are uncertainty of match outcome, uncertainty of seasonal outcome and relatedly championship contention, and the absence of long run domination in a league.

It is clear that these types of uncertainty of outcome could be closely related. Extreme examples of this would be Wigan Rugby League Football Club winning ten championships in succession, or both Glasgow Celtic and Glasgow Rangers Football Clubs winning nine successive Scottish Premier Division titles in various eras. The implication of these track records is that individual clubs facing such opposition would in general be expected to lose. However, the predicted effects of the uncertainty of outcome hypothesis may be more complex.

The presumed impact of intense competition is that ultimately spectator interest is aroused and thus demand and attendance increases and vice versa. However, it is possible that the home attendance of 'dominant teams' may not be reduced. Manchester United Football Club's strength in the 1990s has been matched by sell-out crowds. In turn, clubs that struggle can also retain large crowds. In contrast to Manchester United, Manchester City Football Club has experienced problems throughout the 1990s and, at the time of writing this book, are currently in Division 1 (and previously Division 2) of the football league in contrast to Manchester United's premier league status.[5] However, they consistently achieve higher attendance than Division 1 clubs and even some Premier League clubs. Of course, this implies the need to employ statistical analysis to try to control out the effects of, say, Manchester being a large catchment area which influences average attendance and so on, but the following point is nonetheless important. Committed fans of a particular club may be insensitive to their club's performance over quite substantial periods of time. Ultimately, thus, the interesting feature of the uncertainty of outcome hypothesis becomes what happens to aggregate attendance rather than individual club's attendance over time. This explains the significance of the results discussed in Chapter 4. Moreover, because of the maintained importance of the uncertainty of outcome hypothesis to professional team sports, the next chapter outlines some of the problems of measuring the hypothesis and discusses the results in some detail. For now we note some main themes emergent from the literature.

---

[5] Another association football example is Stoke City, one of the author's own city teams!

As far as the measurement of uncertainty of match outcome is concerned, Hart *et al.* (1975) and Jones and Ferguson (1988) use the differences in league standings between clubs in association football fixtures, and dummy variables involving fixtures with the top three and bottom three clubs in the US and Canadian hockey leagues, respectively. Both of these variables are insignificant. It is clear that these are fairly crude measures of expectations about the results of fixtures. In the former case, the measure presupposes that squads have not changed. In the latter case, it is clear that the categories of clubs are somewhat arbitrary. In contrast, pioneered by Peel and Thomas (1988) in a study of association football, an increasingly popular measure of uncertainty of match outcome is betting odds offered prior to the match. As discussed further in the next chapter, the implication, while often not stated explicitly, is that the betting market is an efficient and unbiased estimator of the true form of the clubs by encapsulating all available information in the odds. Presumably the profit motive ensures that 'bookies' process all available information in offering odds 'professionally'.

While this approach appears to offer a neat solution to measuring uncertainty of outcome, there is a major problem associated with using the raw data. The uncertainty of outcome hypothesis is an inherently quadratic, i.e. u-shaped, relationship that suggests that if clubs' fixtures involve clubs different from their abilities then uncertainty of outcome will diminish. Thus, a mid-table club playing the club at the bottom of the league implies that uncertainty of outcome will be low. The same situation would apply if the mid-table club played a top-table club. In contrast, if the mid-table club played another mid-table club, then one would expect uncertainty of outcome to be higher.[6] The fact that different signs would be expected in the different contexts implies that statistical tests can be misleading. In this respect when Peel and Thomas (1988), who make use of the probabilities of a home win, cite the variable as significant implying that uncertainty of match outcome affects attendance, they are really measuring the probability of success at home and not uncertainty of outcome. In their later paper, Peel and Thomas (1996) acknowledge this explicitly.

One solution to this econometric problem is to model whether or not the relationship between attendance and betting odds is increasing or decreasing. This can be achieved by using a slope dummy variable.[7] An alternative

---

[6] In probability terms, uncertainty of outcome could be measured, for example, by $p_i(1-p_i)$ for the ith team's fixture where p refers to the probability of a win. Uncertainty of outcome will be at a maximum where $p = 0.5$.

[7] A slope dummy variable is constructed by assigning, for example, a value of 1 to the variable if it is felt that the result of the fixture is increasingly uncertain, and 0 otherwise. The dummy variable is multiplied by the betting odds variable and this composite variable included in the regression. This implies that a selection of observations on betting odds associated with increasing uncertainty of outcome are entered into the regression analysis again. If the coefficient on this variable is positive and significant then one has identified uncertainty of outcome.

approach is to enter betting odds into the regression in a quadratic manner. This implies including squared betting odds as well as betting odds *per se* in the regression. The coefficient on the squared term then picks up the 'curved' relationship in the data implied by the uncertainty of outcome hypothesis.[8] An alternative is to create a new variable based on home win probability. Interestingly, Cairns (1988) attempts these approaches using Peel and Thomas' (1988) data and finds no significant relationship between uncertainty of outcome and attendance. Significantly, Kuypers (1996) also adopts this approach in a study of association football and finds similar generally unconvincing results.

This is a pattern that is observed in results associated with other variables that might be argued to measure the uncertainty of match outcomes. For example, while Kuypers (op. cit.) finds that derby matches have a positive and significant effect on association football attendance, Baimbridge *et al.* (1995) find that this is not the case in rugby league. Hynds and Smith (1994) find that increased certainty of cricket *test match* results does not affect test match attendance but increased certainty of *test series*, i.e. set of test matches, results significantly reduce attendance at particular test matches. Wilson and Sim (1995) find that derby matches increase attendance but differences in league points between teams does not in semi-professional Malaysian football. Similarly, making use of the differences between league positions as an indicator of form, Baimbridge *et al.* (1996) find a similar insignificant effect modelling association football attendance in England and Wales. Likewise, in his analysis of 'Euro '96', Baimbridge (1997) finds that international 'derby' football matches do not attract significantly more supporters. In contrast, and essentially returning to the theme of success as a determinant of attendance, Kuypers (1996) finds that the average goals scored for and against a team over the previous three matches in association football fixtures significantly increases attendance. Similarly the number of points earned in the last three home games significantly increases attendance. Baimbridge *et al.* (1995) find that higher home team league position significantly and positively affects rugby league attendance, whereas higher away team league position reduces attendance. In their study of association football, Baimbridge *et al.* (1996) find that a higher previous season's league position can positively affect attendance but that winning a championship implies that attendance can fall. In contrast in 'Euro '96', Baimbridge (1997) finds that matches involving seeded teams and matches that have a significance for the tournament outcome significantly increase attendance. Combined, these results suggest

---

[8] Note that the regression is still linear in the parameters and, as such, ordinary least squares can still be employed. This approach can thus be thought of as trying to fit a line of best fit to the relationship between match results and *squared* betting odds. Intuitively plotting this on a graph would produce a straight line unlike the graph drawn between attendance and betting odds.

that the evidence in favour of the uncertainty of match outcome hypothesis is, in general, mixed to say the least. On balance, it is fair to say that supporters appear to prefer the increased likelihood of their team being successful rather than uncertainty *per se*.

There are similar results for demand studies motivated by the uncertainty of outcome of seasons and championships. Essentially, the measures of uncertainty of outcome adopted in studies seeking to test this hypothesis hinge on trying to proxy contention for a championship, promotion or relegation. In other words, indicators of success or team performance figure prominently. In early work, Demmert (1973) allowed for the average number of teams in contention for baseball championships but found no significant relationship. Similar results follow from a similar approach in Borland's (1987) study of Australian rules football. In contrast, Noll (1974) finds some weak evidence to support the view that ice hockey supporters are attracted to the possibility of their team making it to the play-offs, whereas baseball supporters appreciate a close contest. As discussed in Chapter 5, Jennett (1984) develops a sophisticated model of uncertainty of seasonal outcome in his study of Scottish league association football and finds a highly significant relationship with attendance at fixtures. Likewise, Wilson and Sim (1995) find similar results for their study employing Jennett's measure of uncertainty of outcome. However, this approach has been criticised for overestimating the ability of spectators to calculate the permutations required in identifying the significance of matches. In addition, in as much that the measures are based on *ex post* results, this implies that spectators have perfect information.

Perhaps because of these sorts of criticism and also perhaps because of the time constraints involved in constructing such elaborate measures of uncertainty of outcome, more recent work has tended to emphasise more pragmatic and less information-costly measures of the likelihood of success. This is particularly the case in the longer-term studies of attendance, for example, presented by Dobson and Goddard (1995) and Simmons (1996), discussed further below.

As far as the long-term implications of domination for attendance are concerned, which is the final example of the uncertainty of income hypothesis, it is worth noting that there is a general dearth of insights. Borland (1987), however, attempts to measure long run domination in Australian rules football by including a variable that involves the number of different teams appearing in the finals in the last three seasons divided by the number of places available. There is no significant relationship. As far as uncertainty of outcome is concerned, therefore, the results of more recent work lead one to echo the conclusion aired by Cairns (1990) that:

> . . . there is no evidence that spectators value uncertainty of match outcome, they do value uncertainty of seasonal outcome. But not in its direct form, that is, they do not value uncertainty <u>per se</u>, but that

they are attracted by the prospect of championship success. No firm conclusion should be drawn, at this stage, with respect to long-run domination.

(p. 14, underlining in original)

This would seem to suggest that conclusions drawn from the literature on the management of sporting leagues, that question the uncertainty of outcome hypothesis as a target for policy as discussed in Chapter 4, receive support. The uncertainty of outcome hypothesis thus appears to be a rather overworked theme in the literature.

Having said this, however, it follows that one must address an essential problem that can be identified with the seasonal uncertainty of outcome hypothesis and also the concept of long-run domination before firm conclusions are drawn. It follows, therefore that there are substantial research opportunities in this area particularly.

As noted earlier, the seasonal and long run approaches to the uncertainty of outcome hypothesis essentially argue that if one team begins to dominate a league then overall attendance in the league will fall. Put another way, the hypotheses suggest that a (more) random allocation of winners of league championships would generate extra overall support. Now, one of the main tenets of the above literature suggests that supporters are attracted to their own team because of success. Alternatively they are attracted to their team because of the lack of success and as such are committed supporters. A changed pattern of success would suggest that different types of supporter would choose to watch teams play. This implies that the underlying behavioural patterns of demand are changing, for example, from committed to more 'casual' support. To the extent that this might affect the parameters of the demand functions estimated, this suggests that detecting the effects of uncertainty of outcome is not straightforward. Longer-term changes in the structure of demand may occur following policy changes. Regression analysis may have difficulty in establishing the implied relationship. In contrast a dynamic modelling approach to demand may be more apposite that integrates short run and long run factors influencing demand.

Of the purely sporting factors that have been entered into regression analyses of attendance, variables associated primarily with the quality of the team and/or particular players typically have significant effects as expected *a priori*.[9] For example, in Kuypers' (1996) study of association football, the presence of international players significantly increases attendance. In Baimbridge *et al.*'s (1995; 1996) studies of rugby league and association football attendance the presence of a star player in the home or away team

---

[9] As discussed in Chapter 5, these features of teams and players are usually measured with dummy variables. For example, the presence of an international player in a match or team would be scored 1 or 0 otherwise.

significantly increases attendance. In Wilson and Sim's (1995) study of semi-professional association football in Malaysia, the presence of star players in matches or matches involving clubs from higher divisions both increase attendance. These results are commensurate with Cairns' (1990) survey that concludes that: 'Most studies have found that these measures of expected quality have a statistically significant impact. As (expected) relative quality rises, attendances increase' (p. 15).

In contrast, Cairns (1990) reports that the impact of weather conditions on attendance at sporting events has been mixed. Noll (1974), for example, finds that American football attendance was significantly lower during sunny days and that ice hockey attendance was higher during colder winter days. Geddert and Semple (1985), however, find no significant relationship in the case of ice hockey. Drever and McDonald (1981) find that rain significantly reduces attendance at South Australian football games, whereas Peel and Thomas (1988) find no effect of weather conditions on association football attendance. More recently Kuypers (1996) found no significant relationship between association football attendance and temperature or rainfall. Hynds and Smith (1994) find that, quite naturally, rainfall decreases test match attendance but that sunshine or temperatures did not.[10] Baimbridge *et al.* (1995; 1996) find that cold and windy conditions significantly deter supporters in rugby league matches whereas wet weather does not, while none of these factors affect association football attendance.

A similar 'mixed bag' of results applies as far as the day of the fixture is concerned. Kuypers (1996) finds that mid-week association football matches have significantly less attendance than weekend fixtures. In contrast Baimbridge *et al.* (1995; 1996) finds no significant relationship between attendance and weekend versus mid-week fixtures in rugby league and football respectively. The same is true of 'Euro '96' attendance according to Baimbridge (1997). In contrast Baimbridge *et al.* (1995; 1996) find that attendance is significantly higher on bank holidays. Finally, Cairns (1990) does not address the impact of TV coverage on sporting attendance. This is discussed in some detail in Chapter 8.

Summary

In conclusion it is fair to say that as far as economic factors are concerned, market size is a ubiquitously significant determinant of demand but price and income effects are typically identified as weak influences on attendance. As far as sporting factors are concerned, seasonal success, though not the traditional notion of uncertainty of outcome, and team and player qualities are ubiqui-tously significant forces for increasing attendance. In contrast the timing of

---

[10] For those unfamiliar with cricket as a sport, rainfall very often stops play. Accordingly one would expect a negative association between rainfall and attendance.

fixtures, with the exception of bank holidays, and weather conditions have mixed effects upon attendance. Significantly these results are consistent across the earlier work and more recent efforts. These results should be of concern for economists and sporting policy makers. In the first instance they appear to challenge the major assumptions made about the underlying economic nature of the demand for sports. In the second instance they suggest, perhaps quite reasonably, that the impact of sporting policy should be targeted at managing team success and team/player quality. Consistent with the literature on sporting leagues, moreover, the uncertainty of outcome hypothesis *per se* may not matter.

Before settling on this conclusion, however, in the light of both econometric comments made earlier in the chapter, as well as comments about the scope of the literature, some recent long run studies of the demand for sports are worth discussing.

The long-run determinants of demand: culture, habit persistence and economic effects revisited

Two recent studies of association football in England and Wales have tried to rectify the short run emphasis in the literature by producing long-run insights into attendance. Significantly, moreover, because they also adopt a less aggregate approach, they are of relevance in revisiting the impact of sporting factors on attendance just discussed.

To open the discussion, attention is turned first to the fact that cultural factors have been identified as significant determinants of long-run attendance; the section then outlines how habit persistence has been used to model such effects. Finally, the results of the two studies concerning the role of economic factors upon attendance are discussed.

Of the studies already reviewed, it is interesting to note that Baimbridge *et al.* (1995; 1996) identify that the date of a club's formation and the period over which the club has been in the Super League or Premier league are significant and positive influences on attendance at rugby league and association football matches respectively. Similarly, Kuypers (1996) finds that average home support in the last three years is a significant factor in determining association football attendance. These results are important in that they suggest that longer-term factors, such as social and cultural factors, could be important determinants of demand for professional team sports. Indeed they are implied in notions such as core support employed in, for example, Peel and Thomas' (1996) study of rugby league attendance, as well as the uncertainty of outcome hypotheses discussed at length above. In turn it is interesting to note that Kuypers (1996) makes use of previous years' attendance to represent loyalty or 'habit persistence'. While this is, in fact, a false assertion (the reader should note that the reasons for this are identified in Appendix 5.1), herein lies the importance of the first long run study of attendance discussed in some detail.

Dobson and Goddard (1995) explore association football league attendance between 1925–1992. In this paper they employ a two-stage empirical analysis. First of all they use annual data to estimate the effects of certain medium-term determinants of attendance at football matches. These determinants are specified *a priori* as loyalty, success, entertainment and price. Pre-empting Kuypers (1996), loyalty is proxied by last season's attendance. Success is measured by the overall position of the club in the league. Dobson and Goddard (1995) also include dummy variables in their regressions because attendance and success exhibit 'kinked' relationships when teams finishing at the top of lower divisions have higher attendance than those finishing at the bottom of higher divisions. The total number of goals scored by each team in each season measures entertainment. As Dobson and Goddard (1995) note, this is because goals conceded are unlikely to attract supporters. However, this does rule out the possibility that goal differences may be more important. Price is measured by dividing total gate receipts by attendance. Dobson and Goddard recognise that this rules out some of the other aspects of the full cost of attending matches, discussed earlier in the chapter, but justify this on the basis of lack of data. To control for missing variables that are common to all clubs, they standardise their data on attendance, goals scored and prices by calculating deviations from means divided by standard deviations. They then pool their data to estimate their model.

Initially a fixed-effects model is estimated to produce 'base' levels of attendance in clubs. Basically this procedure involves using a dummy variable for each club as a means of measuring the change in the constant associated with each club after controlling for the medium-term determinants of attendance. The different constants thus represent different average attendance without the effects of the other variables affecting the calculations. In contrast each slope coefficient of the regressions indicates the average affects of the respective variable, over all clubs and for the time period concerned, *ceteris paribus*. Based on their diagnostic tests, the estimates from this equation are corrected for both heteroscedasticity and serial correlation of the residuals.

The main results from their study are a set of rankings of clubs based on 'base' support between 1925 and 1992. It is interesting to note that the top ten clubs over this long time period are: Manchester United, Newcastle, Arsenal, Tottenham Hotspur, Everton, Chelsea, Aston Villa, Manchester City, Sunderland and Liverpool. Most of these clubs still figure prominently in Premier League standings. This suggests, once again, albeit anecdotally, that policies of cross-subsidisation have had little substantive long run impact in association football. In addition Dobson and Goddard (1995) find that loyalty and success are particularly strong determinants of attendance, while the effects of price and entertainment are somewhat weaker. All of the variables have the appropriate impacts expected by prior hypothesis. While the first two results might be expected from the results of many of the earlier studies, it is important to note that as far as price is concerned: '. . . the price elasticity of demand is extremely low; however, . . . this is the first UK study to find strong evidence of any significant price effect' (p. 14).

This suggests that over longer periods of time price does have a significant impact upon demand and, importantly, it suggests that the effect is consistent with the underlying notion that committed supporters would be insensitive to prices. Indeed Dobson and Goddard rationalise the large recent increases in revenue to football clubs on the basis of price rises.

Dobson and Goddard then estimate their model for each of the individual clubs and report that the estimations reveal the same general pattern as before. However, whereas loyalty is significant in 92 of the 94 cases, and success in 85 cases, entertainment and price are only significant in 21 and 19 cases respectively. This suggests that the economic effects are much more heterogeneous. To help to explain this phenomenon, they then take the 94 coefficient estimates as observations on each of the variables: base attendance, loyalty, success, entertainment and price, and regress them upon some long run socioeconomic determinants of attendance. These include the population of the town, the number of other clubs within a 30-mile radius of the club, the age of the league when the club entered, whether or not the club is located in the north or south – of a straight line drawn through Swansea and Coventry – the number of males in the 1961 census in the locality and the number of economically active males in four occupational groups ranging from professional to manual workers.[11] The objective is to try and understand what determines base attendance and the responsiveness of attendance to changes in loyalty, success, entertainment and price.

As there appeared to be contemporaneous variation between the residuals of each of the equations, the set of five equations explaining base attendance, loyalty, success, entertainment and price was estimated as a system of seemingly unrelated regressions.[12] Such a technique is always an option for pooled data sets. Significantly a few other studies noted above have made use of this option. These include, Hart *et al.* (1975), Jones and Ferguson (1988) and Whitney (1988). Wilson and Sim (1995) argue that while the method has attractions, in their case it would have been too expensive in terms of degrees of freedom.

As far as explaining base support is concerned, all of the independent variables are significant and as expected. For example high proportions of males in the population increases attendance, etc. The most statistically significant results reflected the influence of population, which is consistent

---

[11] This is not because the authors' feel that female attendance is unimportant *per se* but simply that the data reflects the historical nature of the data, which focused on collecting male statistics. In this respect the number of members of the armed forces are also included as the study covers the period of World War II, the Korean war and periods of national service.

[12] In statistical terms, this means that the equations were estimated simultaneously because some of the influences on the variables were seen to be common. Estimating the equations simultaneously increases the (statistical) efficiency of the estimates.

with the strong evidence in favour of the impact of this variable detailed earlier in the chapter, and the year in which the club entered the league. This suggests that tradition and loyalties are of particular long-run importance as determinants of base support. In contrast none of the variables were significant in terms of explaining loyalty. This suggests that loyalty is a rather general characteristic with no specific determinants.

Not surprisingly the presence of competitive clubs in the locality increases the responsiveness of attendance to success. Interestingly, the results also suggest that manual workers are more likely to be sensitive to success. This is consistent with the idea that 'terrace-based' support is more result sensitive than, for example, season-ticket support. This is a point emphasised by Simmons (1996) and discussed below. Dobson and Goddard's results also show that price sensitivity is positively affected by the amount of local competition and is greater in the south than the north. Crucially, the results also suggest that manual workers are more price sensitive than their middle-class counterparts. In conclusion, thus, in addition to emphasising the traditional findings in the literature that market size and success are important determinants of demand, Dobson and Goddard (1995) show that in the longer run, tradition and loyalty are important factors. Moreover, economic effects such as the impact of prices on attendance are identified in the longer run and these reflect more working-class segments of the crowd. Crucially their results suggest that price sensitivity will reflect the type of support observed so that aggregate studies will be misleading. Moreover, their results suggest that price sensitivity will be tied to longer-term evolution in social and economic conditions.

The attention to detail in Dodson and Goddard's paper is clearly commendable and substantially moves the literature forward. However, it is worth pointing out some potential problems with their work. The first problem is essentially econometric and stems from some recent work by Peasaran and Smith (1995), who demonstrate that in a pooled- (i.e. panel) data context, with a dynamic model and heterogeneous slope coefficients, then estimates will be inconsistent. The statistical condition of consistency implies that while estimates can be biased in finite, i.e. small, samples, estimates will get closer and closer to the (unknown) true value as the sample size increases. In the first step of Dobson and Goddard's work a dynamic model is employed as loyalty is measured by lagged attendance. Moreover, the dependent variables in the second step of the study were based on the first stage estimates of heterogeneous coefficients. This suggests that Dobson and Goddard's estimates may be unreliable and a more robust method of analysis needs to be adopted.

The second point refers to the conception of the medium-term and long-term effects upon attendance. Data considerations rather than robust theoretical priors essentially drive these effects. For example, price is considered to be a medium-term effect and social class – which proxies income factors as discussed explicitly by the authors – is considered to be a long-term determinant of attendance. There is no obvious justification for this. Nonetheless, the ambitious nature of the study thus provides a very useful benchmark against which to judge the insights of the traditional literature. It suggests that the traditional emphasis in the literature has some support but that the economic factors need more careful investigation in order to tease out their impacts.

In this respect Simmons' (1996) analysis of attendance at 19 large urban-based English football league clubs over the period 1962/3 to 1991/2 draws on a more robust econometric methodology based on establishing the differences between short run and long run relationships between variables. Along with Dobson and Goddard (1995), moreover, Simmons (1996) is explicitly concerned with the problems of identifying, 'Economic determinants such as price and income . . . [because they] . . . will show too little variation to be important in short time-series of pooled data' (p. 139).

Simmons adopts a time-series econometric approach (Hendry, 1992); which employs an 'error-correction' econometric model to represent the demand for association football that is hypothesised to depend, in the long run, on prices and incomes. Because of habit persistence, however, it is hypothesised that equilibrium demands are achieved slowly through time so that the demand equation should also include lagged attendance to capture this feature of support. This is, of course, what Dobson and Goddard (1995) presuppose. As both prices and incomes will also be changing over time, the regression equation implied by the error-correction model thus involves a regression of *changes* in attendance on current and lagged *changes* in prices and incomes as well as the *level* of last period's attendance, prices and incomes. Intuitively, the parameters on the *change* terms indicate the adjustment of economic behaviour through time and the lags indicate the time period over which this adjustment takes place and are essentially given by the data. The parameters on last period's *level* of attendance, price and income represent the equilibrium relationship that attendance is tending towards. Mathematically speaking, if all changes were zero, that is an equilibrium state was achieved, all of the terms in the regression apart from those associated with last period's levels of attendance, price and income would be equal to zero. What would be left is the equilibrium relationship.[13] Tests of the significance of the equilibrium relationship are referred to as tests of 'cointegration'. Appendix 6.1 outlines some of the main issues and concepts implied in this econometric approach.

To measure attendance, Simmons (1996) uses data on both gate and total attendance per club per season (excluding cup and play-off fixtures). The former measure does not include season-ticket holders. So comparison of the results enables him to make inferences about those supporters who might be

---

[13] The reason lagged 'level' terms are involved is because a regression of this period's attendance cannot be done on this period's attendance because this would produce perfect multi-collinearity and the regression would fail.

characterised as 'theatre goers' and in essence decide to attend fixtures on a match-by-match basis, and those supporters who can exhibit their core loyal support by buying season tickets. Price is measured by taking receipts per club per season and dividing by attendance and the retail price index. This gives a measure of the real price of attending a match per season per club. Real average weekly earnings in manufacturing and other industries measure income. As well as these fundamental economic variables, Simmons also includes success, entertainment, promotion and relegation and cup form as sports-specific variables, which are primarily presumed to have short run impacts on attendance. In this respect they are simply added onto the regression equation and do not figure in the derivation of the error-correction model. Success is measured by the minus value of the team's standing in the football league per season. This implies that larger values of the proxy are commensurate with a higher finishing position in the league. Entertainment is measured by goals per game per season. The other variables are measured by dummies and variables that capture the number of rounds clubs have progressed through in cup competitions, respectively.

The main results of the research are that there is a long run equilibrium (i.e. cointegrating) relationship between attendance and its determinants in all cases. Moreover, in 17 of the 19 cases this includes the price variable. This is a highly significant result in that it shows that an appropriate econometric approach, that specifically concerns itself with exploring long run relation-ships, identifies the significance of economic factors as driving attendance in the long run. Also of importance is the heterogeneity of the results. For example, ten of the 19 clubs had long run price elasticities above 0.5, i.e. less than −0.5, and two had price elastic demands in excess of 1.0, i.e. less than −1.0. As Simmons (1996, p. 148) concludes: 'One suspects that pooling or aggregating club-level data results in estimates of price elasticity which are biased downwards by incorporating clubs with low or zero price elasticity'.

Significantly, in employing the analysis to the data excluding season ticket holders reveals that price elasticities increase. This is consistent with the idea that supporters who pay week-by-week are more price sensitive than those buying season tickets.

As far as long run income effects are concerned, five clubs reveal that demands are income elastic. This finding suggests that football can be under-stood as a luxury good in some cases. This again contradicts the findings of previous studies of sporting and football demand. Indeed the results are broadly consistent with Dobson and Goddard's (1995) findings that the higher incomes of say the middle classes may promote more active demands and that the structure of demand is changing away from traditional working-class support. In addition, Simmons (1996) finds that there is a long run equilibrium relationship implied for attendance and league position or success. This is, of course, consistent with the previous literature. Once again, it suggests that long-term domination seems to be a characteristic of professional team sports.

As far as the short run factors are concerned, in general the results on lagged attendance effects are highly variable. There is evidence of short run price effects for five clubs, which are consistently less than their long run counterparts and, as far as the football-specific factors are concerned they, show a diverse pattern.

The importance of Simmons' (1996) work, thus, is that through the use of appropriate econometric techniques, he reverses the conclusions of much of the previous literature. He shows that in the long run the usual economic determinants of demand are significant in explaining association football attendance. In contrast, with the exception of success, the sporting-specific factors are diverse in their impact. This suggests that earlier work that is of a short-term nature, or that aggregates and averages data across clubs, will not only be unable to pick up the impact of economic forces on supporters' choices, but also overstate the idea that the impact of sporting determinants are common. These two alternative interpretations of the demand for professional team sports suggest very different sporting scenarios on which to base policy. In being able to explore both contexts, the implication is that Simmons' (1996) results are more reliable than much of the earlier work. Ironically, however, he does not explicitly explore the uncertainty of outcome hypothesis *per se*. He remarks that:

> Several papers have considered the importance of uncertainty of out-come as a measure of the attractiveness of football matches . . . Here, we explore the minimum essential club-specific variables, partly to preserve degrees of freedom but also to focus on the broader economic deter-minants of club attendance patterns.
>
> (p. 47)

It remains, however, that his results on success are commensurate with the earlier literature. Combined, these results once again cast some doubt on the traditional uncertainty of outcome hypothesis. Nonetheless, integrating this variable into Simmons' approach, and extending his type of analysis to other sports is clearly an important agenda for future research. Currently we are left with the view that admission prices and success are key features in terms of determining attendance in the long run. In as much that team or player quality is essentially reflected in success, this result is not inconsistent with the short run literature. However, Simmons' and Dobson and Goddard's research suggest that ignoring the impact of economic variables such as price on attendance and hence revenues would be a naive option.

Conclusions

In this chapter, the empirical literature on the demand for professional team sports has been discussed. Based on a critical review of the literature we suggest that while there is a diversity of findings upon the determinants of the demand, nonetheless some significant patterns could be understood. As far as economic factors are concerned, while the traditional literature argued that market size was a ubiquitous determinant of demand, price and income effects were identified as weak influences. Moreover, as far as sporting factors are concerned seasonal success, though not the traditional notion of uncertainty of outcome, and team and player qualities appear important determinants of demand. Recent developments in demand estimates for the long run are then discussed. We argue that the more recent long-run studies should be emphasised because of their appropriate econometric methodology, but also because they reflect a changed emphasis from aggregating or averaging results across clubs over short time periods. As longer time horizons are adopted for empirical studies then traditional economic determinants of demand, such as prices and incomes, appear to be more significant determinants than previously had been argued to be the case.

It follows that we suggest that a new research agenda is required that allows researchers to explore both the long run and short run determinants of demand of both a sporting and economic nature simultaneously. Moreover, regressions should avoid averages over clubs. The cost of this approach is the time and expense of the researcher in constructing a data-set. The benefit would be results that are more useful to the sporting commentator and regulator than are currently available.

Appendix 6.1: Time-series econometrics, error correction models and cointegration

This appendix is not meant to be a formal introduction to time-series econometrics. In contrast, it is simply intended to provide the reader with some of the main ideas associated with the approach. To pursue the details of cointegration, as well as the seminal articles there are now many accessible econometric textbooks that the reader should refer to. A very good example is Charemza and Deadman (1997).

The notion of a spurious regression lies at the core of modern time-series econometrics. In a technical paper, Granger and Newbold (1974) showed that ordinary least squares may indicate that there is a significant relationship between a set of variables when in fact there is none. To exemplify their arguments they showed that two independent variables appear to be 'related' if ordinary least squares regression is applied to them under certain conditions. Consequently if these conditions hold then one cannot guarantee that regression results are reliable.

The conditions under which spurious regression can occur are when time-series data are non-stationary. Technically this implies that the means and variances of the data vary through time and that the covariances between time periods do not simply depend on the distance or lag-length between them but also on the point in time in which they are calculated. This is always likely to be the case in time-series work as variables tend to trend through time. For example, simple plots of data reveal that association football attendance has been falling at the same time that gate prices have been rising (Simmons, 1996).

To test for the presence or possibility of spurious regression, researchers conduct 'unit-root' tests. If unit-root tests are accepted, then the series is non-stationary. If unit-root tests are rejected, then the series is stationary. In the case of attendance, for example, if A refers to attendance, Δ to the change in a variable, t to time, B and C to parameters and u a random disturbance term, then the equation

$$A_t = B_1 + B_2 t + CA_{t-1} + u_t, \tag{6.1.1}$$

can be used to test for a unit root in attendance. If $C = 1$ then the equation has a unit root and is non-stationary. It can be shown that, for example, the mean and variance of the time-series A will depend on time. This equation is not a behavioural equation but is simply a means of testing for whether or not a variable is stationary. A similar equation can be used to test for the stationarity of any variable that might comprise part of an economic model. This equation can be simplified to:

$$\Delta A_t = B_1 + B_2 t + u_t. \tag{6.1.2}$$

This equation belongs to a class of models known as a 'random walks'. If non-stationarity characterises all of the data in a model, for example in the case of both attendance and, say, prices, then a regression of attendance on price may simply pick up the 'common trend' that both series depend on time but which is not based on an intrinsic relationship between the two variables.

The most common form of unit-root test is based on a modified version of (6.1.1). Subtracting A_{t-1} from both sides of this equation and rearranging the terms leaves

$$\Delta A_t = B_1 + B_2 t + B_3 A_{t-1} + u_t. \tag{6.1.3}$$

This equation is clearly equivalent to the random walk model with the exception that the lagged value of attendance is included in the regression. Clearly $B_3 = C - 1$. Thus a test of $B_3 = 0$ is equivalent to a test that $C = 1$. Accepting either of these hypotheses implies accepting the random-walk model which, we know, implies that the data are non-stationary. This form of the equation has the advantage of following the usual logic of t-tests in regression models of seeking to test null hypotheses $= 0$. The only modification is that Dickey–Fuller tables have to be used to ascertain critical values because the standard t-values are only valid if the series are stationary.

The implication of these tests is that regression based on non-stationary data will produce spurious results. The solutions to the problem require having to transform the data so that it is stationary or to test for the presence of cointegration. The problem with the former approach is that the variables may enter the equation in a manner in which there is no obvious theoretical rationale. For example, time-series data are referred to as 'integrated of order k' if one has to difference the data k times to produce a stationary series. Thus if attendance was integrated of order 1, the first difference of attendance, i.e. ΔA_t, will be stationary – or integrated of order 0. In contrast if prices are integrated of order 2, then it is likely that the first difference in prices will be integrated of order 1. The second difference in price, for example, $\Delta^2 P_t$, or $\Delta P_t - \Delta P_{t-1}$, will be stationary.[14] If this is the case then a valid statistical result will only follow from regressing the change in attendance on the rate of change in prices.

This is why the concept of cointegration has become so important in econometric modelling. Two or more non-stationary time-series of the same order can be used in a regression model only if they are cointegrated. This means that a linear combination of the variables as of course implied in the regression model itself is stationary. This means that the combination of variables implied in the regression model does not depend on time. As such, cointegrated variables can be interpreted as equilibrium relationships. It follows that tests for cointegration are essentially based on testing the residuals of a regression to check if they are stationary or not.[15]

Thus, given the (equilibrium) demand equation:

$$A_t = B_1 + B_2 P_t + u_t, \tag{6.1.4}$$

it follows that;

$$u_t = A_t - B_1 - B_2 P_t. \tag{6.1.5}$$

The disturbance term u is equivalent to a linear combination of attendance and prices. It is clear that testing for the stationarity of the residuals of a regression – that approximate the disturbances as discussed in Chapter 5 – is a test for cointegration. Cointegration thus means that even though attendance and price are non-stationary they combine in a stationary way. This implies that the regression is valid statistically. More importantly, this

---

[14] Strictly speaking, the tests for unit-roots should be conducted on these data-series to check this presumption.

[15] This approach is often referred to as the Engle and Granger procedure after the two authors (Engle and Granger, 1987). More often today, the Johansen (1991) approach to testing for cointegration is used. The latter approach involves the use of simultaneous tests with each variable being used as the dependent variable. This is known as vector-autoregression modelling. To understand cointegration in this context requires knowlege of matrices which is beyond the scope of this book. The advantage of this approach is that there may be more than one cointegrating relationship in the data. Thus there is an identification problem. The Johansen method identifies how many relationships there are.

result suggests that the variables enter into the regression in a theoretically compatible way.

In economic terms variables that combine to produce stationary residuals will be integrated of order 1 in their levels. This means that one can interpret the cointegrating equation as an essentially long run equilibrium relationship. These relationships, of course, form the core of economic theorising, for example, of demand curves. Thus cointegration produces both statistically and economically meaningful results.

In order to explore the dynamic adjustment of variables towards equilibrium an error-correction model is often employed. This combines a test for cointegration as well as exploring the association between changes in the variables. Thus we might, as Simmons (1996) implies, assume that there is a dynamic context to attendance demand and start with a model such as

$$A_t = B_1 + B_2 P_t + B_3 P_{t-1} + B_4 A_{t-1} + u_t. \tag{6.1.6}$$

Now this dynamic model implies that the long run effect on attendance of a change in prices is $(B_2 + B_3/1 - B_4)$. Thus, in the long run, if $t-1 = t$ then,

$$A_t = B_1 + B_2 P_t + B_3 P_t + B_4 A_t + u_t, \tag{6.1.7}$$

or,

$$A_t = B_4 A_t = B_1 + (B_2 + B_3) P_t + u_t, \tag{6.1.8}$$

or,

$$A_t = \frac{B_1}{1 - B_4} + \frac{(B_2 + B_3)}{1 - B_4} P_t + u_t. \tag{6.1.9}$$

In (6.1.9), the complicated coefficient on the price variable identifies how changes in price will affect attendance in the long run. The top line of this coefficient indicates the direct impact of price changes in periods t and $t-1$. The bottom line captures the (infinite) sum of progressively smaller and smaller effects that changes in one period's attendance has on the next period's attendance. The relationship $(B_2 + B_3/1 - B_4 = z)$ thus implies that z is a scaling factor that translates the short-run effects of P into a long run effect on A. It is akin to a multiplier effect. This relationship can be rewritten as:

$$z(1 - B_4) = B_2 + B_3 \tag{6.1.10}$$

or

$$z(1 - B_4) - B_2 = B_3. \tag{6.1.11}$$

Substituting (6.1.11) into equation (6.1.6) leaves

$$A_t = B_1 + B_2 P_t + [z(1 - B_4) - B_2]P_{t-1} + B_4 A_{t-1} + u_t. \tag{6.1.12}$$

Subtracting A_{t-1} from each side and simplifying leaves

$$A_t - A_{t-1} = B_1 + B_2(P_t - P_{t-1}) + z(1 - B_4) P_{t-1} \\ + (B_4 - 1)A_{t-1} + u_t, \tag{6.1.13}$$

noting that $1 - B_4 = -(B_4 - 1)$ implies that $z(1 - B_4)P_{t-1} = -z(B_4 - 1)$, which in turn implies that (6.1.13) can be simplified to

$$\Delta A_t = B_1 + B_2 \Delta P_t + (B_4 - 1)(A_{t-1} - z P_{t-1}) + u_t, \tag{6.1.14}$$

or,

$$\Delta A_t = B_1 + B_2 \Delta P_t - (1 - B_4)(A_{t-1} - z P_{t-1}) + u_t. \tag{6.1.15}$$

This equation captures the essence of the error correction model. Changes in attendance are driven by changes in price and the extent to which there was no equilibrium in the last period. A stable model requires $|B_4| < 1$, which suggests negative feedback and implies the equation will correct for errors and equilibrium will be achieved. In other words, a continually smaller proportion of any disequilibrium gets carried forward into changes in attendance. If all of the changes are zero, i.e. $\Delta = 0$, then in equilibrium $t = t-1$ and (6.1.15) becomes:

$$0 = B_1 - (1 - B_4)(A_{t-1} - z P_{t-1}) + u_t, \tag{6.1.16}$$

or,

$$(1 - B_4)A_t = B_1 + (1 - B_4)z P_{t-1} + u_t, \tag{6.1.17}$$

or,

$$A_t = \frac{B_1}{1 - B_4} + z P_t + u_t, \tag{6.1.18}$$

or

$$A_t = \frac{B_1}{1 - B_4} + \frac{(B_2 + B_3)}{1 - B_4} P_t + u_t. \tag{6.1.19}$$

This equation is the same as (6.1.9). It indicates the long run impact, i.e. emergent equilibrium relationship, that changes in price will lead changes in attendance too. (6.1.15) thus enables the researcher, such as Simmons (1996), to explore the short run dynamics of the relationship between attendance and, say, prices as well as the long run equilibrium.

Discussion questions

1. Under the assumption that you were thinking of investigating the demand for a sport of interest:
   (a) How would you observe the influence of the price of a close substitute on attendance at your sport?
   (b) How would you measure the 'quality' of a team or player?
   (c) Consider how one might measure 'uncertainty of outcome' in a given sports league; (i) in the very short run, (ii) within a season and (iii) over the longer run.
2. Would you say there is a consensus of opinion on the influence of determinants of demand for sports events?
3. What improvements have taken place in the literature on the demand for professional team sports and still need to be made?
4. Take any econometric study of the demand for professional team sports and carefully assess whether or not:
   (a) The variables used are adequate proxies for the influences on attendance.
   (b) Relevant potential econometric problems have been addressed.
   (c) The results are in line with the findings of this chapter.

7 The uncertainty of outcome hypothesis
Theoretical and empirical issues

Introduction

In the last chapter the empirical literature on the demand for professional team sports was discussed. Based on a critical review of the literature it was suggested that while there was a diversity of findings upon the determinants of the demand, nonetheless some significant patterns could be understood. As far as economic factors are concerned, while the traditional literature argued that market size was a ubiquitous determinant of demand, price and income effects were identified as weak influences. Moreover, as far as sporting factors are concerned seasonal success, though not the traditional notion of uncertainty of outcome, and team and player qualities appear important determinants of demand. Significantly, it was argued that the traditional literature suffered from a short run aggregate and average emphasis. In particular it was argued that as longer time horizons are adopted for empirical studies then traditional economic determinants of demand, such as prices and incomes, appear to be more significant determinants than previously had been argued to be the case – though a heterogeneity of findings remained.

Because of the assumed centrality of the uncertainty of outcome hypothesis for the economics of professional team sports, this chapter re-examines some theoretical and empirical issues associated with the measurement of uncertainty of outcome in more detail. In the next section we briefly redefine uncertainty of outcome, before assessing the empirical indicators of various measures.

We conclude that while there are several problems associated with measuring this concept, nonetheless, in sympathy with the discussions of the last chapter and Chapter 4, long run domination in sports through evolution into a traditionally acceptable form of competition seems to have been the pattern in sports league development. We therefore question the previously assumed centrality of this hypothesis to making leagues work effectively. In the next chapter we argue that this situation *could* change with the growth of TV revenues in sport through their changing the underlying structure of demand. In Chapters 9 and 10 we examine what we perceive to have been the major impacts of leagues attempting to manage uncertainty of outcome.

The nature of uncertainty of outcome

Chapter 2 outlined the uncertainty of outcome hypothesis due to Rottenberg (1956). Chapter 4 argued that the interdependence between providers of team sports suggests the need for a balance between mutual co-operation and mutual competition. It was argued that this has provided a defence of the widespread practice of revenue sharing (cross-subsidisation) and other anti-competitive measures to maintain competitive balance and long run revenue flows. While this hypothesis has been deeply ingrained in the ways of thinking about team sports, as also argued in Chapter 4, less well established is its quantitative impact. We argue that this is partly due to the difficulty of deciding what precisely is meant by 'uncertainty of outcome' and how it may be measured.

To begin with it is worth noting that expressions such as 'technical progress', for example, are in fairly regular use by people who feel they know what the expressions mean, but who would find it hard to give precise definitions. Economists long ago discovered that there was no single practical definition of technical progress and that in consequence attempting to quantify its effects on economic growth is fraught with difficulty. We only begin to appreciate the complexity of heretofore apparently simple and universally recognised concepts when we attempt to apply them. We would argue that uncertainty of outcome is another term used frequently without careful delineation of its precise meaning. This is despite recognising that researchers are ultimately forced to produce working definitions acceptable to other economists and capable of being observed. There is little chance that any writer will produce a definition of uncertainty of outcome that will gain universal acceptance, still less one that wins long-term adherence. As Cairns *et al.* (1986) assert:

> ... it is unfortunate that not only has empirical testing of the key relationship between demand and uncertainty of outcome been limited, but also that the discussion of this central concept has been unmethodical, if not confused. Inadequate attention has been paid to determining the appropriate empirical specifications of the underlying theoretical notions.
>
> (p. 5)

While they refer to earlier literature, despite the best efforts of subsequent researchers these remarks still ring true. We pursue their theme and bring it up to date with the introduction of measures proposed more recently and these comments are organised according to the four versions of uncertainty of outcome distinguished by Cairns *et al.* (1986):

(a) Short run uncertainty related to the outcome of an individual match.
(b) Uncertainty during the season about the identity of the eventual winners.
(c) Uncertainty during the season arising from several teams being 'in contention'.
(d) Long run uncertainty arising from the competition not being dominated by one club.

Short-run match uncertainty

First, short run (match) uncertainty is the notion that spectators prefer close contests, and might be captured by some estimate, if available, of the prior probability (p) of a home win. The closer p is to 0.5 – ignoring the probability of a draw – the more attractive is the match according to this version of the hypothesis. Hart *et al.* (1975), in an early paper on English association football, take teams' pre-match league positions as an indicator of the result. The smaller the absolute difference in pre-match league position, the more attractive the game ought to be to spectators, assuming that they wish to see close games rather than see their own team win irrespective of the quality of play.

Hart *et al.* (op. cit.) included the logarithms of both teams' (home and away) pre-match league standings among the explanatory variables in a log attendance equation, estimated using data on four English clubs over three seasons. They found the home team league standing variable insignificant, largely because the home teams (the four regressions were run separately) tended to hover about fixed points in the table. Multicollinearity would have been less severe had they used data on all clubs in one division in the same regression. This would however have imposed arguably unrealistic restrictions on the elasticity estimates by forcing them to be equal. An alternative, employed by Simmons (1996), would have been to run their single-club regressions over a sufficient number of seasons to permit clubs' rankings to vary more than four seasons showed. They subsequently added (Hart *et al.*, 1975, p. 25) the logarithm of the absolute difference in league standing to the original equation, but without finding it significant.

Cairns (1990) inadvertently gives a misleading impression of the procedure in Hart *et al.* and overlooks the fact that this was subsidiary to the use of the separate league standings. We briefly digress into the rhetoric of economic research, to point out that commentators frequently credit Hart and his associates with having done what Cairns attributed to them, not what they did.

A misattribution comes from Szymanski and Kuypers (1999). Their table (7.6 on p. 278) informs the reader that Hart *et al.* had used the log of the difference between pre-match league standings. It may seem unduly pedantic to comment upon what one assumes to be a typographical error (the essential word 'absolute' has been left out), but the fact is that you cannot take the logs of differences since some will be negative and negative numbers have no logarithms.[1] However it is perfectly feasible to take logarithms of *absolute* differences, which are all positive numbers. Whether team *A* is four places above (+) or four places below (−) team *B* at the kick-off is immaterial; they are simply four places 'apart' in absolute terms. Which is why the original researchers used the logs of absolute differences. Not all of Szymanski and Kuypers' readers will automatically replace the missing word mentally every time they read the passage. Sooner or later the misinformation will appear in student essays and in all probability in articles and books. This is an example of the phenomenon that while errors are easily made (our own included) they are extraordinarily hard to eradicate once they gain currency and, moreover, they may acquire new twists.

Another example of confusion (this looks less like a typographical error) between differences and absolute differences occurs in Wilson and Sim (1995). The authors used the absolute points difference *ABDIF*, and its square *ABDIFSQ* in a study of Malaysian semi-professional association football attendance *ATT*. They selected *ABDIF* in preference to the absolute difference in league standings on the ground that there was greater variation in points than in league standings thanks to the relatively small number of teams involved. Greater variability would give a better chance of picking up any relationship in the data.

ABDIFSQ was apparently included to allow for the possibility of a non-linear relationship between attendance and match uncertainty. In the original authors' words:

> A large value for *ABDIF* implies low uncertainty and thus low attendance. As *ABDIF* falls in value the expected contest is likely to be more evenly fought, thus increasing uncertainty and attendance. After a critical point at which uncertainty is at a maximum, any further fall in *ABDIF* would reduce uncertainty and *ATT*.
>
> (Wilson and Sim, 1995, p. 134, fn. 12)

The *actual* difference in points might indeed have some critical value not too far from zero according to the uncertainty hypothesis. As Cairns *et al.* argue,

> Tests which are based solely on entering the pre-match difference in league positions are not capable of testing the uncertainty of match outcome hypothesis. Consider the difference in league positions. Define a variable *DIFF* which is the home team's league position minus the visiting team's league position. A very large positive value will imply a relatively low probability of success for the home team. As *DIFF* falls the

---

[1] If you think negative numbers do have logarithms, try to get the log of −1 on your calculator. The ERROR message will help you understand why Hart *et al.* (1975) could not have used the logs of differences in league standings in their work.

subjective probability of a home victory increases. At first as *DIFF* falls the uncertainty of outcome will also increase (as the anticipated dominance of the visitor declines). As *DIFF* falls further and the probability of a home win continues to rise a position will be reached where uncertainty of outcome is at a maximum (the teams, *taking home advantage into account*, are evenly balanced).

(Cairns *et al.* 1986, p. 18, our italics)

However the *absolute* points difference is much less informative. A two point *absolute* difference is just as consistent with the away team having a positive lead that offsets home advantage as with it having a negative lead that compounds home advantage. No one-to-one mapping exists from the absolute points difference into the level of uncertainty *taking into account home advantage*, so the inclusion of *ABDIF* and its square cannot be justified by reference to the argument advanced by Cairns *et al.*

Wilson and Sim did not find the points difference variables statistically significant, due perhaps to collinearity between them. The sample correlation coefficient between these variables was 0.92. This seems like a self-inflicted wound, given that there was never any justification for including both *ABDIF* and *ABDIFSQ* in their specification; better by far to use either *ABDIF* alone or the actual differences *DIF* and their squares *DIFSQ* together. *DIF* and *DIFSQ* would be far less correlated than *ABDIF* and *ABDIFSQ*. Also the estimated critical point might suggest the average points value of home advantage in the Malaysian league.

Borland and Lye (1992) measured *UDIFF* as the difference in league standings, but did not conclude that it was significant. In view of earlier remarks about the viability of using actual differences, let us note that Borland and Lye's attendance equation had a mixture of logarithmic and natural variables. Their dependent variable was the logarithm of attendance but the uncertainty variables appeared in natural form. This is why they were able to use a measure that could assume negative values, while Hart and his associates (1975) and (see the next but one section) Dobson and Goddard (1992) could not.

A major problem with using league standings or prior differences in points as a proxy for match uncertainty is that the implied forecast of the result is based on partial information. Knowledge is often available about the first team squad's fitness, which is crucial to spectators and which they would use. League standings also ignore the effect of home advantage, although it is hard to say how that might be quantified. Furthermore, a forecast based on league standings is entirely backward-looking; spectators trying to estimate the probability of a home win will be using available forward looking information, e.g. whether a player will have worked off that three-match suspension in time for the game.

As noted last chapter, Peel and Thomas (1988) provided a forward-looking indicator of the probability of a home win using published betting odds.

Participants in the betting market will have incorporated a range of relevant information that is far wider than the teams' prior league standings. Some of that will be forward-looking, for example, information about the fitness of players currently receiving medical attention. Betting odds ought therefore to be more efficient than prior league standings as predictors of the unknown probabilities of home wins. We may compute an estimate of the prior probability of a home win from the observed betting odds, if we are prepared to make two simplifying assumptions. First, that the probability of a draw is zero; second, that the bookmaker's 'spread' – or margin for covering costs – is also zero.

Under these circumstance a simple relationship exists between the probability of a home win (p) and the betting odds. If, for example, the quoted odds are 3 to 1 against a home win, the implied probability of a home win is 1 in 4, or $p = 0.25$. Peel and Thomas exploited this relationship to obtain a forward-looking estimate of p. Oddly – as Cairns (1990) observes – they did not put the uncertainty hypothesis to the test by trying to establish if match attendance tended to increase as the value of p (*ceteris paribus*) approached 0.5. A potential problem derives from sample selection bias; the population of bettors on a given match may have systematically different expectations from the population of probable match goers.

Peel and Thomas (1997) investigate the efficiency of bookmakers' pre-set handicaps on English rugby league matches as predictors of actual point spreads. In spread betting the bookmaker offers fixed odds on the match outcome, subject to a pre-set 'handicap', which is a number of points allocated in advance to the team the bookmakers regard as less likely to win. The authors are interested, among other things, in whether the pre-allocated absolute handicap (*AHCAP* as they term it) is a sufficiently good predictor of the point spread (*APS* in their terminology) between the favoured team's score and the opponents' score to be useful indices of match uncertainty.

To illustrate, assume that bookmakers fancy team H (home) over team A (away) and accordingly allocate ten points to team A. If the result is 20–0, *APS* is 20 points and *AHCAP* is 10; bookmakers correctly forecast the match result, but underestimated team H's superiority. On the other hand, should the score be 15–40, the bookmakers got the wrong result; *APS* is −25 and *AHCAP* is 10. Naively one might expect a simple linear relationship to hold between *APS* and *AHCAP*

$$APS_m = \beta_0 + \beta_1 AHCAP_m + u_m, \tag{7.1}$$

where the subscript m denotes any given match, the βs are parameters to be estimated and u is a random error term. For *AHCAP* to be an unbiased estimate of *APS* – which, as discussed in Chapter 5, is a desirable property in any estimate/forecast – it is first of all necessary that β_0 should equal 0. A positive value would indicate a persistent tendency of bookmakers to underestimate *APS* when using *AHCAP*. Second, it is essential that β_1 be equal to

1. A value below 1 would indicate a tendency of bookmakers to overreact to small changes in information available, in consequence $AHCAP$ would be persistently more volatile than APS. This is because the information implied in measurements of $AHCAP$ needs to be 'dampened' by $\beta_1 < 1$ to capture APS. Ideally they ought to be equally volatile. Economic forecasts usually prove to be less volatile than the reality they are trying to predict, which might lead one to anticipate that estimates of β_1 should be greater than 1. Peel and Thomas obtained estimates below 1, although not significantly less. Third, the error term u must be a random variable.

While Peel and Thomas (1997) report favourable tests of the restrictions on the βs, they do not test for the normality of the disturbances in their OLS regressions. As discussed in the last chapter, this is an assumption required to justify the use of the approach. In general the assumption implies that OLS is designed for data (on the dependent variable) which can be positive or negative and which can be fractional or integer. It is clear that these assumptions do not exactly fit the models of attendance demand discussed in the last chapter. For example only positive attendance values are observed. However, as an approximation they may be appropriate in that such demand can conceivably vary in small almost fractional amounts. It remains that this is an assumption that needs to be more vigorously investigated than in the past.[2] In contrast, APS and $AHCAP$ can only take positive integer or discrete values and in practice vary in a considerably discrete fashion. Under these circumstances, the researchers might better have applied Poisson regression or negative binomial regression, which are specifically designed to deal with such 'count' data.

Even if correct in their conclusion that $AHCAP$ is an efficient and unbiased predictor of APS, the sample R^2 statistics range from 0.13 to 0.35 dependent on whether the regression is run on all data or by Division. Thus $AHCAP$ may be an unbiased indicator but it is clearly an imperfect one.

The authors report that $AHCAP$ was found to be a significant explanatory variable in attendance regressions. With every one-point increase in $AHCAP$, the authors reckon, about 52 people were lost to a First Division game and 9 to a Second Division game in 1994–95, which is consistent with the hypothesis. This may not seem like a lot but the mean handicap in the First Division sample was about 10 points.

This led Peel and Thomas to infer (1997, p. 569) that equalised team performance ($AHCAP = 0$ for all games) would on average add about 520 to First Division gates, relative to mean attendance of about 5900. However, economic models are linear versions of a more complex world and it is

---

[2] In a similar way, as noted in Chapter 6, only Kuypers (1996) attempts to employ a regression method that explicitly deals with particular features of the dependent variable. As discussed there, he employs a Tobit model to account for the fact that the data on attendance is truncated due to sell-out fixtures for some teams.

dangerous in a non-linear world to infer from the estimated response of some system to a 'small' change in any given stimulus how it will react to a 'large' change. Good examples of non-linearities in markets would be major changes in the way they are organised; say the effect on the UK foreign currency market of the Euro, or the effect of unification on the car market in erstwhile East Germany. A comparable 'regime change' – for example equalisation of team expenditures on players over the last ten years and with no expectation of a policy reversal – may be required in rugby league to give all teams identical prospects. The sport did not experience equality of team prospects in 1994–95, any more than in its more distant past, nor will it in the near future. Having estimated their equations under one set of conditions, the writers cannot reasonably expect to project them into a radically different environment. It follows that even if the reader accepts the 52 as a useful approximation, the 520 must be taken with an extremely generous 'pinch of salt'.

The paper by Kuypers (1996), as noted in Chapter 6, is notable in taking seriously the problems arising from the fact that ground capacities limit the numbers who can attend. Previous authors had largely ignored this issue. His treatment of uncertainty is also of interest. Kuypers used the difference between the maximum and minimum odds quoted on home win, away win and draw to gauge the short run uncertainty of a game. The basic notion is that near-equal odds quoted on all three possible outcomes indicate a most uncertain match; where there is a strongly fancied winner there will be a large gap between the odds offered on winner and loser. Thus one expects the difference between the maximum and minimum quoted odds to be inversely related to the uncertainty of the result. Kuypers (op. cit., p. 33, Table 9) found the odds variable insignificant and wrongly signed, which he interpreted as evidence that spectators prefer to see winning teams than uncertain matches; a theme echoed in other findings as discussed in Chapter 6.

Within-season uncertainty of outcome

The second form of uncertainty of outcome arises when spectators value uncertainty about the identity of the eventual champions, as distinct from uncertainty about the outcome of an individual game. As you will appreciate following the earlier discussion, there is little agreement on how to measure this. Borland (1987) tried four different measures, *UNA*, *UNB*, *UNC* and *UND*, in his annual attendance model of Australian rules football. Each of the four indices was an average of four observations made during the season. The last two were double-weighted on the grounds that a given level of uncertainty is more critical near the end of the season.

Dispersion might be viewed as the spread between top and bottom teams which *UNA* (the difference in the number of wins by the top and bottom clubs) captures. Another interpretation is that dispersion measures the distribution of wins between all the teams. *UNB*, the sum of the coefficients of variation of the number of games won by all teams, captures this. *UNA* and *UNB* measure dispersion in very different ways, *UNB* having the advantage of taking account of all teams, not just the top and bottom ones. *UNC* (the only partially successful version) is the average number of games behind the leader, yet another way to look at dispersion. There is a rationale behind the use of measures like these, the greater the dispersion, the greater the uncertainty, hence (in theory) the bigger the attendance.

These indices involved teams having little prospect of success, which in this context meant finishing in the top five (four prior to 1972) to qualify for the finals. Arguably one ought to look at teams in contention and dispersion does not capture this as a large gap between the clubs at the top and bottom of the league is consistent with a close bunching of clubs near the top. Equally a small gap between the extremes could be consistent with a runaway leader. Borland's *UND* is designed to be an indicator of the number of teams 'in contention'. It is the number of teams either in, or only two games out of, the top five (or four). *UND* and similar measures employed by Demmert (1973), Noll (1974) and other investigators to decide whether a championship race is close or which clubs are in the race are very arbitrary; why for example should *UND* stop at teams either in the top five or only three (or one) game out? How close, in other words, is close?

There is a rationale for trying to model teams in contention by somewhat less arbitrary criteria, if they can be found. Appendix 7.1 considers the application to the problem of a modified version of the Herfindahl Index, used to measure industry structure in the industrial organisation literature. The appendix illustrates just how difficult it is to obtain a good indicator of seasonal uncertainty that is not team specific. Even the Herfindahl Index, for all its merits, is not very good!

The combination of a (probably) unsolvable problem and skepticism about the uncertainty hypothesis perhaps explains why some researchers leave seasonal uncertainty out altogether, even at the risk of specification error. Two recent studies that take this line are Dobson and Goddard (1995) and Simmons (1996), both discussed in Chapter 6. In view of the difficulty of finding a suitable summary statistic for the uncertainty of a whole season, this is probably a sensible decision.

Seasonal (team-specific) uncertainty of outcome

The third form of uncertainty of outcome is seasonal uncertainty where the uncertainty derives, not from spectators themselves valuing uncertain contests as such, but from the presence of several 'contenders for glory'. While there are differences of opinion about how to model this, there seems to be more agreement about how to proceed and slightly more robust estimates than with the other form of seasonal uncertainty. As implied in Chapter 5, Jennett (1984) merits careful consideration here, not least because his method has been adopted and or modified by others, albeit with reservations. Borland

and Lye (1992) used a variation in a study of Australian rules football, while Dobson and Goddard (1992) produced a version designed to be used in logarithmic attendance functions. Kuypers (1996) proposed a modified version which has some interesting if rather disturbing properties of its own, as we show.

Jennett proposed a readily observed variable to capture the development of uncertainty through the season team by team and match by match. While his paper is discussed at some length in Chapter 5, here we focus on his solution to modelling uncertainty. In any given match one or both or possibly neither team will start with a chance of glory. Matches where at least one team 'may' win the championship have the greatest 'championship significance' in Jennett's parlance. In an ideal world the researcher would be able to observe spectators' subjective expectations of their own teams' championship prospects prior to every match, which is clearly impossible. As a substitute Jennett proposed a measure based on the mathematical possibility of winning the title in year X.

To illustrate Jennett's procedure, assume a league that comprises 17 teams, which play each other home and away, meaning 32 matches per team per season, and that the eventual winners in year X had scored 75 points. To derive Jennett's measure of the evolving season X uncertainty, we compute match by match for every team the number of wins it would require to take the title. For those still in with a mathematical possibility, the significance of their next match is simply the reciprocal of the number of games they must win. Thus, if league custom awards three points for a win, and in year X every team begins its 32-game season needing 25 wins (75 points = 25 wins $\times$ 3 points for a win), so teams' starting significance levels are identically $1/25 = 0.04$. Significance levels evolve during the season, increasing numbers of teams dropping out of contention as time passes, and such teams are accorded significance scores of zero.

If a team has won its first 24 matches, its twenty-fifth has a significance score equal to $1/1 = 1$, as it needs only one win to take the championship. If the opposing team in this game had won its first two games and lost the rest, the eight remaining (assuming it had also played twenty-four) are insufficient, even if all are won, to make up 75 points. The championship significance of the twenty fifth match for the second team is thus 0 and must have been so ever since the team lost its tenth game, after which they had only 22 games to win 69 points. They had started that tenth match needing to win it and all subsequent matches, with a significance score of $1/23 = 0.043$. They ended it with a significance score of 0. The bigger the significance score, which must lie between 0 and 1, the greater the attraction of the next game. Once the champions have emerged, all other teams drop out of the running and score zero. To maximise interest requires as many teams as possible to remain in contention right up till the last moment.

Both teams in any encounter (aggregation is at match level) are allocated their significance scores as described, *HSIG* for the home side and *ASIG* for the visitors. In Chapter 5 you will find that Jennett used the same approach to define corresponding indicators of the relegation significance of each game, which we note and pass on. In his attendance (see Chapter 5) regressions Jennett obtained positive and statistically significant estimates of the slope parameters of *HSIG* and *ASIG*, which supported his version of the uncertainty of outcome hypothesis.

Cairns (1990) draws our attention to some unsatisfactory aspects of Jennett's measures. The first is that they capture mathematical possibilities rather than probabilities. A team remains in contention as long as it has sufficient games in hand, irrespective of the probability it might win them all. In our example the team with six points from its first two matches and none thereafter stays in contention until it loses the tenth. Long before that the fans would have written off its championship prospects! Already noted is the implication that all teams start the season equal favourites. This is not too serious a problem since the opening games are unlikely to seem very significant. Cairns also pointed out that to compute *HSIG* and *ASIG* requires the use of information (the number of points that the champions earned) that is never available until the championship is decided. Even though followers look at numbers of points and numbers of games in hand, nobody could calculate *HSIG* and *ASIG* until after the season has ended. It is intrinsically a backward-looking measure of uncertainty of outcome.

Borland and Lye (1992) applied a modified version of Jennett's approach to Australian rules football, although it is not quite clear how they arrived at their results. They did not use separate significance variables for the home and away teams. Instead a single variable termed *UJ* appears in the equations. They define *UJ* as: '. . . the sum of the number of matches required to qualify for the finals for each team playing in a particular game' (p. 1055). We interpret this to mean that *UJ* is a function of the sum of the number of games required by both teams. Most likely what they meant to say is that it is the *reciprocal* of that sum. The positive estimates of the regression coefficients they report would be consistent with this interpretation; by contrast, if their statement is correct then less significant matches, *ceteris paribus*, are better attended. Using *UJ* in place of *ASIG* and *HSIG* discards information about whether a match is significant for both teams or for one only. They add another 'match significance' variable *UD5*, a close relative of *UND* as used in Borland (1987), which is a dichotomous dummy taking the value 1 if both teams are in the top five positions. They find *UD5* significant. A single index of match significance (*UJ*) is justifiable if spectators are attracted mainly by the 'significance' of a game and are indifferent (as for example 'theatregoers') to the identities of the teams. This consideration suggests that *UJ* and *UD5* probably belong in the previous section.

Borland and Lye (1992, p. 1055, fn. 6) mention that *HSIG* and *ASIG* may behave oddly near the end of the season. It is not unknown for the eventual champions to need one win from the last two games and to lose the first. The significance score going into the last-but-one game is 1. Having lost that game, they still need only one win, so the significance score for the last game remains at 1. Supporters might not see things in this light, but of course supporters are looking at probabilities and not mathematical possibilities!

Appendix 7.1 analyses the end of season behaviour of Jennett's index. One might reasonably suppose that the equal 'significance' of a sequence of games means that they are equally important insofar as they must all be won to secure the championship. If this is regarded as a desirable property of a significance index, Jennett's measures do not satisfy it, as the first column of Array 1 in the appendix reveals. The significance scores are 0.33, 0.5 and 1.0, yet all games have to be won. On the other hand if (like Jennett) by equal 'significance' one means that the championship could be awarded given a fixed number of victories, his measure is satisfactory, as the last column of Array 2 shows. The significance scores run 1.0, 1.0 and 1.0. The team loses all its last three games, hence fails to become the champion, but the fact is that it could have won the title by winning any one of those games. In that sense these games have equal significance.

Both concepts of equality of significance have some appeal. If it were possible to build an index that had both properties and if both properties were held to be desirable any index combining them would be preferred to Jennett's, although it does not appear that the properties can be reconciled within the same index. The appendix shows that there is a simple modification of Jennett's index (*WN/GL*) that has the first (but not the second) of these desirable properties. Any researcher who prefers the principle that all games that must be won are identically significant could use the modified index. Those who think equal significance means the target has not altered could stick to Jennett's index. Recall the quotation from Cairns *et al.* (1986), who referred to the 'unmethodical, if not confused' discussion of the central concept. It is not certain that all previous writers have been clear in their own minds which (if any) of these two concepts of equal significance they adhered to.

Dobson and Goddard (1992) use indices of match significance, which are essentially Jennett's. The value taken by the index of significance of the team's next match is based on the relationship between the number of games remaining (z) and the difference ($y - x$) between the number of points needed to win the title (y) and the number of points so far accumulated (x). Three cases arise, A, B and C.

A: If $(y - x)/3 > z$ there are insufficient games left to allow winning the title. The index is set $= 1$.

B: If $(y - x)/3 \leqslant z$, the team is in with a chance and the index value is set at $1 + 3/(y - x)$ subject to a maximum of 2. So with (say) one game left and three points required $(y - x) = 3$, the index value is 2 and the team has got to win the game. With one game left and two points required $(y - x) = 2$, which would make the index equal to 2.5, the team must still win since you get only one point for a draw. The index is set at 2. With one game left and only one point required $(y - x) = 1$, the index would be 4; but the authors limit its value to 2.

C: If $(y - x)/3 \leqslant 0$ the team has already won the championship. The index is set to 2.

Dobson and Goddard's index thus varies between 1 (out of contention) and 2. Between 1 and 2, the closer it is to 2, the more significant the game. But unlike Jennett's index it is restricted to positive values, which is important to Dobson and Goddard because their model is defined in the logarithms of the variables, including the uncertainty ones. In Jennett's version teams out of contention have their *ASIGS* and *HSIGS* equal to 0. But 0 has no logarithm (try log 0 on your calculator). The authors have very neatly reformulated Jennett's *HSIG* and *ASIG* to permit their use in a logarithmic form. Cairns' remarks about the Jennett measures apply also to these.

    To capture seasonal uncertainty, Kuypers (1996) derived measures of match significance superior to Jennett's in that they are based on information available at the time; points behind the leader (*PB*) and games left (*GL*). Spectators could in principle use these (unlike *ASIG*, *HSIG* and *UJ*) to assess the importance of any game in advance. The rationale is that the fewer games a team has left and the fewer points it lies behind the leader, the more significant is its next game. If by winning all the games it has left a team cannot reach the number of points held by the leaders now, it is out of contention. The bigger the value of the indicator, the less significant the match to which it applies.

    In advance of the next match *PB* is known with certainty, as is *GL*; although since the results of future matches cannot be known in advance, the future values of *PB* cannot be exactly predicted. Other things equal, the greater is *GL* the less certain are the team's prospects. As the season draws to a close (*GL* diminishes) an increasing number of teams become aware that they have no prospect of winning the championship, while for the few left in contention the range of possible outcomes from best to worst diminishes.

    Kuypers and Jennett employ different concepts of 'significance'. The former is concerned with uncertainty surrounding a team's final league standing. A value of unity on Jennett's index implies that the team has only to win to be declared champion. A value of unity on Kuypers' index means that it is one point behind the current leader with one game to play. Even a win may not secure the championship; the leaders may meanwhile be winning their own last game, or another team two points behind with two to play may win its last two games. In Jennett's model the team is aiming at a known (*ex post facto*) target, while in Kuypers' model, as in life, it pursues an unknown target. That is why we do not construct 'transition arrays' in the appendix to illustrate the properties of the Kuypers index; what happens to *PB* depends not only on the team itself but also on the other teams.

    Kuypers (1996, p. 18) proposes three indices, A, B and C. His published live-attendance regressions involve B only, and the TV audience regressions A only, without comment on the performance of indicator C in any regressions; although the discussion below suggests that C will not be a good index. His measures are:

A: $PB^{0.75} \times GL^{1.25}$
B: $PB \times GL$
C: $\{(PB/3GL) \times (GL^2 + 2GL)\}$.

GL is most heavily weighted in A and least in C; in B it gets equal weight with *PB*. No justification is offered for these specific expressions, other than that they combine *GL* and *PB* in varying weights and (this is left implicit) that the original author had no strong prior expectation about which is 'best'.[3] We feel very much that since *GL* is the source of the uncertainty it ought to be more heavily weighted. Whichever of A, B or C is used, the current leader is assigned a value of 1 and any team which mathematically cannot win the title is assigned a value 0. A, B and C are computed only after the first 20 games have been played – the first few weeks' play are sensibly regarded as too insignificant to count.

Take the simplest measure first. B is the product of games left and points behind. Because it weights *GL* and *PB* equally it does not pay sufficient attention to *GL* and is thus unable reliably to distinguish between matches that are expected to have different championship significance. To see this, consider the championship significance of the next game of a team three points adrift, with three games to play. We compute this as $3 \times 3 = 9$. The next game of a team that is one point behind with nine games to play (i.e. earlier in the season) is also $1 \times 9 = 9$. Given the much greater uncertainty surrounding the second team's progress, we conclude that B is not satisfactory.[4]

Measure A looks more sensible in giving *GL* greater weight, although one wonders why Kuypers did not try the much simpler and not totally dissimilar $PB \times GL^a$ with *a* being a number (not necessarily an integer) not less than 2. This would give much greater weight to *GL*, which is, after all, the source of uncertainty. Let us check measure A's ability to rank sensibly those combinations of *GL* and *PB* that measure B failed to rank sensibly.

1. Team with three matches remaining and three points behind:
   $A = 3^{0.75}3^{1.25} = 3^2 = 9$
   Remember that $x^a x^b = x^{a+b}$.

---

[3] Szymanski and Kuypers (1999, p. 279) state that, 'Kuypers (1996) develops a new measure of seasonal uncertainty using a championship and relegation significance variable which is just the product of the number of games left in the season and the number of points behind (above) the leader (relegation zone)'. So the author may now prefer his index B.
[4] Just in case you are wondering, a team nine points behind with one to play scores 0. It has no mathematical possibility of catching the leader and is therefore out of the race.

2. Team with nine matches remaining and one point behind:
    $A = 1^{0.75}9^{1.25} = 1(9^{1.25}) = 15.59$
    Remember that $1^a = 1$.

Measure A manages to get different answers, and a sensible ranking. But one's gut feeling is that any match played with nine to go is surrounded by relatively more uncertainty than the ratio of the computed scores suggests. Measure C combines two ideas that each strike the observer as potentially relevant to the spectator's problem; which is to decide if the next game is so significant for their team's championship prospects that they must make every effort to be there. The rationalisation is entirely ours. First, C incorporates the average number of points per game left needed to catch up with the leader's current position (hence the ratio $PB/3GL$). Second, C allows for the impact of games in hand on the championship significance, via the quadratic expression $(GL^2 + 2GL)$. This particular quadratic expression was presumably chosen because the whole expression ensures that the team one point behind with one game to play scores 1 on index C, just as it does on indexes A and B.

We can simplify the expression for C as GL appears in both numerator and denominator. Cancelling GL we find the simpler expression:

$$(PB/3)(GL + 2) = 0.333(PB/GL) + 0.666PB.$$

As noted above, C gives more weight to PB than to GL and we expect this to cause trouble. Let us check how well measure C rates the two teams considered:

1. Team with three to play and three points adrift:
    $C = (3/9) \times (9 + 6) = 5$.
2. Team with nine to play and one point adrift:
    $C = (1/27) \times (81 + 18) = 3.67$.

Measure C actually succeeds in judging the second game to be the more significant. We are reluctantly compelled to conclude that, persuasive as we find Kuypers' approach, the explicit functional forms he used are of limited value. Rather more effective is our suggestion, which we might call measure D, designed to give more weight to GL:

D: $PB \times GL^a$.

We believe that $a \geq 2$ is a sensible restriction to impose on measure D; the higher the power, the greater the effect of uncertainty. We cannot determine an objective (acceptable to everybody) reason for choosing a particular power. The simplest form that yields subjectively sensible rankings (ones that seem about right to the user) is the one to choose. For example, if we use $a = 2$ the team that is three points adrift with three to play scores $3 \times 3^2 = 27$ for its next game. The team that is one point behind with nine to play, gets $1 \times 9^2 = 81$ for its next game, which if anything appears still to under-represent the greater relative uncertainty.

Setting $a = 3$ would give for the first team's next match $D = 3 \times 3^3 = 81$, while the other's would score $D = 1 \times 9^3 = 729$, indicative of much greater relative uncertainty. Kuypers' decision to stick to observable information, *GH* and *PB*, is sound, but requires a little more care in its application.

General long-term uncertainty of outcome

The fourth form of uncertainty is long-term uncertainty of outcome, which has rarely been tested econometrically, although there is plenty of anecdotal evidence, some of which was discussed in the last chapter. Borland's (1987) pioneering paper attempted to model long-term uncertainty in Australian rules football employing a variable called *UNE*, which is the number of teams in the previous three years' finals stage, divided by the number of places available. Available places every year changed from (top teams) four to five. The basic notion is that 12 different teams (say) filling the 15 slots available in the previous three seasons is evidence of more even competitive balance than (at worst) five teams filling those same slots. Three years does not look like a very long run, although the length of the long run cannot be precisely defined. Borland did not have a sufficiently long data set (annual, 1950–1986) to permit him to set up (say) ten lags, because every time he used an observation to create a lagged value he would lose a degree of freedom.

In the event he did not find *UNE* statistically significant, which might mean that long-term dominance was not important in the sample. Or it might imply that three years does not capture the long run. Or there might have been so little variation in *UNE* during the observation period that its partial effects could not be detected. Unless an explanatory variable displays variation within the sampling period we cannot assess the impact of its changes. It is conceivable that in the VFL during the period in question long-term domination was having significant effects upon attendance, but that there was so little variation in long-term dominance that its effects could not be reliably estimated. This is a special case of multicollinearity. The problem is not that sample observations on a variable are closely related to other sample observations, but rather that the sample data on the variable show so little variation that it is virtually collinear with the intercept dummy. It follows that exploring long run uncertainty of outcome is a research issue that needs to be addressed.

Currently, as discussed in Chapter 4, with the exception of Borland's work all that exists is anecdotal evidence. Thus, Quirk and Fort (1992, Ch. 7) provide a battery of data on long run domination in America's chief spectator sports, baseball, basketball, ice hockey and football.

To recap some of their findings, the authors (inter alia) report (op. cit., p. 247, Table 7.1) the average standard deviations of the win/lose percentages decade by decade from 1901 until 1990, for major league baseball, basketball, ice hockey and football. The National Football League got going only in the 1940s; prior to that period American football's organisation was somewhat chaotic. For football, baseball and (to a lesser extent) ice hockey, the average standard deviations have been trending down, suggesting that competitive balance in those sports has tended to improve. In basketball no trend could be detected. They also computed for every sport for every decade the 'idealised' standard deviation of the win/lose percentage; the standard deviation that corresponded to a perfectly balanced league. Having done so they compared the measured standard deviations to the ideal equivalents. In every case the actual value significantly exceeded the ideal value. This means that there is an excess of teams at the bottom and at the top of the league standings and the spread between the champions and the bottom team is greater than equality of opportunity would imply. It confirms our prior expectation that perfect competitive balance has not yet been attained in these sports. They also compute 'lifetime' win/lose percentages for leagues finding that (surprise, surprise) teams like the New York Yankees and the Boston Celtics have attained (very) significantly high lifetime win percents. Necessarily others such as the Saint Louis Browns and the Boston Braves have been lifetime under-achievers (Quirk and Fort, 1992, Tables 7.6–7.11).

Quirk and Fort also examine the degree of concentration of league championships – if sporting leagues were perfectly balanced one might expect to find that every team had a similar number of titles. Their Table 7.4 shows the existence of dominant teams which win far more titles than one would expect if all teams had equal chances. By implication most teams never attain the ultimate goal. The data run until 1990 and show that the celebrated New York Yankees in 88 years won 33 American League titles, while the Boston Red Sox took 10 in 90 years. (The Yankees played two seasons in Baltimore, then relocated to New York.) In the National League, the Brooklyn Dodgers won 9 titles in 57 years before relocating to Los Angeles, where they won another 9 in 33 years. The picture in basketball is similar, with the Boston Celtics winning 16 titles in 44 years in the National Basketball Association. Montreal Canadiens won 23 ice hockey titles (US note!) in 73 years while Toronto won 13.[5] The National Football League looks less unequal in terms of championship wins; Green Bay Packers won 11 titles and Chicago Bears nine to 1990.

If one looks at English association football (Szymanski and Kuypers, 1999, Tables 4.2 and 7.1) 17 teams won league championships during the 47 seasons completed between the start of the Football League in 1889/90 and the start of World War II. League football was interrupted by both world wars. Between the resumption of professional association football in 1946 and the end of the 1998/99 season, 15 teams have won the 53 (Football and Premier) League championships completed. At first glance it appears that dominance has become more prevalent (17/47 >15/53) since 1945. Pre-war 47 wins distributed among 17 teams suggests the average pre-war winner took the title about 2.8 times. Fifty-three wins distributed among 15 clubs suggests that the average post-war winner took about 3.5 titles. Of around 90 teams throughout the post-war era, 75 have never won a championship; in any year only around 20 (those in the topmost division) are eligible to take part in the chase.

'The average winner' of course does not exist. Pre-war, the four (to take an arbitrary number) clubs with most championships were Aston Villa and Sunderland with six each, followed by Arsenal and Everton with five each; 22 in total. Post-war, the four clubs with most wins were Liverpool with 14, Manchester United with ten (they won again in 1998/99), Arsenal with six and Everton with four; 34 between them. Arsenal and Everton are among the top four clubs in both eras, while Liverpool with four titles pre-war only just failed to join them. It looks as if the industry has always been subject to domination by a small number of clubs, with more marked domination during the post-war era. Two clubs have enjoyed exceptional success in both eras. Scottish professional association football is in a more extreme state, Glasgow Rangers having recently won the championship on nine successive occasions, emulating Glasgow Celtic's 'run' of the 1960s and 1970s. Professional association football championships in other west European national leagues are likewise dominated by a handful of clubs (Szymanski and Kuypers, 1999), with Scottish association football, not surprisingly, the least balanced of their sample.

Focusing on the championship to the exclusion of second, third and other nearby places ignores potentially interesting information. Taking this information into account, a very different picture could emerge. However among those English association football teams very often coming second or third since 1946 we find Liverpool, Arsenal, Everton and Manchester United. Newcastle United, Preston North End and Sheffield Wednesday – with ten championships between them prior to 1939, but none since – appear among the runners-up. So do Tottenham Hotspur, Leeds United and Derby County with no pre-war, but seven post-war championships between them. That said, the four most successful clubs in terms of championships appear very often among the leading 'also-rans' since 1946.

English first-class (county) cricket displays a similar tendency to long run domination, according to Frindall (1993). Between 1890 and 1992, with no series in 1915/18 and again in 1940/45, Yorkshire won the annual County Championship outright on 29 occasions, sharing it twice, while Surrey (virtually unbeatable during the 1950s) took it outright 15 times and shared it once. In the early days counties fielded only native players, which may have helped Yorkshire as one of the more populous. In contrast Northamptonshire never won it, although they once (in about 100 attempts!) looked like potential winners. Australia's annual Sheffield-Shield contest between teams representing the several states has been won on 40 occasions by New South Wales (the most populous state) and on 25 by Victoria. South Africa's equivalent – the Currie Cup – was dominated by Transvaal (the most populous province) and by Natal.

In contrast to these essentially sporting leagues, some spectacularly one-sided sporting contests can be identified and, on occasions, attempts to revive competitive balance established. This is particularly in the case of tournaments, which by definition imply less frequent contests. The America's Cup began as a private (amateur) affair between American and British yachtsmen (not formally international). The New York Yacht Club won the first race in 1870 and the America's Cup stayed in America for over a century, in spite of the best four-yearly efforts (wartime excluded) of the British.

To attract a global TV audience, the event was opened during the 1980s to entrants from other countries, since when Australian and New Zealand yachts have won against strong international and US competition. A noteworthy development is that women now compete on absolutely equal terms with men.

In golf, the biennial Ryder Cup was similarly one-sided. Originally a team of American male professionals met (and often annihilated) a similarly constituted team from Britain and Ireland, the first match being in 1927. Swales (1996) shows that to 1995 the US had won 23, lost 6 and halved 2 of 31 Ryder Cup events. Of their six losses, three had occurred since 1979, when they first met a team representing Europe. Opening the contest appears to have succeeded in improving competitive balance. The amateur equivalent trophies, the Curtis Cup (women) and the Walker Cup (men), remained closed to all except US and Irish/British teams. To 1995 the US had won 20, lost 5 and halved 3 Curtis Cups, while they had won 30, lost 4 and drawn 1 Walker Cup. Should organisers seek to generate more widespread public interest, although there is less immediate financial pressure when athletes' services are free, these cups may need to be opened to include other countries' performers.

Thus, careful assessment of the empirical evidence suggests that the evolution of long-term domination looks like being the natural order in sports leagues to date and this is despite the effects of league management policies. As discussed earlier in the book, however, it remains that the processes by which this arises are not well understood and need further investigation. As such domination is typical of many industries other than sports, it may well be that analogies can be drawn from the process of competition there. As discussed in chapter 4, exploring the details of the dynamics of competition between teams would seem to be an urgent line of enquiry for future research.

The current environment would seem to be a particularly opportune moment for this type of work. As discussed in Chapter 3, 'policy regime' changes have occurred with the advent of TV revenues and elite leagues in UK, and likely to be European, sport. In the next chapter we analyse the historical context of these changes in some detail and try to indicate the likely impacts they will have on professional team sports.

Conclusions

We conclude this chapter, therefore, with the observation that there are several problems associated with any measurement of uncertainty of outcome. Nonetheless, the existent evidence suggests that uncertainty of outcome has been an overworked hypothesis in explaining the demand for professional team sports. Moreover, long- run domination in sports into a traditionally acceptable form of competition seems to have been the pattern in sports league development. We therefore question the previously assumed centralityof this hypothesis to making leagues work effectively. This is because short of radical action to equalise revenue it is hard to see how competitive balance can be improved in European team sports. While Americans share revenue to an extent that is only a dim memory in Europe, they still find their team sports dominated over long periods. In the next chapter we argue that this situation *could* change with the growth of TV revenues in sport through their radically changing the underlying structure of demand.

Appendix 7.1: Some properties of uncertainty of outcome indicators

This appendix is aimed at the reader who might be thinking about doing a piece of empirical work on the role of seasonal uncertainty of outcome in the demand for sport. Alternatively, it may be of interest to the general reader interested in quantifying the 'significance' of events.

The issues discussed throw light on how far it can be said that economists have succeeded in capturing the notion of uncertainty of outcome and in detecting its effects on attendance. Students of sports medicine or sports psychology will find parallels with research in those fields. We look first at the end-of-season behaviour of Jennett's and of a closely related index and second at the problems in trying to capture generalised seasonal uncertainty using a modified Herfindahl Index.

We look at two arrays recording how Jennett's index of significance behaves in the closing period of the season. It is defined as $1/WN$, where WN refers to the number of wins needed. The first shows how 'significance' behaves as the team wins successive games ('win transitions') and the second how it responds as the team loses successive matches ('lose transitions'). For the purpose of placing illustrative numbers in the arrays we assume teams initially have three games left and require from one to three wins for 'glory'. Scores other than the zeros for teams out of contention ought to increase as one moves *down* and *rightwards* through the arrays.

In the body of the chapter, we contrasted two equally plausible concepts of 'match significance'. One is Jennett's, whereby two successive matches score 1 if the team has the possibility of leaving the field as champions at the end of either. The second is based on required future 'average' performance. It scores two successive matches 1 if the team has to win both to become champions at the close of the second game. Win and lose arrays are also presented for this model. The arrays illustrate the relationship between these two concepts.

Array 1: Win transition array (Jennett ≡ 1/WN)

$WN = 1$ $GL = 1$ Index = 1	$WN = 0$ $GL = 1$ Index = 1 Champions	$WN = 0$ $GL = 1$ Index = 1 Champions
$WN = 2$ $GL = 2$ Index = 0.5	$WN = 1$ $GL = 2$ Index = 1	$WN = 0$ $GL = 2$ Index = 1 Champions
$WN = 3$ $GL = 3$ Index = 0.33	$WN = 2$ $GL = 3$ Index = 0.5	$WN = 1$ $GL = 3$ Index = 1

Any box (there are three) in Array 1 with $WN = 0$ and Index = 1 means the team in question has already won the championship. Clearly if $WN = 0$ we cannot compute $1/WN$; so the index is set to 1 when the championship has been secured. Now consider the bottom left-hand box, which tells us that a team needs three wins ($WN = 3$) from its last three games ($GL = 3$). The first of the three matches has significance level $1/3 = 0.33$. Should it win it moves up a row, needing two wins in two games, the implied significance level being 0.5. Having won the second match the significance level for the third is 1. Since it becomes the league champion only at the end of the last game, the first match it starts as champions will be next season. These figures demonstrate that Jennett's measure accords increasing significance as WN diminishes. Given that 'coronation' cannot occur before $WN = 0$, there is a clear logic behind attributing most significance to the last game, despite the fact that if the team loses the first one the others will be totally insignificant.

A team that requires one victory (bottom right-hand box) goes into the first of the three games with significance level 1. Having won, it moves up a row and plays its last two games as the championship winner. Jennett's *CHAMP* variable would be accorded the value 1 for the last two games. No other researchers using Jennett's approach to modelling seasonal uncertainty report having used *CHAMP* to pick up the possible 'glory' effect on attendance. In that sense nobody else has replicated Jennett's approach entirely.

Array 2: Lose transition array (Jennett ≡ 1/WN)

$WN = 3$ $GL = 1$ Index = 0	$WN = 2$ $GL = 1$ Index = 0	$WN = 1$ $GL = 1$ Index = 1
$WN = 3$ $GL = 2$ Index = 0	$WN = 2$ $GL = 2$ Index = 0.5	$WN = 1$ $GL = 2$ Index = 1
$WN = 3$ $GL = 3$ Index = 0.33	$WN = 2$ $GL = 3$ Index = 0.5	$WN = 1$ $GL = 3$ Index = 1

In Array 2 the team moves up one row every time it loses a match and as soon as $WN > GL$ it drops out of contention and the index is set to 0. Starting in the bottom middle box, a team needs two wins from three games. The first match has significance level 0.5. Once this is lost the second game also has significance level 0.5. The team's second defeat puts it out of contention and the last match scores 0 on the index. The last column displays to best advantage the feature picked up by Borland and Lye (1992). The significance score is identically 1 for a team needing one win from (successively) three games, two games and one game. Each successive game lost 'ought', one would think, to make the remaining ones more significant, because the chance of glory is diminishing, but 'significance' in Jennett's model is not a probability measure and should not be judged as if it were. The match significance scores are perfectly consistent with the Jennett model. As the team will be declared champions if it wins any one of those three games they are all equivalent in Jennett's sense.

To capture the other concept of 'significance' one could use a close relative of Jennett's index, namely (WN/GL), the average future performance needed for glory. Array 3 and Array 4 show that (WN/GL) meets the criterion that two successive games are equally important if they must both be won.

Array 3: Win transition array (index $\equiv$ WN/GL)

$WN = 1\ GL = 1$ Index $= 1$	$WN = 0\ GL = 1$ Index $= 1$ Champions	$WN = 0\ GL = 1$ Index $= 1$ Champions
$WN = 2\ GL = 2$ Index $= 1$	$WN = 1\ GL = 2$ Index $= 0.5$	$WN = 0\ GL = 2$ Index $= 1$ Champions
$WN = 3\ GL = 3$ Index $= 1$	$WN = 2\ GL = 3$ Index $= 0.67$	$WN = 1\ GL = 3$ Index $= 0.33$

In Array 3 when $WN = 0$, WN/GL equals 0, suggesting the team that has won is out of contention! To prevent this we define Index $= 1$ when $WN = 0$ and the title has been won. The team that enters the closing stages needing to win all three games has a significance score of 1 attached to each game, as the alternative logic requires. A team that needs fewer than three wins would play at least one game as champions, but the team needing to win them all must wait until next season to start a match as champions. The team requiring two wins from three has an initial significance score of 0.67, having won its first match the significance score for the second drops to 0.5. It ends that game as championship winner and plays the last game of the season in glory. The corresponding lose transition array appears next.

Array 4: Lose transition array (index ≡ WN/GL)

WN = 3 GL = 1 Index = 0	WN = 2 GL = 1 Index = 0	WN = 1 GL = 1 Index = 1
WN = 3 GL = 2 Index = 0	WN = 2 GL = 2 Index = 1	WN = 1 GL = 2 Index = 0.5
WN = 3 GL = 3 Index = 1	WN = 2 GL = 3 Index = 0.67	WN = 1 GL = 3 Index = 0.33

In Array 4 the team needing three wins but losing its first game drops out of contention after the loss. Note that whenever $WN > GL$ the team is out of contention. We do not therefore compute values where $WN/GL > 1$, but set the index to zero. The last column shows that the club that requires one win, but hits a losing streak, faces increasingly 'significant' games, as the alternative criterion requires and as a 'probabilistic' approach suggests. That said the desire to be there when one's team achieves glory and indeed to watch its progress from earlier stages (Jennett) is a plausible motivation for attendance.

The essence of this discussion is that there are as many reasonable definitions of 'significance' as there are views on what is a reasonable requirement for an index to meet. Put simply, there is no perfect solution. We find that a close relative of Jennett's index meets an alternative concept of 'reasonableness', one which might better describe the patterns of behaviour of supporters who take, as Cairns (1990) indicated, a probabilistic view of their teams' prospects. The alternative measure is not objectively better than Jennett's, it is merely different; some might think it decidedly inferior. For the purpose of capturing the notion of significance that Jennett had in mind it most certainly is inferior.

A modified Herfindahl indicator of uncertainty of outcome

This section illustrates the problems that continue to plague researchers looking for simple measures of the general level of competitive balance during a season. A simple summary statistic of the level of inequality during the season could be based upon the sum of squares of team's shares of the total number of wins, the Herfindahl Index (HI), usually met in discussions of market structure in the industrial organisation literature, defined as

$$HI \equiv \Sigma(\text{team's share of total wins})^2. \tag{7.1.1}$$

We modify the Herfindahl Index, multiplying through by N, the total number of teams in the league, so that in a perfectly balanced season the Modified Herfindahl Index (MHI) would always equal unity, however many teams the league contains

$$\text{MHI} \equiv N \ \Sigma(\text{team's share of total wins})^2. \tag{7.1.2}$$

The more unequally balanced is the league, the greater is the value of MHI. It takes account of the relative performances of all the teams, is simple to compute and behaves 'sensibly' (relatively speaking). Indeed its original is preferred as a measure of market structure to concentration ratios which (a) ignore most of the firms and (b) cannot indicate whether there are several big firms or one 'giant' and a few 'pygmies'. These considerations suggest that our MHI may be able to distinguish (imperfectly of course) between a close race (the leading teams all have more or less similar shares) and a runaway race (only the leaders have a large share). Despite its virtues, the main one being simplicity, we will see that MHI is unlikely to obviate the need experienced by Borland (1987), Borland and Lye (1992) and others for separate if arbitrary measures.

For illustrative purposes assume a league of 20 teams, each of whom plays the others twice a season. The most perfectly balanced season (like perfect competition this is an ideal state) would produce every team winning the same number of games. If they all play 38 games, they might win 19 games each and lose the same number (somebody has to lose every game that is won). MHI would rate this season's inequality as equal to:

$$\text{MHI} = 20 \ \Sigma(0.05)_j^2 = 20[20(0.0025)] = 1, \tag{7.1.3}$$

where we sum over the $j = 1, 2, 3, \ldots, 20$ teams and every team obtains 19 (5%) of the total of 380 wins recorded by all teams. The value 1 indicates the most balanced season possible, thus 1 is the lower bound of MHI. Another case of perfect balance occurs if every game is drawn. Now there are no wins at all and of course you cannot divide by 0, so you cannot calculate the index as above. But since the (zero) total of wins is uniformly divided between teams, we set the index to 1, consistent with perfect balance.

The most unequally balanced season (in win terms) sees the leaders win all their 38 games. The other 19 teams lose two each to the winners and draw all their 36 other games. MHI would take the value

$$\text{MHI} = 20[(38/38)^2 + 19(0/38)^2] = 20[1] = 20. \tag{7.1.4}$$

Note there are only 38 wins, every other team loses two matches to the winners and draws 36 with other losers. All losers share this dismal record. There could be no clearer winner – the winners take 100% of the wins. In this case the MHI score equals the number of teams. This is its upper bound; the top team cannot win more than 100% of the games won.

Suppose two teams both win all their games against the rest of the league and draw against each other – a perfectly balanced two-horse race in other words. The leaders each win 36 games, drawing the other two, while every other side loses four against the two leaders and draws the other 34. The MHI yields

$$\text{MHI} = 20[2(36/72)^2 + 18(0/72)^2] = 20[2(0.25)] = 10. \tag{7.1.5}$$

Note that *two* teams win 36 games out of 72, leaving 18 teams with no wins. MHI roughly shows the number of teams 'in contention'. Dividing the number of teams in the league by the MHI gives a rough indicator of the number of equally balanced winners. If there are four teams who draw with one another and beat all the others, who obligingly draw their other games, then MHI = 5 (each team has 25% of the total number of wins). But the indication is exact only in extreme cases like those above, as the next example shows.

Consider another extreme case, where there are no draws at all. The champions win 38, the runners-up win 36, and so on, right down to the bottom side that loses every game. The MHI equals

$$\text{MHI} = 20[(38/380)^2 + (36/380)^2 + (34/380)^2 + \ldots + (0/380)^2]$$

$$= 20[\, 0.01000 + 0.00898 + 0.00801 + \ldots + 0]$$

$$= 20[0.06842]$$

$$= 1.37, \tag{7.1.6}$$

rounded to significant figures. Now, 20 divided by 1.37 gives about 15 'equally balanced' teams and wins are much more evenly distributed here. Every team is separated by two wins from its neighbours in the rankings, seemingly 'close' in the first few weeks but not at the end. Is the eighth team, for example, with sixteen fewer wins, really in contention? One should not regard the MHI as an infallible indicator of the number of teams in contention!

Compared to the one- and two-horse race(s), this looks like a closely fought season on the basis of their MHI values, twenty and ten, respectively. Also nineteen teams have at least one victory as opposed to one or two teams only in the other extreme cases. If one looks at the distribution of points, assuming that wins bear two points, draws one and losses none, the top team ends the season with 76 points and each successive team gets 72, 68, 64, and so on down the standings to the bottom team which gets none. Teams are separated from their closest rivals above and below by only four points. By comparison in the extreme one-horse race case the leaders finish with 76 points from their 38 wins, while the runners-up (all the other teams) finish with 36 points, a gap of 40 points. In the two-horse race, the front runners gain 72 points from their 36 wins plus two more from their drawn games, making 74 in all. The runners-up get 34 points from their draws. The one- and two-horse race(s) are extremely close for all teams not in contention, but 40 points separate the leaders from the pack.

In another sense, however, the one-horse race (7.1.4) is far more equal. The spread of points between the champions and the bottom club when there are no draws (7.1.6) is at its maximum. The former with their 38 wins gain 76 points, while the bottom team gets none. This is wider than the range from 76 to 36 or 74 to 34 that the one- and two-horse race(s) produce. A summary statistic that concerns itself only with the range of wins (or points) scored between bottom and top clubs (Borland's UNA for example) will rate the one- and two-horse race(s) closer competitively than the case where there are no drawn games, while MHI would reverse the rankings. Summary statistics frequently give conflicting impressions of the same data, so it is important to be aware of the behaviour of any particular summary statistic.

Discussion questions

1. Explain Jennett's (1984) assertion that the operation of uncertainty of outcome does not require all spectators to be risk lovers.
2. Cairns *et al.* (1986) argued that the optimal pre-match points (or position) differential need not be zero. Why? Explain with the aid of a simple diagram why these authors hypothesised a quadratic relationship between these variables.
3. Carefully consider the relative advantages of pre-match betting odds over pre-match league positions as indicators of match uncertainty. Use a simple diagram to explain why Peel and Thomas (1988) misspecified the hypothetical relationship and indicate simple alternative procedures.
4. Attempt to assess[6] the 'overall' performance of the set of uncertainty indicators used by Baimbridge *et al.* (1996) in their study of the effect of 'live' TV broadcasting upon Premier League attendance.
5. To what extent can it be said that there is evidence in favour of the uncertainty of outcome hypothesis in any of its four (Cairns *et al.*, 1986) forms?

---

[6] Ask yourself such questions as whether the variables, singly or collectively, seem to be statistically significant, whether their coefficients are 'correctly' signed, whether the variables are defined sensibly.

6. Over the long period it appears that many team sports have prospered in spite of markedly unequal team performance records, for example in the distribution of championship wins. Explain carefully why this is not necessarily disproof of the long-term uncertainty of outcome hypothesis.

8 Broadcast demand and the impact of television

Introduction

Having discussed at length the attendance demand for professional team sports, in this chapter we turn our attention to the TV coverage of sport. A brief history of the origins of televised sport in the US and the UK is presented. Broad economic reasons explaining these developments are offered. The economic consequences of 'broadcast' demand are then discussed. The impact of TV coverage of fixtures on attendance is examined to extend some of the insights already discussed in Chapter 6.

In more detail, the feedback effects of TV on the financing and supply side of professional team sports are discussed. While we have already stressed the interdependence of demand and supply issues for the economics of professional team sports, as discussed in Chapter 3, the advent of huge increases in TV revenues in, for example the UK, has produced an 'exogenous' shock to historically more stable relationships. As such it is of interest to revisit some of the main themes of the economics of professional team sports. In particular the potential impacts of the redistribution of revenues on uncertainty of outcome are discussed. Some contrasts are identified between the US and UK literatures.

Finally, the advent of pay-per-view, and TV companies making direct investments into sporting clubs, are discussed. Much of this discussion is centred upon recent public policy and legal discussion in the UK concerning BSkyB and the English football league.

A brief history of televised sport: the US and UK

The history of televised sport, for example in the US and the UK, is essentially characterised by suspicion between sporting league authorities and broadcasting media over the potential effects on the popularity of the sport. On the one hand, it is argued that the profile of the sport is raised. On the other hand, it is argued that interest, and particularly attendance at fixtures, will fall. At the same time, however, there has been a conflicting incentive for sports authorities to avail themselves of the revenues that broadcasting media could bring to their sports. Thus, as Cashmore (1994, p. 133) notes, in the US:

> There was money available for sports. For example, as far back as 1910, the motion picture industry paid major league baseball (MLB) $500 for the right to film and show the World Series. Such was the commercial success of the arrangement that in the next year, the fee was increased sevenfold to $3,500. While MLB accommodated this, team owners claimed that simultaneous information, such as that transmitted by Western Union, which paid $17,000 per annum for five years from 1913, would deter fans from attending games. The view persisted; as late as 1932, the three New York Teams banned radio. But, in 1939, all MLB teams consented to a radio contract and rights for the World Series sold for about $400,000.

Likewise, when television emerged as an economically sustainable medium, $65,000 captured the rights to broadcast the World Series to fewer than 12% of US households in 1947.

Nonetheless, over the next ten years televised live MLB games were seen to be instrumental in reducing attendance at both MLB and minor league events. This was even with, for example, only the north east of the US having access to MLB up to 1958 (because of the geographic coverage of the teams). Similar sentiments were echoed in other sports. Between 1949 and 1953, the National Collegiate Athletic Association (NCAA) limited the number of televised fixtures for college football to help to counter reductions in attendance. In general, TV coverage of sports was discouraged.

In a development that has parallels with recent events in the UK, US sports broadcasting received renewed impetus with the advent of ABC's aggressive attempt to build interest in sports coverage that previously had been shared relatively peacefully between CBS and NBC (Cashmore, 1994, p. 135). ABC pursued an aggressive drive to promote sport to a wider demographic population than simply men. For example, they focused on personalities, and coupled with technical innovations such as the introduction of slow-motion replays, close-ups and split screens, ABC received increased sponsorship and advertising revenues that, ultimately, led, for example, to ABC bidding successfully for NCAA football in 1960/61. This was a significant event as college football was more popular than the NFL. Moreover, as discussed in Chapter 3, ABC helped to finance the emergent, weaker, AFL in 1960 in direct competition with the NFL.

Prior to this the only real concession to TV coverage in professional football occurred in 1958 when the NFL had previously introduced 'television time outs' to allow for commercials. The objective was to encourage CBS to promote the popularity of football through wider coverage following the increased commercial interest in advertising during sporting coverage.

In contrast, the AFL was essentially constituted with sponsorship and advertising revenues in mind. The AFL's increased success ultimately led it to negotiate independently and in 1965 a deal with NBC was struck for $42 million over five years. Such success and national coverage of the sport through the AFL was coupled with the merger agreement of the NFL and the AFL in 1966. The NFL had only managed to negotiate local and regional TV deals. This suggests that financial pressure as much as the uncertainty of outcome hypothesis *per se* helped to promote the 'monopolisation' of this sporting league.

This progress towards an increased role for TV in sports has continued. By the mid-1980s other competitions had been devised to meet TV's desire for sports coverage to encourage advertising revenues. The ABA and the World Hockey League were examples of successes. In contrast, the USFL failed after losing a lawsuit against the NFL. The former claimed that the NFL had a monopoly over network broadcasting payments. The suit failed because the Sports Broadcasting Act 1961 enabled teams in the NFL to negotiate as a cartel with the TV companies. The stronger established NFL was thus protected from competition. Thus, as discussed in Chapter 4, sports were treated differently from the tenor and tone of competition legislation generally.

Similar, but perhaps less pronounced, patterns of events can be charted in the UK. Thus, in their analysis of association football, which as noted earlier in the book, is by far the most popular professional team sport in the UK, Dobson and Goddard (1998) note that the first televised football matches were England versus Scotland and the Football Association cup final in 1938. Subsequent to this, regular coverage of association football did not commence until 1964 when the BBC began to show highlights of matches in 'Match of the Day'. Significantly, as a public broadcasting service the BBC retained the right to show major sporting events. This was a right based in law when commercially funded TV began in the UK with ITV in 1955. This right remained in force through the 1981 and 1984 Broadcasting Acts. Such legislation did not exist in the US, though such major events remain on national TV.

As Whannel (1992) notes, however, the fragmentation of the franchised commercial opposition to the BBC arguably left ITV initially in a relatively weak position when trying to make deals in comparison with the BBC. From its inception the network essentially comprised a series of relatively autonomous regional franchises. In contrast in the US, regional stations are affiliated to the major networks and buy programmes from them and sell advertising time to them. In 1966, however, and arguably prompted by the success of the BBC in televising the England football team's exploits in the World Cup, ITV set up a special unit to acquire broadcasting rights and plan overall programming. The result was that ITV won contracts for the Gillette Cup in county cricket, and association football's league cup. It also developed its own set of regionally-based football highlights shows. Moreover, ITV essentially imitated ABC's approach to presenting sport in developing new camera angles, running replays and so on. As Cashmore (1994) notes, the instant replay was used to devastating effect by the BBC in the World Cup – and particularly the final in which England won the cup but one of the goals was highly disputed (and still is!).

Notwithstanding these developments, however, as far as association football is concerned, as Dobson and Goddard (1998) note, throughout the 1970s the BBC and ITV effectively acted as a cartel. The growth of finances in UK sports was thus far less dramatic than in the US. The cartel arrangement kept fees for televising matches down and clubs received equal and modest sums in return. Thus, in 1967 individual clubs received £1,300 from TV sources. In 1978, the amount had only risen to £5,800 – over a period dominated by unprecedented inflation since 1945!

Initially, the TV cartel received implicit support from the courts. In 1978, London Weekend Television – an ITV company – attempted to secure the exclusive rights to televise and distribute association football around the network. While the Office of Fair Trading ruled against this arrangement going ahead, a qualitative shift in the relationship between sports and TV occurred in the UK. The economic pressure from this attempt to break up the existing arrangements led to more highly valued contracts. In the very next season each club received £23,900 compared to £5,800 in the previous season. This increased 'commercial edge' to contract negotiations continued to gather pace. Ten live league fixtures were televised for the first time in 1983 and again in 1984. This two-year contract between the BBC and ITV and the football league was worth £2.6m per annum. However, tensions started to be revealed by the increased commercial stakes. As discussed in Chapter 6, association football was experiencing a long-term fall in attendance and hence gate revenues overall. TV revenues were increasingly seen as a welcome source of extra funds by clubs. However, disputes between the larger and smaller clubs developed over the distribution of funds – a factor revealed further with the advent of satellite television. In these circumstances the 1985/86 season saw only £1.3m being earned from a six-month contract. Subsequently, a further two-year deal worth £3.1m per annum was negotiated.

Nonetheless, the now-shaky TV cartel arrangement finally collapsed in 1988. New potential competition existed from two subscription satellite broadcasting companies – British Satellite Broadcasting (BSB) formed in 1988 and Sky in 1989. In contrast to the existing 'free-at-the-point-of-consumption channels', these channels were financed partially by subscriptions. Not surprisingly to overcome consumer resistance to paying for what was previously a 'free' good, such services needed to offer attractive products. Sport was an obvious candidate and not surprisingly this suggests that these TV companies were willing to pay more for the opportunity of televising live sport and particularly association football than previous suppliers. This prompted ITV to break free of the existing pattern of negotiations and effectively outbid the BBC for exclusive live coverage of association football matches. A four-year deal worth £11m per annum was agreed. Significantly, the larger more successful clubs received most of the funds. Thus, £8.25m of the £11m funds went to Division 1 of the football league. In addition £3.5m of this went to Arsenal, Everton, Liverpool, Manchester United and Tottenham Hotspur (Dobson and Goddard, 1998).

Moreover, as discussed in Chapter 3, the bargaining power of larger clubs ultimately led Division 1 to break away from the football league to form the Premier League for the 1992/93 season. The tendency towards increased commercial aspirations for the top clubs was no doubt fuelled by the commensurate emergence of even stronger economic competition for the rights to televise live football as BSB and Sky merged in 1990. One of the first actions of the Premier League was to set up an auction for the TV rights to broadcast live football. BSkyB ultimately won the contract, despite legal attempts to prevent the deal by ITV. Consistent with the idea that sport was to be the 'battering ram' to promote satellite broadcasting, the contract reflected BSkyB's interest in sport.[1] A deal worth approximately £43m was agreed for the live coverage of 60 fixtures. As part of the deal the BBC were left with the rights to supply recorded highlights of matches. Moreover, as with earlier developments in the US, an implication of such TV involvement in sports meant that, 'a significant alteration of the traditional fixture schedule was required, with matches being played on Sunday afternoons and Monday nights almost every week' (Szymanski and Kuypers, 1999, p. 60). More recently, BSkyB renegotiated their deal in 1997. These authors report that two other subscription TV companies submitted bids as well. The effect was that contract values increased substantially again.

Coupled with the changes in contract associated with BSkyB, formulae that allocated the TV revenues between clubs have been established. Unlike the US TV deals discussed in Chapter 4, BSkyB's formula consistently skews financial rewards towards successful clubs. As noted above, however, the formula really consolidates an already established tendency of the larger clubs to bargain hard for a larger allocation of TV funds. For example, while all clubs in the Premier League receive an equal fixed fee from 50% of the TV revenues, for example £743,500 in 1993/94 and £3,040,278 in 1997/98, the remaining 50% of revenues are allocated unequally. Twenty-five per cent of the TV revenues are allocated according to the teams' positions in the league. This is known as a merit award. In 1993/94 the Premier League champions, Manchester United, received £856,240. In 1997/98 the champions, Arsenal, received £3,250,000. Likewise, Swindon Town, the team relegated in 1993/94, received £38,920 and Crystal Palace, relegated in 1997/98, received £162,500

---

[1] There is some evidence that this strategy is working. For example a recent MINTEL report, *The Football Business* (1 August 1998) argues that up to one in ten adults cite televised football as a reason for subscribing to satellite television.

(Baimbridge *et al.*, 1996; Findlay *et al.*, 1999). The remaining 25% of TV revenues are allocated according to the number of live matches that a team is featured in. Each team must appear in at least three live fixtures. This is known as the facility fee. Not surprisingly, above the minimum number of televised matches, fixtures involving more successful teams are broadcast more often. Consequently, for the seasons noted above, Manchester United and Arsenal received facility fees of £1,011,375 and £3,030,984, respectively. Likewise, Swindon Town and Crystal Palace received £243,150 and £1,010,328, respectively. The implications of such funding arrangements are considered further below.

The above developments are not simply confined to assocation football. In rugby league, the UK's other traditional professional team sport, TV coverage used to be confined to the regional networks in the north of England – the traditional heartland of its support. Since 1995, BSkyB have had the contract to televise live league fixtures. The BBC has televised the major cup competitions. The process by which BSkyB won this contract reflects similar developments to the case of football. As Thomas (1997) notes, in key policy documents issued by the Rugby Football League (RFL) in the early 1990s the opinion was aired that, rather like association football, the traditional sources of finance in the sport were lacking and that facilities needed upgrading. In addition it was felt that the game needed more wide-spread promotion. By 1995, BskyB had tabled an offer for the exclusive rights to show matches for £87m over five years. Key aspects of this deal, which were accepted, were that the game should switch to the summer, that a super league similar to the Premier League should be established and that clubs should be expanded to population centres outside traditional catchment areas. Finally, some existing clubs should merge to create 'superclubs'. All but the final aspect have been implemented. This proposal raised severe hostility from traditional support bases. Moreover, attempts to expand the support to London and the north-east and even Paris have met with mixed success. In the latter case Paris St Germain has folded. In the north-east a merger of Gateshead Thunder with financially struggling Hull Sharks has occurred. Moreover, while London Broncos have been relatively successful on the field, their gates are dwindling. Despite these setbacks however, it is clear that TV has increasingly set the administrative agenda for sports leagues in the UK.

BSkyB's hegemony of sport is not confined to football and rugby league. Concurrent with the turn of rugby union from an amateur to a professional team sport, both English rugby union premiership fixtures and cup fixtures are broadcast exclusively by them. In addition, the England rugby team's matches in the five (now six) nations are shown exclusively by BSkyB. The emergent European Cup competition has remained televised on terrestial TV however. The same applies to the World Cup, though this is unlikely to be the case with association football in the future. Similarly, elsewhere in the world, after protracted battles with other media suppliers, BSkyB through their parent company, News Corporation, dominate sports coverage. For example, they have the exclusive rights to televise both codes of Rugby in Australia – the current world champions of both sports. The same is true of the prestigious 'Tri-Nations' and 'Super-12s' rugby union series. This said, however, changes in the technical environment of broadcasting suggest that the BSkyB's hegemony may change. These are examined after first outlining the economic principles that could be said to explain the rise of BSkyB to its position of prominence.

The economics of broadcasting and sport

The above developments can be understood in terms of the discussion in Chapter 2. It can be argued that the broadcasting supply of professional team sports has historically evolved as a process of 'internalising' an externality. An externality arises when the true costs and benefits of a transaction are not reflected in the price of the transaction. Consequently resources get mis-allocated.

In his seminal work, Neale (1964) argued that professional team sports confer a major positive externality on the media via the 'league standing effect'. Widespread interest in the performance of sporting teams is jointly produced with the live event. Consequently, while games could occur without any media input, the media cannot benefit from interest in league standings if the league does not exist. Thus, professional team sports leagues create an externality in the form of income for the media at no cost to them. Accordingly while the team's gate revenues could measure the team owner's private benefit from production, the social benefit includes the revenue generated in the media as a by-product of the team's activities. This suggests that team sports may be undervalued from the social welfare perspective, since the private benefit of their activity is substantially less than the social benefit. The result would be that teams and players would receive less revenue than is justified by their activities in producing sports events.

As discussed in Chapter 4, Coase (1960) stressed that if property rights can be established for the 'free' resource and if a market can be organised to price that resource correctly, optimal allocation or something akin to it should follow. As the property rights to broadcast sporting fixtures can be easily established, because of restricted access to sporting stadia, it follows that there will always be the option to supply sports by such media. What ultimately matters, therefore, is the technical ability to supply broadcast coverage and an economic incentive to do so. In a market economy, with the general growth in broadcasting technology, the scale of financial demand for sports has provided the economic conditions for the growth of sports broad-casting. The long-term growth in broadcasting revenues in professional team sports reflects the perceived long-term profitability of doing so.

Historically, then, it is not surprising that sports leagues have acted collectively to sell the rights to broadcast live matches and highlights. This 'internalises' a portion of the external benefits. Notably, more recent developments in sports leagues can be understood in these terms too. As technology changes, the clamour for a share of previously unattainable 'external' income changes. Thus, the advent of cable or satellite broadcasting presented media suppliers and sports leagues with the necessity of further 'internalising' the externality. The rise of BSkyB required explicit subscriptions to the appropriate technology to access the media. As an expression of the derived demand for sport, broadcasters had to channel these funds towards sporting leagues to provide the incentives for leagues to supply them with access to fixtures in opposition to rival broadcasters.[2]

From a classical economic perspective, therefore, the need to pay for media access to sporting fixtures is an inevitable outcome of the professional nature of team sports. Indeed, as discussed in Chapter 3, these developments can be thought of as a necessary consequence of the organisation and supply of sports on a professional basis. It follows that the economic consequences for professional team sports ultimately impinge in four interconnected areas. The first is the effect of broadcasting media on alternative sources of clubs' revenues, particularly gate attendance. The second is the effect on competitive balance and hence overall revenues in sporting leagues. The third concerns the potential changes in league structure and management and the long-term characteristics of the sport. The final area concerns the evolution of the media market. Each of these issues is now discussed.

Television and the demand for professional team sports

As noted in Chapter 6, gate attendance has been the traditional source of most revenue in professional team sports. For example, in the UK sponsorship and advertising only really began to grow as a source of finance for football clubs in the 1980s commensurate with the development of sports broadcasting (Szymanski and Kuypers, 1999). Thus, in his relatively recent survey of the demand for professional team sports, Cairns (1990) does not address the impact of television coverage on sporting attendance. On one level this may be an entirely legitimate omission as Cairns' work was prior to the large-scale increase in both television revenues and coverage of sport in Europe with the advent of BSkyB. However, as Zhang *et al.* (1998, p. 108) argue for primarily the US too:

> Traditional beliefs in the relationship between the two primary revenue sources of professional sports (i.e. game attendance and broadcasting) have been based mainly upon professional insights but have lacked support data. In fact the quantitative knowledge base is very limited.

---

[2] For more discussion on derived demand, see Appendix 9.1.

This suggests that the lacuna may simply be due to a presumption about the likely effects of television broadcasting on demand as discussed in the opening statements in this chapter. Consequently, it is instructive to examine the economic literature that has begun to focus on assessing the impact of television on attendance demand.

The basic method for assessing the effects of television coverage of fixtures on attendance demand has been to make use of dummy variables. In particular, based on a sample including both televised and non-televised fixtures, an attendance function is estimated in the manner discussed in Chapter 5. As well as including variables measuring the influence of other likely effects on attendance, a dummy variable is included in the analysis as an independent variable to identify the effects on attendance of a fixture that is televised relative to a non-televised fixture. As discussed in Chapter 5, dummy variables are typically assigned a value of 1 or 0. In this case either value can be used to indicate whether or not a fixture was broadcast. The estimated coefficient on the dummy variable thus measures the average increase or decrease in attendance due to televising the fixture and allowing for other influencing factors on attendance. This approach is an improvement on those that simply assert that falling attendance and television are related. Cashmore (1994), for example, has a tendency to do this. Consideration of UK association football attendance provides an example of the importance of this issue. As discussed above, preceding, but becoming commensurate with the increase in television coverage of sports, association football has experienced a long-term decline in attendance. Assessing the impact of television on attendance thus implies controlling for the influence of this and other factors.

To illustrate the role of dummy variables in this context, one can assume that there is a simple demand function for a professional team sport that suggests that attendance will be related to spectator incomes. (8.1) illustrates this simple model:

$$A_i = \beta_1 + \beta_2 I_i + u_i. \tag{8.1}$$

Here, A refers to attendance, I to incomes and u is a random disturbance variable that captures all other effects on attendance than income. i is the index of observation. β_1 is the intercept of the equation and β_2 is the slope of the equation. Recall from Chapter 5 that the equation represents the hypothesised relationship between income and attendance. The parameters that measure the hypothesised relationship between the variables could be estimated from data. If this exercise was undertaken, from a sample of data, the intercept would indicate the average attendance at fixtures when incomes are zero. There is, thus, little economic significance to this potential statistical result. More importantly, the slope coefficient on income, β_2, would measure the average change in attendance following a unit change in income. Figure 8.1 is drawn reflecting a positive association between these variables.

To assess the impact of television on attendance, (8.1) would have to be

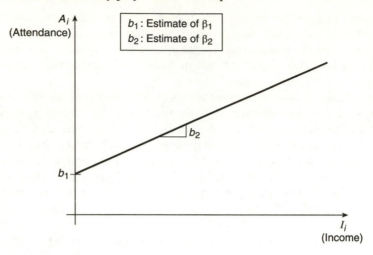

Figure 8.1 Income and the demand for professional team sports

augmented by, for example, the inclusion of a dummy variable like *TV*, as defined above. (8.2) represents this model, v_i represents the (random) influences on attendance not due to television or spectator incomes in this model

$$A_i = \beta_1 + \beta_2 I_i + \beta_3 TV_i + v_i. \tag{8.2}$$

If the variable *TV* was assigned a value of 1 when a fixture in the sample of data was televised, and a value of 0 otherwise, then (8.2) really measures two equations from two 'subsamples' of the data – televised fixtures and non-televised fixtures. Thus, (8.2) would apply for televised fixtures given this definition of the dummy variable. For non-televised fixtures, i.e. when *TV* takes a value of 0, (8.1) is implied.[3] Importantly, the difference between the two equations would measure the difference in attendance due to televising fixtures. This is given in (8.3).

$$(\beta_1 + \beta_2 I_i + \beta_3 TV_i + v_i) - (\beta_1 + \beta_2 I_i + u_i) = \beta_3 TV_i + v_i - u_i. \tag{8.3}$$

---

[3] Note that if the dummy variable was assigned a value of 0 for televised matches and a value of 1 for non-televised matches the opposite would apply. Hence assigning particular values of the dummy variable does not matter in analysis. One should note that the interpretation of the slope coefficent on the dummy variable measures the average increment/decrement in the dependent variable from values that would obtain if the dummy variable was equal to 0.

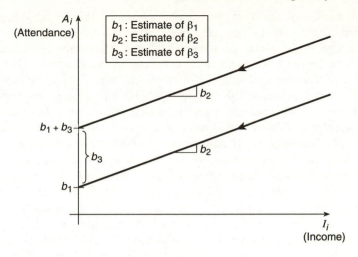

Figure 8.2 TV and the demand for professional team sports

As TV_i is equal to 1, this reduces to:

$$\beta_3 + (v_i - u_i). \tag{8.4}$$

This states that the hypothesised change in attendance due to televising matches is measured by the slope coefficient on the dummy variable. As the term in brackets is a linear combination of the two random variables from the regression equations, it captures the random variation that is likely to be observed as well. This is due to a theorem concerning probabilities.[4] In estimating the parameter correctly, for the reasons discussed in Chapter 5, these random effects on average will be 0. Thus, the estimated average effects of television on attendance can be identified from the estimate of β_3.

Figure 8.2 illustrates the information identified by the estimate of the coefficient. Note that while Figure 8.1 presents (8.1), Figure 8.2 also adds the graph of (8.2) under the assumption that attendance is *increased* by television coverage. The vertical difference between the two lines measures the magnitude of β_3. Note that the lines retain the same slope relating spectator income to attendance. For this reason, the above dummy variable analysis is sometimes referred to as 'differential intercept' analysis.

[4] The properties of the random terms in regression models are discussed in Chapter 5. They are assumed to follow a normal distribution. A statistical theorem states that linear combinations of normal distributions will be a normal distribution (see any intermediate statistics textbook).

In general, studies of the effects of television broadcasting on attendance demand offer mixed results. These studies question the often-stated league concern that live broadcasting of fixtures reduces attendance at matches discussed above. In the US, for example, early studies by Demmert (1973), Noll (1974) and Thomas and Jolson (1979) are supported by more recent studies by Fizel and Bennett (1989), Wilson (1994) and Zhang and Smith (1997) that television coverage reduces attendance at live matches. In contrast however, Kaempfer and Pacey (1986) and Zhang *et al.* (1998) find that broadcasting is positively related to attendance. Their argument is that broadcast and live demand are complementary goods that raise fan interest. Finally, Seigfried and Hinshaw (1979) and Hill *et al.* (1982) find that television has no effect on attendance. Similarly, in the UK, Kuypers (1996) finds no significant relationship between television coverage and association football attendance. Baimbridge *et al.* (1996) find that televising live matches on the TV on Monday nights will decrease attendance at association football matches. They also find that this is not the case for traditional Saturday afternoon fixtures. Baimbridge *et al.* (1995) find similar results for their study of rugby league as well. In addition, Carmichael *et al.* (1998) support these results, which suggest that traditional weekend fixtures are unlikely to be affected by television coverage. While more work needs to be done on this issue, it appears that there is some resistance to an alternative source of the consumption of sports provided by television companies.

Television and competitive balance

The rapid growth of television revenues in UK sports has produced much discussion about the likely impact on competitive balance. Rather like the case of concern over the effects of television on attendance, there is a general presumption that competitive balance will be adversely affected in the UK. Typical of these claims is that:

> A key factor that determines the overall success of a league is *league balance* or *competitive balance* . . . It is for these reasons that most sports leagues operate regulatory systems that aim to promote league balance by redistributing revenues from stronger to weaker teams.
>
> (Findlay *et al.*, 1999, pp. 125–126, italics in original).

The problem with such arguments is that they take a rather uncritical perspective on the effects of cross-subsidisation policies upon competitive balance. As we have argued in Chapter 6, the demand for professional team sports is not simply driven by the uncertainty of outcome hypothesis. It may not be the organising principle around which support can be galvanised. Indeed traditional patterns of support, as noted in Chapter 6, appear to produce partisan concern for success. It follows that this support may be undermined by policies that make the results of fixtures more random. More importantly, as discussed in Chapter 4, it is by no means clear that the results of league management policies, often justified on the basis of promoting competitive balance, have the desired effect. Chapter 4 illustrated the statistical evidence on the effects of various policies directed at the promotion of competitive balance.

Crucially, as noted in Chapter 4, there is no firm evidence from the US on the effects of television deals on competitive balance or league revenues. This is for two reasons. The first reason is that traditionally local television revenues are not shared between clubs. They are also small in magnitude. Fort and Quirk (1995), however, provide some descriptive evidence that, as far as local television revenue sharing arrangements are concerned, more equal distribution of revenues could produce less concentration in win percents in leagues. This was the situation in the NFL that carried over its generous gate-revenue sharing arrangements to local television revenues. Nonetheless, an important theoretical result stemming from Fort and Quirk's research is that gate and television revenue sharing rules interact in a complicated way. While gate-sharing rules *per se* have no effect on competitive balance, the simultaneous presence of, for example, local television revenues, complicates matters greatly. They argue that a rational policy would be to adopt the same sharing rules for both local television and gate-sharing arrangements.

The second reason for the lack of evidence on television revenues and competitive balance is that, as far as national television revenues are concerned, in the US payments are independent of results and are typically negotiated at a league level under a one-team-one-vote system and shared equally. As noted in Chapter 4, Fort and Quirk report that revenue rose by 33% when the NFL began collective negotiations. Consequently, there appear to be demonstrable benefits to this policy and under these rules there should be no effect on win percents. However, Fort and Quirk argue that in as much as the league may be able to negotiate greater television audiences and hence revenues by encouraging particularly strong teams to compete, this could produce incentives for leagues to promote policies that work against competitive balance.

While in European sport there is no distinction between local and national television deals, by analogy Fort and Quirk's theoretical and tentative empirical results suggest that television revenue sharing in combination with gate-revenue sharing arrangements could be the only policies that do affect the competitive balance of sporting leagues. By implication, the skewed nature of television revenues in European sport would seem to suggest that a lack of competitive balance, which historically seems to be the case, would be either, at a minimum, consolidated or, at a maximum, accelerated.

Of course, whether or not any of these developments are desirable really hinges on the ultimate effects of the move towards and away from traditional competitive balance on traditional sources of revenue. Much more research needs to be done on this issue before firm conclusions are offered.

From the point of view of the analysis of this book some potential developments can be identified. If we accept the argument from Chapter 4 that uncertainty of outcome has not been strongly affected by league management policies but has *de facto* evolved in some acceptable way, then rapid movements away from these norms will eventually change the underlying structure of team sports. If left unchecked, an unequal distribution of television revenues might lead to the evolution of the sport beyond existing arrangements and management. This could happen framed by a desire to promote more competitive balance, or simply to pursue greater television revenues. Alternatively, if sports leagues share television revenues more equally, then greater uncertainty of outcome than traditionally experienced might follow. This could jeopardise traditional sources of finance and support.

A potential check on this latter development could be to target the redistribution of funds at tempering the evolution of competitive balance from traditional levels. However, if the costs to some clubs, either literally or in terms of foregone earnings, could be offset by greater television revenues elsewhere, then the current administration of the sport will still face incentives to change.

Change is not inevitable however. A final factor that needs to be taken into account is that coupled with the growth of television revenues, the costs of professional team sports have also risen following changes in the players' labour market. The details of these changes are presented in the next two chapters. If these costs and revenues increase at similar rates then the effects on club profits could be neutral. Better players simply cost the better teams more money from their increased revenues. In these circumstances, there is no necessary effect on competitive balance or a compelling incentive for clubs to seek changes in league structures.

Nonetheless, given these potential changes it is not surprising that there is much speculation about future developments in European association football. It follows, as discussed in Chapter 4, that more research needs to be done on the impact of league policies on funds and competitive balance and, in particular, the dynamics of their evolution. It also appears to be the case that changes in the media market will be an increasingly important influence in the development of European sports. This latter issue is now discussed.

Potential changes in league structure: European Super League

As we discussed in Chapter 2, Fort and Quirk (1995) point out that at the end of 1994 monopoly leagues characterised all four major US team sports (football, baseball, basketball and ice hockey. It was argued in Chapter 3 that this trend could be understood more clearly in viewing sporting leagues as cartels. As discussed in Chapter 3 and above, faced with media influences, European sports have evolved in a similar manner to the US. Significantly, as far as the monopoly outcome is concerned, the effects of media finances on European association football suggest further consolidation of sporting leagues. Thus, the arrival of satellite television revenues and the Premier League discussed earlier have also heralded changes in European association football competitions. Previously, European competitions between clubs involved various (knock-out) cup competitions. For example, domestic league champions contested the European cup. Runners up to each league contested the UEFA cup. In turn, winners of domestic cup competitions contested the Cup Winners cup. In many respects these competitions were seen to be expressions of national pride and some additional income.

While in the past the incentives have clearly not been significant enough to promote changes in these competitions, the rise of television revenues in association football has changed this outlook. The first development involved changing the knock-out status of the European cup into the 'Champions League'. This involved entrants in an initial 'league' stage involving groups of teams. The winners and best runners-up then moved forward into a knock-out stage. Many international tournaments now follow this pattern. Indeed, in spirit, it follows the logic of the organisation of some US sports as noted above. While seemingly innocuous, this development is motivated by pressure on UEFA to guarantee a certain number of fixtures against European rather than domestic opposition. Such pressure increased in 1998 with an approach from Media Partners, a company controlled by Silvio Berlusconi, to 16 of the top football sides in Europe to found a European 'Super League'. In essence television revenues helped clubs to put pressure upon league authorities once again. Given that the Premier League in the UK was formed under such circumstances, the European Super League remains a very clear possibility. Indeed it has been reported that the Premier League demanded written undertakings from top clubs by which they agreed not to work towards developments that would threaten the Premier League. A failure to respond led to threats of legal injunctions to prevent clubs entertaining such prospects. In turn, it has been reported that the Super League proponents have considered actions against potential restraints of trade that 'prevent clubs maximising their earning potential' (*The Times*, 30 July 1998).

Currently, in the face of such pressures, UEFA has extended the number of domestic clubs that can enter the 'Champions League'. Teams have also been given extra revenues from participating. Moreover, the UEFA cup has been transformed into a 'second-tier' champions league for those clubs not making it through to the knock-out stage of the 'first-tier' competition and for further clubs from the domestic leagues. It is clear, however, that matters are not settled. However, if the US experience is followed it is likely that European football will be transformed into something whereby domestic leagues resemble US conferences and European competition resembles play-offs for championships.

This may be a fairly benign development for spectators. Tradition is satisfied and yet extra more casual interest is promoted through European football. Both television revenues and increased gates could coexist. Indeed a MORI poll conducted on 14–18 August 1998 suggested that British association football fans supported replacing the existing UEFA arrangements by a ratio of 4 : 1. The results also indicated that there was no gender bias, nor did the results differ between those that did have satellite/cable TV and those that did not. Crucially, however, the results did hinge on pledges of the league not to interfere with domestic fixtures and more terrestrial TV coverage of sport. In addition, qualification to the league should be based on merit and money should be fed into grass-roots association football.

However, the basic problem of managing resources within leagues remains. To the extent that revenues are distributed unequally, there is the possibility that particular teams' success becomes entrenched and moves away from traditional bases. Under such circumstances it is difficult to see how weaker clubs and stronger clubs could comfortably coexist and incentives for a complete break away of some clubs cannot be discounted. In turn, television interest may require more fixtures between the bigger clubs. This is to attract and retain the more casual media spectator attracted to more unique, big events, as well as the committed fan. Paradoxically, therefore, uncertainty of outcome may be the result rather than the cause of league evolution as leagues evolve away from their traditional structures and opponents in a much more radical manner than previously experienced.

It has been argued that open access to a European super league is important as it provokes competition between teams for players so that teams can compete on a more equal footing (Szymanski and Kuypers, 1999, p. 306). The discussion of Chapter 4 suggests that this is unlikely to be the case. However, there are likely to be implications for domestic teams. If all teams face the possibility of gaining access to more lucrative association football fixtures, either through promotion domestically or ultimately through European association football, then team owners might face incentives to incur high playing costs in the short run in the pursuit of revenues and/or success in the long run. In the language of Chapter 3, utility maximising behaviour and profit maximising behaviour might intertwine over time. Moreover, teams in fear of relegation might resist the potential restructuring required.

In contrast profit oriented clubs have the option of scaling up or down their operations to meet particular targets. Overall, having some flexibility in activity is engendered which gives owners and players some bargaining room and outside options in pursuing their respective objectives. The precise outcomes remain an empirical, i.e. historical, issue.

In contrast, if a super league broke with the policy of, say, the Premier League and became 'closed' to entry and exit, then different dynamics would be set in motion. Bargaining would become more intense between stronger clubs and players. The effects on success and profits nonetheless remain an empirical question. However, as access of owners to top association football clubs is restricted, this suggests that clubs may be subject to takeover bids more than in the past. This is, of course, the experience of US sports.

As discussed in Chapter 3, in the US, leagues grant local monopolies to teams by issuing franchises. Competitive markets for the ownership of clubs exist and teams have readily moved location in response to owner objectives (and indeed incentives offered by local authorities). These developments have occurred in rugby league as discussed above. While these have met with limited success, because the franchises have been 'forced' into areas by Super League authorities trying to raise the profile of the game, it is by no means clear that such constraints apply to the most popular professional sport. Whatever the actual outcome, it seems clear from the above analysis that club-level association football is likely to become more internationally oriented and television revenues will be an integral element of this development. It is also possible that uncertainty of outcome will be more important to sports evolution than suggested by the evidence of previous experience. One feature of this would be because the nature of sports demand might need to evolve from its traditional basis to one of a more casual nature induced by the media, whose own interests may be similarly mercurial.

The evolution of the media market

Having made these arguments, it is clear that constraints on their likelihood will be introduced by developments in media technology. The major technical innovation that will affect European sports is the introduction of digital television. Digital television is essentially part of a more efficient communications system. As well as allowing clearer reproduction of pictures and greater sound quality, digital-data processing, in comparison to existing analogue systems of communication, will provide more flexible interfaces between suppliers and consumers of information, for example through computer systems, cameras and telephones. In addition, the carrying capacity of telecommunication systems will be greatly enhanced. The upshot of these developments is that there are likely to be radically more avenues for suppliers of, for example, television programmes to meet their audiences than before. As discussed below, this might involve sports teams themselves. The economic incentive required to underpin this potential increased supply in broadcast sports is likely to revolve around pay-per-view (PPV) television. This concept involves spectators paying a fixed fee for specific events. As such it differs from terrestrial television that is free at the point of consumption, or BSkyB's initial strategy of paying a subscription fee for particular bundles of broadcast media.

PPV television is not something necessarily allied to digital media. The first sports event to be shown on PPV television was the Sugar Ray Leonard versus Roberto Duran fight. This was, in commercial terms, a success. A number of other boxing matches have been sold under these terms including fights involving, for example, Mike Tyson, Evander Holyfield and George Foreman. As Cashmore (1994, p. 142) notes however, many other events have met with relatively limited success:

> Perhaps the biggest debacle was NBC's 1992 Olympic Triplecast, a 15-day package of Olympic events, 24 hours a day for a total of $125, or $19.95

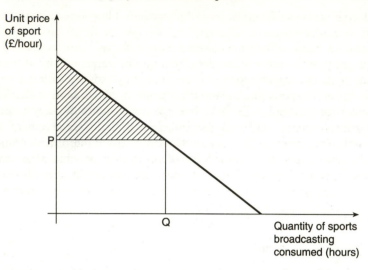

Figure 8.3 Consumer surplus

by the day. About 20 million US homes were then cabled and so had access to PPV; only 165,000 took the whole package and 35,000 took the single days.

The crucial issue, as far as making PPV a success is concerned, is thus the elasticity of demand for the event. With price inelastic demand, extra fees can be demanded of spectators to extract 'consumer surpluses'.

Chapter 2 discussed the definition of consumer surplus in examining the costs to society of monopolistic supply. Consumer surplus represents benefits above the market price paid for a good or service that accrue to the consumer. The shaded area of Figure 8.3 illustrates consumer surplus for a market price and quantity of hours of sport watched of, say, *P* and *Q* respectively. Note that for fewer hours of sport consumers would, in principle, pay a higher price than the current market price. This implies that given the current market price of sports consumers receive benefits that they have not effectively paid for.

Clearly, consumer surplus could form a revenue target for a sporting industry. If the industry could match its price to what each consumer would be willing to pay then its revenues would increase. Industries do this under the banner of price discrimination. It explains why, for example, we pay higher prices for peak-time rail or air travel and why different prices for the same good or service often exist. Technically, price discrimination can be employed if there is no possibility of consumers buying a good or service at the low price and then selling it on themselves for the higher price. This is a process of *arbitrage*. Processes such as these are very efficient in, for example, financial markets. This explains why share prices for particular companies are the same in any market at any time.

Basically therefore, price inelastic demands can be charged a higher price than price elastic demands.[5] Providing the markets can be separated there is no possibility that competition will drive the prices together. Clearly broadcast sporting events provide opportunities for price discrimination as part of a package of media products; PPV is thus a form of price discrimination. If a broadcasting company has the sole rights to televise a particular sport, then it follows that subscribers with inelastic demands can be forced to pay a higher price than simply their subscription to watch a particular fixture. To make PPV work thus involves the media companies targeting inelastic demands. This would suggest that the television companies cannot simply ignore the traditional and committed nature of support.

As discussed in Chapter 6, it seems that as far as live attendance is concerned demand is price inelastic for professional team sports. If this characteristic carries over to broadcast demand then media companies will be able to exploit this demand profile. If broadcast and gate demands for sports are complementary goods, then this would be possible. The earlier discussion, however, also suggested that attendance and broadcast demand are not necessarily complementary goods. There is an element of substitution. This suggests that PPV sports provision would need to look for inelastic demands elsewhere. Indeed this is the possible basis under which television radically reshapes the demand for professional team sports. This is because inelastic demands would seem likely to reside in larger-scale unique events that attract the more casual spectator because of the event's general significance. If this is the case then it is clear that sporting leagues and competitions will need to evolve at a greater and greater speed. Likewise, it could also be that PPV could be successful at a more regional or parochial level where particular rivalries are emphasised. Thus US college football embraces PPV.

As far as European sport is concerned, therefore, it seems that two possibilities arise with digital broadcasting and PPV. On the one hand, it may reinforce the current moves towards BSkyB's hegemony – the development of BSkyB Digital is clearly an element in this possible development. In contrast, it follows that there is potential for the media market to break up in attempting to meet the demands of more specific markets. Under both of

---

[5] The formula for the price elasticity of demand is, of course, the percentage change in quantity demanded divided by the percentage change in price. As prices and quantities are normally negatively related, it follows that price elasticities greater than 1 in absolute terms are described as elastic demands, and price elasticities between 0 and 1 in absolute terms are described as inelastic demands. Thus a given percentage increase in price will produce a larger percentage fall in demand, *compared to the price increase*, in an elastic case and a smaller percentage fall in demand, *compared to the price increase,* in an inelastic case. Consequently revenues will fall following a price rise with elastic demand but rise with inelastic demand, *even though in both cases prices increase and demands fall.*

these circumstances, but perhaps particularly the latter, professional team sports leagues are likely to fragment and change at a much greater pace than in the past.

An important factor affecting these developments is thus who supplies professional team sports to the media consumer. A number of teams, for example, in the Premier League have already launched their own television channels. Whether or not leagues or teams will be part of future developments depends on current legislation in the media market. If this begins to break up the existing collective bargaining arrangements between leagues and particular media distributors, then the content of television programmes rather than the distribution network is likely to matter most in the future of broadcasting. This would be a very strong challenge to BSkyB's hegemony.

Recent developments in the UK media market, for example, reflect this likely greater competition to supply broadcasts of football. As Szymanski and Kuypers (1999) note, two other media companies, Carlton and MAI submitted bids for the 1997/98–2000/01 rights to televise the Premier League. The latest offer from BSkyB for the next contract is reported to be in the order of £1bn. The auction process for television rights is thus far from being constrained. Part of the reason for this demand-led increase in the value of contract rights is that currently the Premier League's television rights are negotiated collectively – as in many US sports and, for example, German association football. The implication is that some exercise of monopoly power is possible under the current arrangements and this makes it profitable to make such bids.

In contrast, in Dutch association football, the competition authorities recently upheld an argument by Feyenoord that they should be able to negotiate their own television deals. Indeed, in the UK a similar argument has been put forward by the Office of Fair Trading (OFT). The OFT argued that the current arrangements acted in such a way as to restrict live coverage of Premier League games to only 60 out of a possible 380 games on BSkyB – with the highlights on BBC – and prevents other broadcasters from showing the rest of the games. The restrictive practices court, however, upheld the current arrangement. In a statement on 28 July 1999 (see www.oft.gov.uk/html/new/premier.htm), John Bridgman, Director of Fair Trading argued:

> This was a proper case to bring to court. The court has confirmed that these agreements needed to be examined. But it has decided that on balance the wider public interest is better served by allowing the main restrictions to continue. It has accepted though that without them there might have been benefits in some areas including greater choice of TV coverage for fans . . . My job is to protect the consumers' interest. I put considerable weight on unfilled consumer demand – in this case from fans who want to see more of their favourite clubs on TV. Unfortunately, the court did not feel able to attach much weight to this point . . . I had a legal

duty to ask the court to examine the exclusive tie-up between the Premier League and two broadcasters . . . In general the court agreed with me that competition has been restricted in these markets but has no power to prescribe an alternative under the restrictive Trade Practices Act . . . This Act will be repealed next year when new competition law comes into force. This judgement contains some interesting groundwork for future competition analysis.

It is clear, therefore, that matters are not entirely settled. The potential break up of the existing collective arrangements cannot be ruled out in the future. Perhaps in anticipation of such developments, recent events in the media market involve attempts by media companies to buy actual clubs. This enables the companies to retain a stake in the industry. This is not an uncommon experience outside of the UK. Thus News Corporation, BSkyB's parent company, owns the Los Angeles Dodgers, has shares in the New York Knicks basketball and New York Rangers ice hockey teams. Canal Plus, a French PPV channel, had bought into the Paris St Germain rugby league team and Silvio Berlusconi owns AC Milan (Lee, 1999; *Financial Times*, 9 April 1999).

The most publicised example of these developments has been BSkyB's attempt to buy Manchester United. Lee (op. cit.) details a lot of the background to this case. If this merger had gone ahead it would have combined the two giants of the media and association football industries. To the joy of traditional fans, the move was blocked by the Monopolies and Mergers Commision (MMC) on 8 April 1999. The argument against the takeover was essentially that it would have given BSkyB an unfair advantage in future sports television rights negotiations. Getting back a sizeable portion of its revenues from a bid to televise football by already owning Manchester United would, it was argued, have allowed BSkyB to bid more aggressively than other TV companies in auctions for television rights (Szymanski and Kuypers (1999)) already note how attractive BSkyB's bids for the Premier League have been relative to European league deals). Little faith thus appears to have been placed in assurances that United could have kept information on rival bids secret from BSkyB, or that auctions would not have been reopened if more money was on the table (*The Economist*, 20 March 1999, p. 35). Similar to the discussions of Chapter 4, it is recognised that economic incentives might undermine attempts to regulate the market. News of this decision has dampened financial market expectations about football, though it remains that media companies are currently taking minority stakes in various sporting clubs. These investments are presumably hedges against future changes in the media market.

In short, the MMC decision seems to have been taken in line with the emphasis of the OFT decision on the collective selling of sports broadcasting rights. Another factor that appears to have been important in the MMC decision was the desire to prevent the gulf between the largest and smallest clubs from widening (*Financial Times*, op. cit.). This could result from the largest clubs openly competing with smaller clubs for television revenue and perhaps accelerating some of the changes towards European association football discussed above. Both regulators' decisions can thus be seen as a partial attempt to retain elements of the existing arrangements in association football. It remains to be seen if they can arrest the pressures for greater internationalisation of club association football – and professional team sports in general – driven by the potential mass markets and finances that television bring. These may accelerate the historical process in sporting league development discussed earlier in this book.

Conclusions

In this chapter a brief history of the origins of televised sport in the US and the UK is presented. Broad economic reasons explaining these developments are offered, together with an analysis of the economic consequences of these changes. In particular it has been argued that more research needs to be done on the effects of television on sports generally. It is suggested that the evidence that is available implies that the impact of television coverage of fixtures on attendance is not likely to affect traditional fixtures. However, the feedback effects of television through the financing and supply side of professional team sports could be profound. The advent of huge increases in television revenues in, for example, the UK has produced an 'exogenous' shock to historically more stable relationships. It is argued that whatever the precise outcome it seems that such vast skewed television revenues will change the structure of leagues at a previously unknown speed. Competitive balance may thus change at a previously unknown speed, and despite the previous discussion in this book, may thus matter much more in the future than in the past.

Perhaps more than before, the future of professional sports leagues will reflect the relative bargaining power of a variety of constituents. It is this more than anything else that makes predicting these developments more difficult. Having begun these discussions by contemplating the demand for professional team sports, the growth in the bargaining power of players as a key component of the supply of professional team sports is now discussed. We will show that in the labour market the effects of league management policies have been much more consistent.

Discussion questions

1. What do you consider to have been the major effects on professional team sports of television coverage? Suppose that the next round of exclusive television live broadcasting deals for soccer increases the annual payments by 20%. Indicate what you expect (*ceteris paribus*) would happen to: club revenues, club profits, wages, competitive balance.

2. Explain why the attractiveness of pay-per-view to broadcasting providers (potential and current) is related to the price elasticity of viewer demand.
3. Writers have frequently asserted that broadcasting sports events reduces the demand for attendance. Is there a consensus on this question among researchers?
4. An economist investigating the effect of broadcasting on attendance proposes an attendance demand function of the form:

$$A = b_0 + b_1 D_1 + b_2 (D_1 P) + b_3 P + \text{other variables.}$$

D_1 is a dichotomous dummy taking the value 1 if the match is simultaneously broadcast and zero otherwise. A is attendance at the match. P is the price of a ticket. $D_1 P$ is an interaction term that measures the change in the responsiveness of attendance to changes in price because of matches being broadcast.

   (a) What *a priori* expectations might you entertain about the signs of b_1 and b_2?
   (b) What expectation might you entertain about the sign of b_2 if it is your conviction that televising games is a good substitute for watching them? (Hint: what does increased substitutability imply?)
   (c) Suppose you held firmly to the view that live broadcasting has no effect on attendance? What expectation would you have about the values of b_1 and b_2?
   (d) Explain what will happen to the process of estimating the bs if the researcher instead of proceeding as above specifies *two* dummies: D_1 exactly as above and a companion, D_2, that equals zero if the match is broadcast and 1 otherwise.

5. An assumption made when specifying a dummy to capture the effect of broadcasting on attendance is that the dummy itself is a random variable. Does this seem reasonable? If not, would you anticipate that existing measures have systematically underestimated or systematically overestimated the effects of television upon attendance? Explain.

Section C

The labour market in professional team sports

9 The traditional view

Theory and evidence

Introduction

As we noted in Chapter 4, sporting labour markets are a source of much interest in discussion about the management of sporting leagues. In this and the next chapter, we begin to explore the main themes and evidence associated with sporting labour markets.

In particular the idealised labour market is outlined illustrating the close relationship between product and labour markets. The theory of monopsonistic competition that has figured prominently in the traditional literature is then outlined. The theory is exemplified by exploring, in some detail, some of the early studies of monopsonistic exploitation in US baseball. The next chapter examines institutional changes in US and European sporting labour markets, explores the role of bargaining in salary and transfer fee determination and then outlines some of the main recent empirical findings.

Some benchmark economic concepts of labour markets: the case of perfect competition

In order to understand wage determination a useful starting point is the elementary model of perfect competition noted in Chapter 2. As discussed there, it was argued that it provides a 'benchmark' from which we can develop models that we suggest capture the main features of reality and hence be able to evaluate alternative institutional arrangements.

Recall that in the perfectly competitive model it is assumed that all of the firms in an industry are profit maximisers who sell a homogenous product (sporting or otherwise) to perfectly informed utility maximising consumers. Profit maximisiation occurs where the firm's price or marginal revenue equals the firm's marginal costs. This point determines the supply of goods or services such as sports in the market.

Because the demand curve is given to the firm by the market, in perfect competition, it was argued in Chapter 2 that the marginal cost curve is essential to understanding how much output firms supply. In sporting terms, if output is measured as wins for a club, then marginal cost essentially determines how many matches a club will win when faced with the prevailing price it can charge for fixtures. Chapter 2 defined marginal costs as

Wage rate/marginal product of labour. (9.1)

In other words, marginal cost measures the money cost of an extra employee, or extra work provided by an additional employee, divided by the output produced by the extra worker or work done. It should be remembered that in perfect competition, the market for labour as a whole sets the money-wage rate. Like the market for the firm's output, prices are set outside the firm. If this is the case, then the only reason marginal costs can rise for a given money wage rate is because the marginal product of labour falls. In the theory of competitive markets this is assumed to be the case and is known as the assumption of 'diminishing marginal productivity'. It clearly echoes the concept of diminishing marginal utility discussed in Chapter 5.

Having discussed the supply of products we are now in a position to understand how much labour firms hire in order to maximise their profits. We can show that the demand for labour is a 'derived demand' from the demand for the firm's output.[1] An elementary chain of logic shows us this:

(1) We assume that firms maximise profit.
(2) Profit maximisation implies price = marginal cost.
(3) Price = marginal revenue.
(4) Marginal cost = wage rate/marginal product of labour.
(5) This implies that marginal revenue = wage rate/marginal product of labour.
(6) Rearranged this means that either:
     marginal product of labour × marginal revenue = wage rate
     or,
     marginal product of labour = wage rate/marginal revenue.

Both of the conditions described in point 6 imply that firms' hire labour up to the point at which workers earn enough for the firm to cover their wage rate. For example, the marginal product of labour × marginal revenue is known as the marginal revenue product of labour. Basically it measures the amount of revenue earned for the firm from the last unit, produced by the worker, being sold at the market price. The second expression means the same thing but is expressed in 'real' terms. The implication of this result is that workers get a 'just' wage. They effectively get paid what they produce (and contribute to revenues). It is worth noting, as implied in Chapter 2, that *in general* the price

---

[1] The principles of derived demand were first formulated by the English economist Alfred Marshall. Marshall's four principles of derived demand, and a sporting example of each, are given in Appendix 9.1.

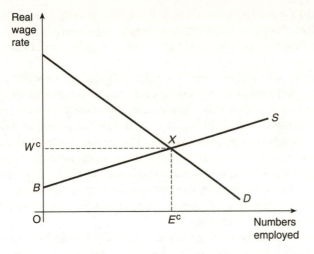

Figure 9.1 The labour market in perfect competition

at which output is sold is not equal to marginal revenue. Thus, *in general*, the marginal product of labour multiplied by the price of the firm's product, known as the Value of Labour's Marginal Product (VMP), is not equal to the marginal revenue product. For example the VMP of a monopoly would be greater than the MRP of a monopoly (why?).

Nonetheless, in this the simplest of cases in which there is perfect competition in both the product and labour markets, one can represent the market for labour as shown in Figure 9.1. Firms are price takers in both the labour and product markets, so the industry demand for labour is D (the marginal product of labour curve).

The supply of labour to the industry is S (an individual firm can always hire more labour at the same wage). Equilibrium occurs at point X, where D and S intersect, and the marginal product of labour equals the real wage rate (W^c) giving E^c and W^c as the competitive employment and real wage respectively. As drawn, S implies that intra-marginal workers, those to the left of point E^c, receive real 'economic rents' totalling the area of the triangle $W^c XB$.

Economic rents can be understood in the following terms. The supply curve, S, measures the minimum real wage that must be paid in order to obtain and retain the services of an employee. The supply curve thus charts the employee's 'transfer earnings'. These, by definition, cannot be less than what they could obtain in their next most preferred occupation. If they receive a wage in excess of their transfer earnings, as workers to the left of E^c clearly do, then an 'economic rent' arises. This reflects the fact that the employee's remuneration, given by W^c, is greater than the amount the employee would have been prepared to work for. Nonetheless, it should be noted that in this simple case of perfect competition, economic rents accrue solely from differences in workers' willingness to enter the industry, not from the possession of rare skills.

If workers are identically averse to entering the industry, in the sense that they share the same preferences over income and leisure, the labour supply curve (*S*) to the industry is perfectly elastic and the (uniform) wage rate comprises transfer earnings only. If hiring is by order of increasing aversion to the work, labour supply is imperfectly elastic. The uniform wage rate then includes an element of economic rent accruing to intra-marginal workers. The marginal worker earns transfer earnings only. The less price elastic the supply of the input, *ceteris paribus*, the greater its potential economic rent; hence the importance of economic rents to professional team sports players, musicians, actors and other possessors of rare skills.

In the context of professional team sports this implies that athletes' wages reflect the revenue they earn for the team by attracting spectators to come and watch the team play and pay the admission price to do so. It is clear that from an empirical context, one can explore whether or not players get a 'just' wage. We have seen from Chapter 6, that data on admission prices is available. In the US, if not the UK, players' salaries are known. Thus, if we can calculate the contribution of a player to the results of a team, that is calculate their marginal product, then we can test whether or not players receive their marginal revenue products. Later in this chapter we look at the seminal attempts to do this in US baseball. Before this, however, we elaborate on some of the other theories of the labour market that can conceivably be used to understand current developments in professional team sports.

Theories of player labour markets

The essence of the perfectly competitive model is that both clubs and players have no economic power over the price of output or the wage rate. This is because products and worker are assumed to be of the same quality and that there are a large number of them. In other words, there is no uniqueness about either of them. In a sporting context this implies that all teams produced performances of the same quality and the players within teams were of the same quality. Moreover, there would be a large number of teams and players in leagues. Under such circumstances this would suggest that match results would be entirely random and hence uncertainty of outcome would be at a maximum. This implies that profits would be maximised for the league.

Clearly, however, as discussed at length in previous chapters these assumptions about teams and leagues are not credible approximate descriptions of sporting leagues. This is despite the apparent financial attractiveness of the outcomes. Significantly, if we challenge some of the key assumptions of the perfectly competitive model, then essentially three other alternatives to under-

HIGH	Monopoly: 'star model'	Bilateral monopoly: 'bargaining over rents'
LOW	Perfect competition: 'just wage'	Monopsony: exploitation of players
Player power/ Club power	**LOW**	**HIGH**

Figure 9.2 The players' labour market structure

standing wage determination become possible.[2] Figure 9.2 provides a simple taxonomy to characterise these alternatives.

The axes of the taxonomy reflect player and club power, respectively. Thus, at the bottom left-hand corner of the diagram is the perfectly competitive case just outlined. Moving horizontally, the diagram indicates increasing club power with player power remaining constant. Essentially we are assuming that either the number of clubs is smaller than in the competitive case or that particular clubs are perceived to be so good that players want to play for the club. It is clear that these assumptions are closer to sporting leagues than the perfectly competitive assumptions. At a rudimentary level, there will always be more players than there are clubs. Basically this implies that monopolistic power in the product market implies bargaining power for the club in the labour market. This puts the clubs in a relatively strong position compared to the many equally good players wishing to play professional sports. In this respect, the competitive pressure really applies to the players rather than the clubs. The limiting case of this scenario is a monopsony. A monopsony is concerned with a sole buyer among many suppliers of a product. As we will see in detail below, historically sporting labour markets have been understood in these terms. The implication of clubs having power over athletes is that

---

[2] There are, of course, other possibilities depending on the nature of the product market as well as the labour market. For example, assuming that product markets are monopolistic – that is in the language of Neale (1964) that leagues are monopolies – then if labour markets were still competitive – that is, players could be hired in a perfectly competitive market – then firms must lower price to sell additional output. The revenue lost on intra-marginal sales implies that $VMP > MRP$ for a monopolistic firm. The imperfectly competitive firm's demand curve for labour will be below the perfectly competitive case (*ceteris paribus*). This implies that in imperfectly competitive equilibrium firms would employ fewer people and pay lower wages than perfectly competitive firms. In terms of Figure 9.1, one could draw a new demand curve, D^m below D to show that labour is hired up to the point where D^m intersects S (the money wage is equated to the marginal revenue product). In this case it is easy to show that the industry employs fewer people at a lower wage rate.

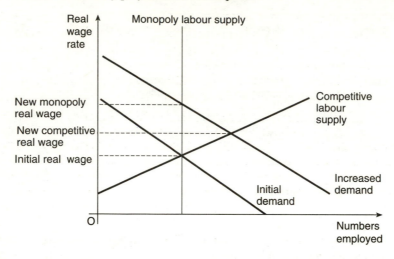

Figure 9.3 Wage increases for competitive and monopoly labour supply following an increase in demand

players have faced monopsonistic exploitation. This implies that they have received salaries *below* their marginal revenue products.

Moving vertically from the perfectly competitive case indicates increasing player power with club power remaining low. We are essentially assuming that particular players have unique talents and are monopolies as there is no effective substitute for them. In this case competitive pressure applies to clubs wishing to hire the player. One can think of many examples of such sporting monopolies: Mark McGuire, Deion Sanders, Jerry Rice, Michael Jordan, Shak O'Neal, Ronaldo (though his change in form and injuries since the 1998 world cup are noticeable). In the case of sporting monopolies, as Neale (1964) points out, the supply curve of the athlete is vertical and, as a consequence, wages are demand driven. As noted above, in this case economists refer to such earnings as economic rents.[3] Figure 9.3 illustrates that if demand increases wages have to rise more than in the competitive case because the supply of the players is different. The evidence on 'superstar' salaries is discussed in the next chapter.

---

[3] As can be seen from Figure 9.1, in the industry as a whole economic rents would be earned by some players prepared to work for less than the competitive wage-rate. The *MC* curve for the industry is given by the supply curve and indicates the 'transfer earnings' of athletes (not to be confused with the idea of a transfer fee which is discussed in the next chapter). This is the wage at which the athletes find it acceptable to offer their labour services to clubs rather than work in their next best paying occupation. The vertical distance between the prevailing wage rate and the *MC* curve indicates the economic rent. However, the implication of the competitive model is that at the margin athletes receive their marginal product. There is no exploitation.

The final quadrant of Figure 9.2 refers to the case of bilateral monopoly. Here both clubs and players have market power. The interesting thing about this scenario is that it is difficult to predict the impact that bargains will have on wages and salaries (and related features such as contract length and so on). In the case of perfect competition, wages will equal marginal revenue product. In the case of monopsony, players will receive salaries below their marginal revenue products. As far as bargaining is concerned one can only infer that salaries will lie somewhere between these two possibilities as the parties bargain over 'economic rents'. Bargaining theory and evidence are discussed in more detail in the next chapter.

For now it is worth noting that traditionally sports labour markets have been described as monopsonistic. However, as institutional arrangements such as the move to free agency in the US, and the Bosman ruling in Europe have occurred then labour markets have evolved. One can identify an evolutionary path that has moved from monopsonistic labour markets to bargaining structures and then competitive outcomes. Significantly with the general rise of player power commensurate with these earnings, wage bargains that approximate perfect competition, in the sense that the outcomes of bargaining mean that salaries now reflect marginal revenue products, have occurred.[4] To move towards a more detailed understanding of these issues the remainder of this chapter explores the seminal work on players' labour markets in baseball that illustrates the exploitation experienced by athletes and also the empirical approach adopted by researchers. As will be seen, the approach employs the regression method used to study the demand for professional team sports.

Case study: US baseball

As noted above, firms can enjoy monopsony power in the labour market to complement monopoly power in the product market. Unlike price takers who can hire as much labour as desired at the current wage, monopsonists can attract more labour only by raising wages. As illustrated in Figure 9.4, firms' marginal labour cost (MCL) exceeds the wage paid to the marginal worker since the intra-marginal workers also receive the higher rate of pay.

The relevant labour supply to the industry is MCL, everywhere above S. Profit maximising equilibrium is where MCL intersects D^m – the marginal cost of labour equals its marginal revenue product. Firms employ E^m people and pay a real wage equal to W^m. The implication of this model is that the wages of athletes are lower than in the competitive case. It is precisely these predictions that prompted one of the first systematic

---

4 It is important to note that this is 'on average'. The experiences of individual athletes may be very different. Issues such as these are discussed in the next chapter.

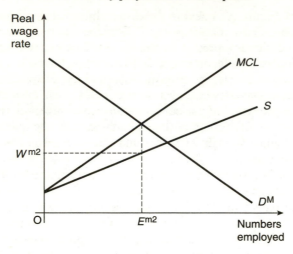

Figure 9.4 Monopsony labour markets. At W^m firms can attract labour by paying the competitive wage given the firms' desired employment E^m. The competitive wage is lower than the monopsony could pay.

econometric investigations into athletes' remuneration by Gerald Scully (1974).

Scully's paper was written against the background of the 1972 baseball players' strike – nominally[5] about pensions, although there was a long-running history of player discontent over the game's standard year-long 'renewable' contracts, discussed in Chapter 4, as a feature of league management policies. Prior to signing, the player was a free agent (able to negotiate with any team). On the player signing the owner acquired the exclusive right to bargain with him under the reserve-option clause. On expiry of the existing contract the owner might renew, sell or terminate it. The player offered another contract by his employer could only sign or bargain for a better deal. Once the owner's final offer was made, the player's choice was stark – accept what was offered or leave the sport permanently.

The obvious asymmetry of the treatment of employee and employer would be expected to reduce the former's earnings below his marginal revenue product. In a perfectly competitive labour market a player currently earning less than his marginal revenue product simply moves to a club willing to pay

---

[5] Industrial disputes, as all students of labour economics rapidly learn, are only rarely (if indeed ever) wholly about the issues reported in the media. Furthermore, it is not usually possible to determine whether a given dispute is a strike or a lock-out, as the compilers of official British labour market statistics recognise by referring to all disputes by that title and no other. If this comes as a surprise, you might reflect that to the firm an occasional strike may be a good way to 'discipline' the workforce. From the public relations angle, a strike beats a lock-out hands down; the media and the general public are liable to blame the union.

the full value. As this might differ from one club to another, *ceteris paribus*, being greater at a club with greater drawing power, the player moves to where his marginal revenue product and earnings are maximised. The reserve clause in baseball effectively tied him to one employer for an indefinite period.

Scully's major aim was, 'to crudely measure the economic loss to the players due to the restrictions of the reserve clause' (Scully, 1974, p. 915). This he set out to accomplish by first obtaining estimates of the marginal revenue products of pitchers and batters in major league baseball, then comparing these to players' earnings in order to determine what percentage of a player's marginal revenue product was retained by him. Other things equal, the more effective the reserve clause in weakening players relative to owners, the less the proportion of his economic rent a player would retain.

Scully's procedure is worthy of detailed examination both in its own right and as the starting point for a whole sub-literature within the economics of professional team sports. His proposed causal model directly determines both the marginal effect of player performance upon team success and the marginal effect of the latter upon team revenues. Given estimates of these marginal effects it is possible to estimate the player marginal revenue products.

In the model a team's success, measured by its win percent, depends on player performances and on other inputs, for example managerial and coaching talent, and finance. In turn, the team's revenues depend upon its playing success and other variables. There are, thus, two 'dependent' variables, playing success and revenues. As proposed it is not a simultaneous equation model; in such a model the independent variables would determine both revenue and sporting success simultaneously. Scully proposed a causal chain (recursive) model. In the first stage a subset of the independent variables determines the team's success. In the second stage, team success and the independent variables then determine the team revenues. Team success is conceived of as 'more' independent than team revenue. Whether a model is simultaneous or recursive has implications for estimation as will be seen below. Scully's estimation method – the application of OLS regression to both equations – is inappropriate unless the model is truly recursive. To this question we return after setting out and discussing Scully's estimated equations.

(9.2) is the linear equation Scully derived from theoretical considerations which is intended to explain team performance ($PCTWIN_t$) in year t, estimated using data from the 1968 and 1969 seasons:

$$PCTWIN_t = \alpha_1 + \alpha_2 TSA_t + \alpha_3 TSW_t + \alpha_4 NL + \alpha_5 CONT_t$$
$$+ \alpha_6 OUT_t + u_t. \tag{9.2}$$

The alphas are coefficients to be estimated. *TSA* is a measure of batting prowess, the team's slugging average (the number of bases gained per match) regarded as an index of its attacking success. *TSW* is the team's strikeout-to-walk ratio, a measure of its pitching (defensive) success. One would anticipate that α_2 and α_3 should be positive (better batting and pitching should improve the team's percent wins). Scully's data set comprised all teams in the American and National Leagues. *NL* is a dichotomous dummy variable taking the value unity when the team is in the National League, otherwise zero, introduced to capture the author's belief that standards of play were consistently higher in the National League. He might alternatively have computed regressions for both leagues, but at the cost of halving his degrees of freedom. On the assumption that the standard of play in the National League was higher, α_4 should be negative.

The dichotomous dummy variables *CONT* and *OUT* were introduced to capture the idea that team success depended not only on batting and pitching but on other factors such as morale, quality of managerial decisions and quality of decisions on the field. With data available on none of these, the author sought to differentiate between teams 'in contention' for the championship, those in the middle and those (possibly demoralised) by lack of success. *CONT* = 1 for the winning team and for teams finishing within five or fewer wins of them; otherwise it is zero. *OUT* = 1 for all teams more than twenty games behind the winners; otherwise it is zero. Notice that all the teams 'in the middle' score 0 for both *CONT* and *OUT*. *Two* dummies will neatly separate teams into *three* categories, just as two cuts in a length of string will produce three separate lengths. You would expect α_5 to be positive and α_6 to be negative. Clearly the specification of *CONT* and *OUT* is rather ad hoc, there is no valid reason for choosing five games out and twenty games out as the bounds, rather than six and fifteen. As noted in Chapter 7, uncertainty of outcome has only been measured similarly in a problematic way. Consequently, the equations estimated above, and those in general by economists, should be seen as a compromise between the ideal and the practical.

The remaining variable u is a random error term intended to pick up the effects of errors in the measurement of *PCTWIN*, missing variables (e.g. the managerial decisions not observed) and the inevitable unpredictability of life. In effect *PCTWIN* is modelled as the outcome of a systematic (predictable) process and an unpredictable (random) one. As discussed in Chapter 5, for OLS regression to yield unbiased estimates of the αs, all the right-hand side variables must be independent of u. As noted in Chapter 6 also, this is scarcely ever true in economics. In contrast it may be closely approached in the laboratory where the right-hand side variables are held constant in successive experiments.

Scully's estimate of the *PCTWIN* function is given in Table 9.1. It suggests that, *ceteris paribus*, another one point slugging average would augment the win percent by 0.92 points. Of two teams enjoying equal playing skills, the one in the American League would be expected to finish about 39 points higher in percent wins, thanks to generally inferior opposition. All the coefficients have the signs expected by the original author. The *t*-ratios indicate that the explanatory variables are statistically significant at the 1% level or better, while

Table 9.1 Scully's estimates of PCTWIN

Variable	Estimated coefficient value	T-ratios
Constant	37.24	0.39
TSA	0.92	4.37
TSW	0.90	5.92
NL	−38.57	−4.03
CONT	43.78	3.77
OUT	−75.64	−6.17
Other statistics	*Value*	
R^2	0.88	
Degrees of freedom	38	

the value of R^2 suggests that within-sample variation in the explanatory variables (*TSA* and the others) could account for 88% of the within-sample variation in the dependent variable (*PCTWIN*).[6] The linear team revenue function specified by Scully is (9.3),

$$REVENUE_t = \beta_1 + \beta_2 PCTWIN_t + \beta_3 SMSA_{70} + \beta_4 MARGA$$
$$+ \beta_5 NL + \beta_6 STD_t + \beta_7 BBPCT_t + v_t. \tag{9.3}$$

Comparing (9.2) and (9.3) you will notice that while *PCTWIN* appears as an explanatory variable of *REVENUE* in (9.3), *REVENUE* is not listed among the explanatory variables in (9.2). This is a necessary (but not a sufficient) condition for the pair of equations to constitute a causal chain model; it rules out systematic feedback from *REVENUE* to *PCTWIN*. The other condition that must be met is that *PCTWIN* is independent of v; this condition rules out non-systematic feedback from *REVENUE* to *PCTWIN*. This in turn depends upon the two errors (u and v) being mutually independent.

Given that factors such as managerial quality which influence performance on the field (*PCTWIN*) are also likely to affect the team's earnings (*REVENUE*) this condition may not be met, in which case Scully's estimation

---

[6] Note that this does not mean the exaplanatory variables do account for 88% of the within-sample variation in *PCTWIN* – association does not prove causation. Equally, it does not imply that 88% of without-sample variation in *PCTWIN* could be accounted for by without-sample variation in the explanatory variables. This point may strike you as somewhat academic, but it has very great practical significance, within and without economics. A naïve economic model, for example a simple 'Keynesian' consumption function, nearly always gets R^2 in excess of 0.95, but is always absolutely useless for predicting future levels of consumption. The development of alternative consumption theories testifies that R^2 is useless as a guide to predictive power, although Scully interpreted his R^2 statistic that way.

method is inappropriate. Furthermore, teams enjoying larger revenues have the potential to pay higher wages and thereby to obtain a higher level of performance on the field. Finally, had Scully specified *REVENUE* to be an explanator of *PCTWIN*, the model would clearly have been simultaneous and he would not have used ordinary least-squares regression.

REVENUE is defined as attendance times mean ticket price plus income from the sale of broadcasting rights. This both understates by ignoring concession revenue such as sales of refreshments and overstates by ignoring the share of the gates paid to the visiting team, actual team revenues. One would expect β_2 to be positive; successful teams should attract both attendance and broadcasting revenues. $SMSA_{70}$ is the population in 1970 of the standard metropolitan statistical area in which the team is domiciled. As discussed in Chapter 6, it can be viewed as a proxy for the value to the team of the local (much larger geographically in the US than in Europe) monopoly, which the team enjoys as a member of the relevant league. In line with studies that suggest that 'big city' teams tend to enjoy more sporting and more economic success than 'small city' teams, one would expect that β_3 is positive.

MARGA attempts to measure inter-city differences in team support which arise from causes other than the size of the catchment area. It is the estimated coefficient (derived from time-series regressions) of team-specific attendance levels on current and past success (*PCTWIN*) and other variables, not reported by Scully. He expected β_4 to be positive; *ceteris paribus*, a higher degree of team support ought to increase revenues. NL is already familiar; to the extent National League teams out-performed American League teams Scully expected β_5 would be positive. *STD* is another dummy variable equal to one if the home stadium is located in a poor neighbourhood with limited car parking. Again this is rather ad hoc as there is not universal agreement on what constitutes a 'poor' neighbourhood or for that matter 'limited' parking, although one would expect paying customers to take these factors into account when deciding whether to attend. The expectation is that β_6 would be negative.

BBCPT attempts to allow for possible racial prejudice on the parts of baseball spectators in the period under study. It is defined as the percentage of black players in the team. A negative value of β_7 would be consistent with racial prejudice on the customer's part. Not everybody has found evidence of customer discrimination. Gwartney and Haworth (1974) estimated that teams employing more blacks during 1952–1956 had won more games than others, and that the presence of black players had had a positive influence on attendance. This might not necessarily imply that customers were unprejudiced however; the rapid decline of the black baseball game once the major leagues began to employ black players may have brought about a substitution of black for white spectators, possibly suggestive of racial discrimination operating in both directions. The variable v is the error term, introduced for the same reasons as u in (9.2). The original author's estimate of (9.3) is given in Table 9.2.

Table 9.2 Scully's estimates of REVENUE

Variable	Estimated coefficient value	T-ratios
Constant	−1,735,890	−1.69
PCTWIN	10,330	6.64
$SMSA_{70}$	494,585	4.61
MARGA	512	4.28
NL	580,913	1.84
STD	−764,248	−2.42
BBPCT	−58,523	3.13

Other statistics	Value
R^2	0.75
Degrees of freedom	36

These suggest that a one-point increase in percent wins would have added about $10,000 dollars to the team's annual revenue, while membership of the National League would have added about $580,000. It looks as if (on a fairly naïve interpretation) spectator prejudice against black players would have cost the team about $580,000 following a 10% increase in the proportion of black players. Operating from a stadium in an inner-city area might have cost about $760,000 a year. About 75% of the within-sample variation in *REVENUE* might have been accounted for by within-sample variation in the explanatory variables.

The coefficient estimates of most interest to Scully (and to us) are those on *TSA* and *TSW* in Table 9.1 and that on *PCTWIN* in Table 9.2. These three estimates are used in the computation of values for the marginal revenue products (*MRP*s) of batters and pitchers.[7] The estimated rates of change of *PCTWIN* with respect to *TSA* and *TSW* are respectively 0.92 and 0.90, while the estimated rate of change of *REVENUE* with respect to *PCTWIN* is 10,330. This suggests that the *MRP*s in batting and pitching performance levels are respectively $10,330 × 0.92 = $9504 per unit increase in *TSA* and $10,330 × 0.90 = $9297 per 1/100 unit increase in *TSW*.

To convert these (average) *MRP*s into *MRP* per player, Scully assumed further that the team's performance was the sum of the individuals' perform-ances, i.e. an unusually good/bad performance by *A* never had 'spillover'

---

[7] You might wonder why we spent so much time on the equations and the underlying theory if only three of 13 reported coefficients are central to Scully's argument. The reason is that unless we understand and have confidence in the methods employed by researchers we cannot have confidence in their results. Researchers must inform readers exactly how they reached their published conclusions. In turn, the reader has a corresponding duty to take pains to under-stand the methods employed. The ideal in presenting research findings is that anybody who applies the same methods to the same data should reach the same results.

effects on *B*'s performance. This was not a terribly attractive assumption (as he admitted) but he saw no obvious alternative. Team rosters carried about fifteen batters of whom about twelve would have batted in a match, and ten pitchers of whom about eight would have played in a match. Hence a 'mediocre' batter with a career average *SA* of 270 contributed about 22.5 (270/12) points to (the team's) *TSA*. Taking each point to be worth $9504 to the team, his *MRP* was estimated as 22.5 × $9504 = $213,840. By the same logic a 'star' pitcher with a career average *SW* of 3.4 contributed 0.425 (3.4/8) points to *TSW* and (remembering *TSW* is measured in 1/100 points) his *MRP* works out at 0.425 × 100 × $9297 = $395,123. Scully's Table 1 (ibid., p. 923) stacks estimated *MRP*s and salaries for average career length players of varying degrees of competence, which enables you to check the accuracy of the *MRP*s presented here.

Scully regards these as 'gross' *MRP*s since they do not allow for costs associated with putting players onto the field. Thus he calculates a corresponding set of 'net' *MRP*s by making deductions. For example, the sum total of transport and equipment and related costs per away game came out as at least $800,000 for 81 away games per team per season. Per member of the typical 30-man travelling squad (team roster plus coaching staff), that came to $26,700 a player if one accepts the crudeness of a simple average. More controversial is training cost per man; the teams had estimated this as $300,000 over the player's entire major league career, average span seven years, giving $43,000 a year estimated training cost. This figure had been arrived at by dividing the entire costs (fixed and variable!) of the minor leagues by the number of players promoted every year to the majors. Obviously it is a very considerable overestimate. Only teams' variable (i.e. avoidable) costs should be taken into account when adjusting the estimated *MRP*.

Making a series of adjustments on the basis of the data available to him, Scully reckoned that the annual cost of fielding (salary apart) an average career length player came to about $128,300. We deduct this from the estimates of (gross) *MRP* above to arrive at a net *MRP* for a mediocre career length batter (*SW* = 270) = $213,840 − $128,300 = $85,540; check this against Table 9.3 below, an abbreviated version of Table 1 in the original. The numbers are Scully's, rounded to the nearest $1000, rather than ours above. Ours are presented in that form so as to enable you to replicate them directly to satisfy yourself that we (and Scully) are proceeding correctly.

The last column in Table 9.3 stores estimates of the salaries that would have been paid to players in the various categories. These were estimated from separate salary regressions for batters and hitters using data on 148 players in the 1968 and 1969 seasons. Since our main interest lies in how Scully estimated the players' *MRP*s we deal briefly with how the salary data were obtained. *A* batter's salary was modelled as a function of his (previous) career average *SA*, the number of times he batted relative to its theoretical maximum, the number of years he had spent in the major leagues and other variables.

Table 9.3 Estimated *MRP*s and salaries of average career length players

Career SA/SW	Gross MRP	Net MRP	Salary
		Batters	
270	213,800	85,500	31,700
370	292,700	164,400	44,400
470	372,600	244,300	57,400
570	451,400	323,100	70,600
		Pitchers	
1.60	185,900	57,600	31,100
2.60	302,200	173,900	46,000
3.60	418,400	290,100	59,800

Similarly a pitcher's salary was modelled as a function of his (to date) career average *SW*, the number of years he had spent in the majors and the percentage of innings he pitched.

Although the data in Table 9.3 are suggestive of exploitation, the computed salaries could not be directly compared to the *MRP*s as the players they represented (like the average family with 1.7 children) did not exist. Batters capable of 340 a season (a) are more frequently used and (b) spend more years in the majors than batters whose *SA* is 250. The same goes for pitchers. But in Table 9.3, as in the original Table 1, everybody has the same (average) career length in the majors. Scully was able to overcome this problem by estimating *MRP*s and salaries for players of varying capabilities (measured by their lifetime *SA/SW*) and varying years in the majors, and proportion of innings batted/pitched.

These are reported in his Table 2 (*ibid.*, p. 928) which also presents his estimates of the rates of exploitation. The computed rate of exploitation relative to the player's gross *MRP* is simply the difference between the estimated gross *MRP* and the estimated salary, divided by the estimated gross *MRP*. The bigger the ratio, the greater the degree of exploitation. A value of 0 would indicate that the player gets the whole gross *MRP*, a value of 1 would suggest the player got none of his *MRP*. Scully's Table 2 suggested that average players got about 20% of their net *MRP*s and about 10% of their gross *MRP*s, while stars got around 10% of their gross *MRP*s and 15% of their net *MRP*s. Mediocre players appeared to have negative *MRP*s, which could reflect their shorter careers and lower use rates. Or perhaps it is due to the industry's overestimate of its own annual average training costs alluded to above. Table 9.4 above stacks a few of the entries in the original author's Table 2 to give you a flavour of his results.

Perhaps not surprisingly, these estimated rates of exploitation seemed implausibly high to some scholars at the time. The problems identified by

Table 9.4 MRP, salary and rates of exploitation for average batters and pitchers

Career SA/SW	Gross MRP	Net MRP	Salary	Gross exp. %	Net exp. %
			Batters[a]		
305	231,900	103,600	14,100	94	86
350	266,100	137,800	32,700	88	76
375	285,100	156,800	39,000	86	75
			Pitchers[b]		
2.00	260,300	132,000	16,500	94	88
2.22	288,200	159,900	33,000	89	79
2.46	316,000	187,700	43,700	86	77

[a]Average batters played seven years in the majors and batted 8% of possible innings.
[b]Average pitchers played seven years in the majors and pitched 14% of possible innings.

commentators on Scully's results lie with two interrelated issues associated with either the data employed or the underlying model. In the first case, for example, there were no data available on other vital inputs into baseball. In the latter case, the model and estimation method employed by Scully assumed a recursive chain of causation, which required that the disturbance terms in (9.2) and (9.3) should be independent of one another. This is an important statistical assumption and, as such, was the primary focus of concern with Scully's results. Thus, as discussed above, if certain baseball inputs are not included specifically in the equations (because no measures were available to Scully) such as managerial skills, these would be expected to increase both *PCTWIN* and *REVENUE*. If teams grossing large revenues might be teams able to pay higher wages and obtain greater values of *PCTWIN*, then again *PCTWIN* and *REVENUE* are related. Thus, if the disturbance terms in these regression equations are not independent, indirect feedback between the relationships that Scully was attempting to measure with assumed independent equations would make *PCTWIN* dependent upon *REVENUE*. This would bias the ordinary least-squares regression estimates of the β coefficients in (9.3). It therefore seems likely that the errors u and v are positively correlated and that, by implication, β_3 was overestimated by Scully. That implies a possible overestimate by the original author of the *MRP*s of both pitchers and batters, hence a possible overestimate of the degrees of exploitation made possible by the reserve clause.

Largely because of these problems Medoff (1976) reports findings consistent with the view that Scully had overestimated the degree of player exploitation, although their estimates are not directly comparable. Medoff changed the model specification slightly and updated the study period from 1967–1968 to 1972–1974, so his parameter estimates would differ from Scully's even if the original author's model had been the 'true' model. The crucial difference between Medoff's results, and those of Scully, is that

Medoff estimates the revenue equation by Two Stage Least Squares (2SLS). This procedure, as the name implies, involved two stages. The first stage involved Medoff estimating the *PCTWIN* equation. Based on the estimated parameters of this equation and given the values of the independent variables, predicted values for *PCTWIN* were calculated.[8] The second stage then involved using these estimated values of *PCTWIN* rather than the actual values of *PCTWIN* in the estimate of the *REVENUE* equation. The intuition behind this approach is quite clear. As detailed in Chapter 6, a regression equation calculates the conditional average value of the dependent variable for a given set of values of independent variables. As an average value, the random influences on the dependent variable, that are included in the original data, are removed. This means that the set of average values calculated in step one of the procedure do not include the random elements that could affect *PCTWIN* and hence *REVENUE*. This is clearly an improvement on the Scully procedure.

Statistically speaking, using terms defined in Chapter 5, the improvement can be noted by saying that while 2SLS gives biased but consistent parameter estimates, OLS, which Scully had used, give estimates which are both biased and inconsistent. *Ceteris paribus*, an unbiased estimator is preferable to a consistent estimator. As discussed in Chapter 5, an unbiased estimator on average estimates a true value. The property of unbiasedness applies at any sample size. As discussed in Chapter 6, the statistical condition of consistency implies that while estimates can be biased in finite, i.e. small, samples, estimates will get closer and closer to the (unknown) true value as the sample size increases. As the bias of an inconsistent and biased estimator does not diminish as the number of observations increases, while the bias of a biased but consistent estimator does then one can conclude that theoretically Medoff's application of a 2SLS estimator would produce superior statistical results to the OLS estimator.[9]

Table 9.5 reproduces Medoff's estimated revenue equation. Based on these results, it appears that a unit increase in *PCTWIN* adds only $7295 to team revenue and not $10,330 as Scully reported. The reduced estimate of the *PCTWIN* coefficient estimate supports the view that indirect feedback from *REVENUE* into *PCTWIN* is a serious problem and that Scully's estimates of player marginal products were upward biased as a result of ignoring the problem. Nonetheless, the fact that Medoff estimated that players in his sample received between 30 and 50% of their *MRPs*, rather than the 10 to 20%

---

[8] Econometric computer packages have this procedure as a routine facility now.

[9] It has to be admitted, however, that in any given sample the bias of an inconsistent parameter estimate may actually be smaller than that of a corresponding consistent parameter estimate. Consistency is a 'large sample' property but no researcher really knows what constitutes a large sample in any context of interest. This is why the results are stressed in theoretical terms.

Table 9.5 Medoff's estimates of *REVENUE*

Variable	Estimated coefficient value	T-ratios
Constant	2,174,333	1.18
PCTWIN	7,295	1.96
SMSA	320,615	3.24
SUB	−359,989	−2.41
NL	1,038,160	2.39
STAD	−647,191	−1.78
BBPCT	−24,330	−1.34
Other statistics	*Value*	
R^2	0.58	
Degrees of freedom	35	

suggested by Scully, does not detract from the qualitatively similar conclusion found by both researchers. This was that significant exploitation of baseball players existed and that this must be attributable to the operation of the reserve clause in US baseball. As we noted earlier, this reserve clause underpinned a monopsonistic labour market. Moreover, the explosion in player salaries that followed the abolition of the reserve clause suggests that player exploitation had indeed been a problem in major league baseball, whatever its degree.

Conclusions

This chapter has outlined some of the key economic concepts associated with the economic analysis of labour markets. In particular, it has argued that traditionally sporting labour markets have been characterised by monopsonistic exploitation as a result of the league management policies discussed in Chapter 4. Some of the seminal empirical work on baseball earnings has been discussed to provide some detailed understanding of this issue. In the next chapter we examine the major institutional changes in US and European sporting labour markets and explore the role of bargaining in salary and transfer fee determination. Some of the main recent empirical findings are then discussed.

Appendix 9.1: The principles of derived demand

The English economist Alfred Marshall was the first to analyse the relationships between the demand for a product and the 'derived' demands for the factors required in its production. Marshall's four principles of derived demand may cast light on those factors that determine how the total income paid to professional team sport is divided between owners and players. It should be borne in mind that Marshall's analysis assumes profit maximising firms. As discussed in Chapter 3, owners of professional sports teams may not be profit maximisers but may pursue a range of goals among which profit takes its place with team performance in terms of league position, cup success and – at the bottom of the heap – bare survival.

Marshall's principles may be set down (we do not attempt to derive them herein) as follows.

Ceteris paribus, the more inelastic the demand for the product, the more inelastic the derived demand for the input. Thus we might expect that while successful teams are able to enjoy wider profit margins (thanks to inelastic product demand) than other teams, players who are organised into a union may be able to extract some of that monopoly profit in the form of higher wages.

Ceteris paribus, the less important the cost of an input relative to the total cost of production, the less elastic is its derived demand. This favours the team owners, given that the biggest single item in the running costs of professional team sports tends to be players' wages. While owners may not concern themselves too much with a 5% rise in the price of paper clips, an attempt by players to extract a 5% wage rise will be resisted.

Ceteris paribus, the less the degree of substitutability between an input and co-operating inputs, the less elastic is its derived demand. The best substitute for player *A* on Saturday afternoon may be player *B* on Saturday afternoon, but given the degree to which skills are person-specific, player *B* may not be a close enough substitute. More subtly, the best substitute for player *A* on Saturday afternoon may be player *A* on the following Wednesday evening. In many industries the lost sales and goodwill imposed by a dispute are quickly recovered by means of overtime working. This strengthens the employer's hand. In professional team sports the replay always occurs, but lost revenue is not always replaced. The league may timetable the game to minimise possible effects on the promotion/demotion prospects of other members, rather than to accommodate the preferences of intending spectators.

Ceteris paribus, the less price elastic the supply of co-operating inputs the less elastic the demand for a given input. In December 1995, the European Court of Justice outlawed the Union of European Football Associations' (UEFA) quota restrictions on the number of foreign players a club could field, ruling that these contradict Article 48 of the Treaty of Rome which guarantees free movement of labour throughout the European Union. All players originating in EU countries must be regarded as 'domestic' players. The immediate effect was to increase the number of substitutes available to each team owner for the current playing staff. This might – temporarily – lower (raise) the price elasticity of supply of talent available to teams operating in high (low) wage leagues. In the longer run, the tendency towards free agency ought to reduce wage differentials across European leagues.

Discussion questions

1. Outline the theory of wage determination in competitive markets. Do you think that this model applies to sporting labour markets? If not, how would you characterise the labour market in professional team sports?
2. Scully's pioneering study of baseball earnings suggested major league players might be grossly exploited by club owners. What theoretical ideas motivated his work?
3. How did Scully arrive at his conclusion? Can we accept his estimate that baseball players might be paid around 30% of their true worth – and if not, why not?
4. Is it likely that pro athletes receive their marginal products?
5. On what grounds do owners of teams justify labour market restrictions?
6. Do you think that these are valid arguments?
7. Assume that the output of a sporting tournament is measured as the number of spectators attracted, multiplied by the number of days' duration (spectator days).
    (a) If getting Venus Williams to play at a given tournament adds 1000 spectators a day over two weeks (assuming she wins), find her marginal physical product.
    (b) If entrance costs £10 a day and the ticket price does not have to be reduced to sell the extra tickets, what is the maximum amount that profit maximising tournament organisers would be prepared to pay Venus to appear?
    (c) If the tournament organisers have to reduce the price of a ticket to £9.90 to sell the extra 1000 tickets a day, and if 40,000 'intra-marginal' tickets could be sold at £10, what is the maximum the organisers would be willing to pay Venus?
8. You observe that footballer A earns twice as much money as footballer B. Does this imply that *any* or *all* of the following three propositions is or are true? A is not being exploited. B is being exploited. A is not being exploited but B is. Carefully explain the reasoning behind your conclusions, (Hint: think about other things that are not necessarily equal.)
9. If the Bosman ruling were to be reversed, what do you think would happen, *ceteris paribus*, to: players' wages, competitive balance, employment contract lengths, team profits in English soccer?

10 Recent developments
Theory and evidence

Introduction

The previous chapter outlined some of the key economic concepts associated with the economic analysis of sporting labour markets, in particular the theory of monopsonistic competition that has figured prominently in the traditional literature. The results of the seminal studies of monopsonistic exploitation in US baseball were then explored in some detail.

In this chapter we examine the key institutional changes that have taken place in US and European sporting labour markets. The changes involve the movement to free agency in both US and UK sports. The 1995 Bosman Ruling made by the European Court of Justice will also be explored. It is argued that these developments reflect increased player power in the labour market. As a result players are now more able to bargain over their salaries and contracts. To provide an economic understanding of these processes, the chapter also explores bargaining theory and then examines the application of this theory to sporting markets. In particular salary levels and contract duration in US sports are examined. In the European context, transfer fee determination is discussed. Some implications of increased player power for league management policy are then discussed.

The move to increased player power: the rise of free agency in the US

As discussed in the last chapter, prior to the mid-1970s the market for baseball players could be characterised as a monopsony. The institutional arrangement that led to this characterisation was the 'reserve-option clause'. As noted in Chapter 4, the main motivation for the introduction of the reserve-option clause in baseball in 1880 was to try and control player mobility. It is probably fair to say that initially team owner profits were a key consideration in this policy. This said, however, as Fort and Quirk (1995) note:

> Over time as the reserve clause faced court challenges, owners of sports teams developed the argument that, whatever the consequences of the reserve clause on players' salaries, it was needed to preserve competitive

balance. Owners argued that free agency would allow the richest teams to acquire a disproportionate share of the playing talent in the league. Competitive balance would be destroyed, driving weaker franchises out of business.

(p. 1274)

The argument increasingly put forward by advocates of the reserve-option clause was that controlling players' movements and, by implication their salaries, would enable poorer teams, in principle, to be able to afford the best players as well as the larger, richer clubs. In this way the competitive balance or uncertainty of outcome of the league would be retained.

To recap, the main feature of this clause was to bind a player to the club owning the contract. Effectively once a player had joined a club the owner had the unilateral option to extend his contract for a further year; the player however was bound to his club for as long as it chose to exercise the reserve option. In the event that the player would or could not agree to the next set of terms offered by the owner of the club, and the owner refused permission for the player to negotiate with a fresh club, the player's only option was to retire from the game. Given that his next best alternative earnings (as noted in the last chapter referred to by economists as reservation wages or transfer earnings) might be substantially lower than his most recent offer, the player had little choice but to accept his employer's latest offer. In effect the player appeared to be tied to his present club for a single season but in practice the system tied the player to the club indefinitely.

It is clear that this is a considerable restriction on the mobility of players in terms of jobs. In fact, as discussed in Chapter 4, all players in the main four US sports, baseball, basketball, grid-iron football and ice hockey, were subject to similar restrictions on their mobility and ability to negotiate their terms of employment with sporting clubs. All of these major US sporting leagues have employed a version of the reserve clause, although the details do vary.

As Sanderson and Seigfried (1997) note, the move towards free agency in US sports began in the 1970s. With the exception of baseball since 1922, the other professional team sports in the US were subject to US laws prohibiting collective action to restrict competition. In the late 1960s and 1970s legal challenges to some of the restrictive practices employed by clubs saw labour relations evolve in a complex way involving collective bargaining agreements between teams and player unions. By the 1990s the situation had developed to the extent that, in effect, 'rookie' players were subject to monopsonistic exploitation, but veteran players had substantial freedom to contract. A similar pattern of development occurred in baseball, though it provides a very interesting example in that this has occurred despite being exempt from US competition law.[1]

---

[1] For a highly readable account of these developments, see Dworkin (1981).

In 1970, a forceful baseball players' union negotiated a collective bargaining agreement that brought into existence an impartial arbitrator to help sort out contractual grievances. Some crucial developments followed. By 1973 final offer-arbitration for salary grievances was instituted. In final-offer arbitration, the two sides to a dispute, the players and the team, make salary offers and then the arbitrator picks one of the two offers as the settlement. This is distinct from conventional arbitration settlements in which the arbitrator is free to impose any settlement they deem fit. Moreover, in 1975 two players, Andy Messersmith and Dave McNally, two star pitchers, refused to sign contracts, played a year without contracts for their clubs, and at the conclusion argued they had worked off their clubs' reserve-option periods and asked to be regarded and treated as free agents. Crucially, the arbitrator, Peter Seitz, favoured the players and was consequently sacked by the team owners. However, the courts refused to reverse the decision. In this respect the Messersmith and McNally ruling marks a significant challenge to the reserve-option clause. The outcome of the Messersmith–McNally judgement was to give the club an exclusive six-year option on the player's services, after which time he automatically becomes a free agent. Nonetheless, while this principle remains, one of the issues that has dominated labour relations in baseball is eligibility for final-offer arbitration prior to becoming a free agent. For example, there was a two-day strike in 1985, a 32-day lock-out in 1990 and the 1994 season was not completed because of disputes over this issue.

However, since 1986 it is fair to say that major league baseball players can be grouped into three institutional or contract environments. Rookies of one or two years' experience are subject to a reserve clause. Intermediate players of between three–six years' experience are eligible for final-offer arbitration and veterans of seven or more years' service are free agents or eligible for final-offer arbitration. In short,

> By the 1990's, labour relations in each of the four professional team sports leagues in the United States had evolved into a situation where teams maintained limited power over entry-level players with substantial freedom to contract for veteran players. The iron grip of monopsony had been relaxed.
>
> (Sanderson and Seigfried, 1997, p. 8)

The widespread use of the reserve clause in US sports has, of course, been combined with the other labour market polices such as the salary cap and the rookie draft discussed in Chapter 4. Indeed these developments are not unrelated. In the same way that the reserve clause potentially impinges on both the remuneration and mobility of players, it is clear that drafting systems are intended to reinforce the control of player mobility between clubs and hence their ability to bargain for higher salaries. As noted in Chapter 4, the ability of clubs to restrict player movements appears to be small given the lack of effect on competitive balance of these policies. It seems likely therefore, that the major impact of restriction is upon salaries and, by implication, clubs' profit levels. Thus, it is notable that much of the impetus for salary caps, for example in the NBA in the 1980s and the NFL in the 1990s, came from the asserted financial difficulties experienced by clubs following the rise in player salaries after the move to free agency.[2] Indeed the increases in salary have been quite extraordinary. As Sanderson and Seigfried (1997) note, average baseball salaries rose by approximately 730% between 1975 and 1985. Between 1967 and 1977, basketball salaries rose by approximately 615%. Between 1967 and 1977, grid-iron football salaries grew by 120% and between 1977 and 1987, ice hockey salaries grew by approximately 180%. It is clear, therefore, that a shift away from monopsonistic labour markets increases salaries. This suggests that the economic rents previously extracted by teams were being reallocated to the players. Whether or not clubs can afford the salary increases is a matter returned to below. What is clear is that the salary hikes are always met with claims that wage demands could put clubs out of business and jeopardise sports. Later in this chapter the evidence on this issue is discussed.

Free agency in the UK and the Bosman ruling

As noted in Chapter 6, in much the same way that baseball has dominated both academic and general sporting discussion in US sports, so association football has been the counterpart in European sport. This is particularly because the increased commercialisation in sport in Europe and the UK has centred on association football, which is by far the largest spectator sport. This is not to say that other professional team sports such as rugby league and rugby union do not have active labour markets. The top rugby league clubs have always bought and sold players, though the most publicised of these involved amateur rugby union players 'going north'. Similarly, the recent change of rugby union from amateur to professional status has been accompanied by the emergence of a transfer market and the subsequent return of previous union players from league. Nonetheless the focus of discussion on association football in the UK and Europe is unquestionable.

In this respect it is interesting to note that in the case of association football, there are strong parallels with the development of US sporting labour markets. In particular labour market restrictions have applied to both player

---

[2] Similarly, in the UK, the Rugby Football League currently employs a salary cap with the explicit intention of helping teams to cope with the problems of increasing player salaries in the post-Bosman era. Likewise in rugby union and association football there is concern being expressed over the enormous rise in player salaries. Rugby union clubs in general have much smaller financial bases than football clubs and this has manifested itself in clubs such as Gloucester, for example, releasing large numbers of players from their contracts during the close of the 1999 season. As discussed earlier in the book, salary caps are on the agenda for rugby union.

remuneration and player mobility. For example, as Szymanski and Kuypers (1999) argue:

> At its foundation in 1888 the Football League expressly set out the twin aims of imposing a maximum wage and preventing the movement of a player from one club to another without permission of the former.
>
> (p. 99)

In the former case, as Szymanski and Kuypers (op. cit.) note, the origins of professionalism in association football are furtive. However, with the advent of the Football League in 1888, players earned about four times the average wage of skilled manual workers. Moreover, rather like US sports debate raged about the merits or otherwise of letting markets determine wages – though a maximum wage was instituted in 1900. There was also debate about the efficacy or need for players to belong to a union. Thus, while by 1910 the players union was recognised on the understanding it withdrew from the emergent (wider) Trades Union Congress, 'The Union had little success over the next fifty years in confronting the massed authority of the football hierarchy and the maximum wage' (Szymanski and Kuypers, 1999, p. 90).

Despite this state of affairs, the post-war boom of interest in association football, with attendance figures at their all-time high (Dobson and Goddard, 1995), coincided with increased player and union militancy. In 1960, Jimmy Hill, a player at the time who became a famous television pundit in the UK, co-ordinated a campaign that led to the abolition of the maximum wage. By 1978, more freedom of contract, as discussed below, was agreed by the clubs and, '. . . led to a wage explosion in the late 1970s and early 1980s. Between 1977 and 1983 wage expenditure by clubs trebled in the First, Third and Fourth divisions, while it more than doubled in the Second' (Szymanski and Kuypers, 1999, p. 95). As in the US, this led to much concern over the financing of association football. Indeed the 1983 Chester Report in particular examined the growing indebtedness of association football clubs.

With respect to player mobility, in association football this was controlled by the 'retain-and-transfer' system. Only a player registered with the Football Association can play professional football. Because the registration is held by a club, historically, it could control the players' movements much in the same way as the reserve-option clause in US sports. At the end of a season, for example, a club could retain players if it wished, or let them leave. In principle it could retain the registration of a player even if it did not renew the contract. Moreover, clubs could charge a fee – a transfer fee – for allowing the player to move to another club. Note that this could apply even in the absence of the maximum wage, so, effectively, the terms and conditions of the players' contracts lay with the club under this system.

The first effective challenge to the transfer system came in 1963 when George Eastham took his club, Newcastle United, to court for refusing to let him leave the club on a transfer. The courts upheld his claim.

> From then on, the club holding the registration had to offer a new
> contract at least as remunerative and of the same duration as the expired
> contract . . . in order to retain the player's registration; if such a contract
> was not forthcoming, the player became a free agent.
>
> (Dobson and Goddard, 1998, p. 776)

Moreover, in 1977 players were awarded the right to decide on a move at the
end of their contracts. However, if the club wanted to retain the player or
demand a fee the player could go to arbitration to the Football League
Appeals Committee. As this 'freedom to contract' took place, not surprisingly,
like salaries, transfer fees escalated rapidly as larger clubs competed to sign
talent. This situation has reinforced a desire to keep transfer fees in the game
because of their revenue-generating ability for smaller clubs. These latter,
which rely on youth policies, active scouting and player development because
of a lack of funds for simply signing talent, staunchly defend the transfer
system because of the transfer of funds it brings. There is also economic
evidence that this is the case (Dobson and Goddard, 1998, p. 777).

It is perhaps for this reason, more than most, that the Bosman ruling has
received much attention. It is also worth noting that while the case of the UK
has been discussed, the general thrust of institutional developments has been
similar:

> In other countries similar though not identical arrangements apply. Thus,
> under the rules of the Union of European Football Associations (UEFA)
> a board of experts makes a binding judgement in the case of a disputed
> fee . . . but differences remained. Thus within France a transfer fee is
> payable only in the case of a player's first change of club and within Spain
> players aged 25 or more can transfer freely without a fee being required.
>
> (Campbell and Sloane, 1997, pp. 2–3)

It is clear, therefore, that sporting labour markets in European association
football, and by implication other sports, are closely linked.

The main details of the Bosman ruling concern Jean Marc Bosman, a
former player for RC Liege in Belgium, whose two-year contract was due to
expire in 1990. His club offered him a new one-year contract with a much
reduced basic salary. On refusing these terms, Bosman was transfer listed.
Based on the transfer fee set by Liege, no other clubs approached Bosman.
Consequently, he agreed his own terms with a French club, US Dunkerque, at
a much reduced transfer fee. This was to be for an initial period as a loan
player and then as a full-time player. RC Liege and US Dunkerque failed
to agree terms and the contracts lapsed. Bosman thus took the clubs to the
European Court of Justice under Article 177 of the Treaty of Rome, which
enshrines the free mobility of land, labour and capital in the European Union,
for damaging his employment opportunities by fixing a transfer fee. The court
declared that, in the absence of pressing reasons of public interest, the

transfer rules did constitute an obstacle to the free movement of workers. Thus, the important outcome of the Bosman ruling was that *no* fee could be expected by clubs on the transfer of an out-of-contract player.

It is interesting to note that, following the discussions of Chapter 4, the advocate general (Lenz) accepted, in principle, the need for leagues to maintain competitive balance and uncertainty of outcome. In addition he also accepted that smaller clubs often covered financial losses through transfer fee income. However, he argued that using the 'means' of the transfer system to achieve these 'ends' was not justifiable. This was because there were other methods of achieving competitive balance that did not restrict player mobility. Moreover, the evidence cited in Chapter 4 was referred to in arguing that the policies appeared largely ineffective. The advocate general argued for limits on player salaries and more equal gate-revenue and television-revenue sharing arrangements. Moreover, the advocate general argued that justifying transfer fees as a means of recovering training costs was invalid. This was because transfer fees often reflected earnings rather than training costs and took place even in the context of experienced players. However, it was argued that restricting fees to first-club transfers, as in the case of France, could be justifiable as well as linking them to players' development costs.[3]

Implications of free agency for professional team sports

The likely implications of the movement towards free agency in professional team sports can thus be understood in terms of the direct effects on the labour market and, by implication, the indirect effects on sporting leagues. In this section we re-examine the direct impacts on the players' labour market, which has been subject to some detailed academic scrutiny. We then re-consider the more indirect implications of free agency for league policy.

The players' labour market

As already noted, there is widespread agreement and indeed descriptive evidence that the movement towards free agency raises players' salaries. Coupled with this rise in salaries it is observed that the disparity between top and bottom players' salaries has widened as noted by Campbell and Sloane (1997),

---

[3] While the advocate general may well be right in his sentiments, there is a degree of contradiction in his reasoning here. In a competitive model, as noted last chapter, wages will reflect performance. In this respect, the 'costs' of player development and player earnings are naturally and closely related. In a non-competitive labour market this is less likely to be the case. While there is dispute in the empirical literature for the UK as to whether or not the sporting labour market has outcomes consistent with the competitive model, the US empirical results seem to suggest that this is the case under free agency. This contradiction thus can be seen as a failure to take into account the economic aspects of the transfer market and a focus on its accounting aspects.

Sanderson and Seigfried 1997, Simmons (1997) and Szymanski and Kuypers (1999).

The explanation for these developments reflects bargaining power. On the one hand, generally increased player bargaining power will, on average, raise salaries above the levels previously established under monopsonistic levels. However, it is also likely that particularly talented players will have greater bargaining power and hence receive higher salaries still. Of course, this does not necessarily imply players generally, or star players particularly, exploit their clubs. The crucial issue concerns whether or not their salaries are commensurate with their contribution to the teams' revenues.

A related issue concerns the duration of players' contracts. Under the monopsony conditions of the reserve-clause or traditional association football contract, clubs faced no potential financial loss from losing a player to a rival bid for the player's services from another team. In essence, as noted above, there was a 'one-way' long-term contract between the club and the player – though a particular contract might be 'nominally' specified for a set number of years. However, in moving towards a more competitive environment, 'nominal' contract lengths begin to assume a real economic impact.

Commensurate with the risks faced by players of injury and loss of earnings, clubs face the real economic risk of losing their better players with no recourse to 'compensation'. It is clear that in a context of relative aversion to risk then contract lengths would lengthen generally as a form of insurance.[4] Once again there is descriptive evidence to support this claim according to Simmons (1997) and Szymanski and Kuypers (1999).

Despite these descriptive accounts of developments in sporting labour markets, it remains that an adequate test of these hypotheses needs to be established. As we discussed in the Introduction and, indeed Chapter 5, it was argued that economists needed to be careful not to draw spurious conclusions based on purely qualitative or descriptive insights. It was argued that regression models provide the quasi-experimental conditions under which they attempt to test theories. Crucially, to facilitate unambiguous predictions economists also require theories to produce the appropriate hypotheses to test. In the next section the theoretical model underlying recent economic tests of the labour market is discussed. Some of the main empirical findings are then presented.

Bargaining theory

In the case of perfectly competitive or monopsonistic labour markets, outcomes to decisions over, say, wage determination are relatively easy to

---

[4] The widespread coverage of insurance markets is testimony to the extensive incidence of risk aversion.

establish. In the former case, impersonal market forces determine wages. In the latter case, an established cartel of purchasers decide the wage for a large number of employees. In theoretical terms individuals and their groups are not hypothesised to take into account the affects that their decisions may have on other parties to a deal or transaction.

In the context of the movement to free agency discussed above, in which players' power has increased, this is a dubious assumption. In contrast, it is clear that decisions are made with explicit attention being paid to the likely responses of other parties. As discussed in Chapter 3 with reference to sporting leagues, theorising about the likely reactions of participants to a transaction thus becomes necessary. As discussed in Chapter 3, this procedure is much more involved and complicated and ultimately involves game theory. A simple example of a game – the prisoners' dilemma – was presented in Chapter 3.

More generally, game theory is a modelling tool employed to explore how economic parties to a transaction interact. Essentially economists specify utility functions for economic agents, identify a strategy or set of actions that agents are likely to undertake and, based on a notion of equilibrium, try to predict the likely outcome that will emerge. In many respects the underlying methodological procedures in game theory are no different from conventional economic theories. The complexity and difficulty lies in trying to adequately capture the essential characteristics of the transaction taking place.

Thus 'games' can involve conflict or non-conflict. In a sporting context one can see that signing a new player to strengthen a team may not produce conflict between clubs and players. However, if the new player is seen as a replacement player, then the context is different – conflicts of interest arise. Likewise games can be characterised as co-operative or non-co-operative. Co-operative games imply that agents can make binding commitments on one another. Non-co-operative games do not. It is clear that in the former case, players' labour markets, which are governed by the law of contract, have this characteristic. Two competing companies in a market, however, imply a non-co-operative situation. Game theoretical models can also account for differences in the information possessed by parties to a deal. Thus, it can be assumed that information is symmetrically distributed. In contrast, it is possible that games might be characterised by asymmetric information in which one party to a deal has more information than the other. In the former case it is likely that, *ceteris paribus*, an experienced player will know their true ability relative to the competition. Moreover, because of the scrutiny of sports players it is also likely that teams will have an accurate perception of established players' abilities. Under such circumstances it seems plausible to think of the players' contractual circumstances as being characterised by symmetric information. However, in the case of a relatively new talent, then clearly the situation is different. Clubs will be more suspicious of committing themselves to lucrative or long-term deals for players whose track record is not established. Finally, these different types of game also have different solution concepts. Solution concepts try to identify situations of stability in which agents do not have incentives to change their strategies.

In non-co-operative games an often-used solution concept is a 'Nash equilibrium'. This is the set of strategies in which each agent optimises their behaviour against each other. The Cournot model discussed in Chapter 3 employs this concept. It is entirely possible under this definition that more than one possible set of behaviours constituting an equilibrium exists. In the co-operative concept, an 'axiomatic' approach to solving the game can be adopted because binding commitments can be formally incorporated into the solution to the game. A common approach adopted in co-operative games thus is to invoke the 'Nash-bargaining' solution. The assumption underpinning this solution is that the bargained outcome will maximise the product of the incremental utilities of all parties. Basically this solution makes the value judgement that parties to a bargain will settle on a solution that maximises overall utility rather than that of a particular individual.

Based on this discussion it seems plausible, as an approximation, to identify players' contractual negotiations with a co-operative game and symmetric information. If this is the case then we can make predictions about the implications of the movement towards free agency using the Nash-bargaining solution. Thus, if we return to the case of monopsony, discussed in the last chapter, we can note that the difference between the salary paid to a player and the revenue received by the club, in the form of the marginal revenue product of the player, represents an increment of income that could be reallocated to the player. Clearly there is a disagreement point based on the current level of players' pay from which bargains can be made.

To illustrate the idea underlying the bargaining solution we can begin by assuming that agents seek to maximise their utility when making decisions. This raises the issue of how we can measure utility – a matter discussed in Chapter 5. There we indicated that a variety of mathematical forms could be employed. If we take the highly simplified case that one unit of utility corresponds to £1, then we can proceed. Under these circumstances we can assume that each £1 of the potential income to the player, and currently realised revenue contribution going to the club under the monopsony wage agreement, measures the 'utility' or economic satisfaction of the respective economic agent. If the player's current wage ($W0$) is £20,000, and the marginal revenue product of the player (M) is £40,000, then this implies that there is £20,000 of income to be bargained over. The Nash-bargaining solution would be to divide this extra gain equally so that the player received £10,000 extra salary, that is a new wage (W) of £30,000 and the club retained £10,000 of the player's marginal revenue product. The reason for this is that £10,000 × £10,000 produces a higher measure of utility than say £8,000 × £12,000; £6,000 × £14,000; £5,000 × £15,000; or any other combination by which the increment of income could be split.

It is important to note here that the measure of utility adopted is simply for convenience in producing a numerical example. Moreover, the equal split that occurs reflects this assumption about the utility function. As shown in Appendix 10.1, in general the split of incremental income will depend on the form of the utility function. Nonetheless, the model predicts that the new agreed wage will lie somewhere between the player's marginal revenue product and their monopsony wage. Thus, while all of this may seem a rather abstract set of ideas, it nonetheless illustrates the important result that bargaining theory predicts that there will be some sharing of the gains from any deal to be made. It follows that more specific theoretical or empirical investigation can explore the detail of these gains and how they are dispersed. As an aside, it thus seems to be an approach that would lend itself to discussing the evolving nature of sporting leagues and their relative domination in the light of changes in funding arrangements, etc. as discussed in Chapters 4 and 7.

The implication for the labour market in professional team sports is that as player power increases with the movement towards free agency, one would expect player wages to rise above the monopsony level and, in the limit, approach the competitive level where wages reflect marginal revenue products. It is to this issue that we now turn in exploring econometric studies of the players' labour market.

Empirical findings

Salaries, contracts and exploitation

Most of the econometric work on the implications of moving towards free agency in players' labour markets has, for the reasons discussed in the last chapter, focused on baseball. Most of these studies invoke a bargaining explanation of wage determination as discussed above. As will be shown, there appears to be some consensus of evidence that monopsony exploitation has fallen.

The first econometric attempt to explore the impact of free agency was made by Sommers and Quinton (1982), who compared the salaries and marginal revenue products of the first 14 free agents at the end of the 1976 season. They essentially adopt a two-tier model of bargaining by comparing the wage and marginal revenue products of free agents and non-free agents. They estimated marginal revenue products following the Scully–Medoff approach discussed in the last chapter, though there was some re-specification of variables. Their results show that, for pitchers rather than hitters salaries and marginal revenue products were very similar. Raimondo (1983) adds weight to these findings by examining the salaries of 216 non-free agents and 46 free agents and comparing these with estimates of their marginal revenue products made by Scully and Medoff. The estimates were inflation adjusted. The results suggest that the rate of exploitation substantially decreased for free agents. Likewise, Hill (1985) and Hill and Spellman (1983) identify similar effects of free agency in a two-tier bargaining framework.

Despite their common findings, there are a number of interrelated problems with these earlier studies that need to be taken into account in reaching conclusions concerning the impact of the changed institutional features of sporting labour markets. These stem from their proximity to the institutional changes that took place. On the one hand, they are based on rather small data-sets. On the other hand, it is unlikely that the fuller implications of the movement towards free agency will have taken place. This can have both statistical and theoretical consequences.

The process of salary negotiations, like any other economic process needs to be learned by the respective participants and, as econometric models look to identify average or typical relationships, one should be sure that the underlying processes are sufficiently stable to make the econometric results meaningful. As discussed in Chapter 6, structural stability is important if econometric results are to make sense. Related to this issue is that the earlier studies did not simultaneously take into account final-offer arbitration. As discussed above, this institutional mechanism has been as important as the move to free agency and as such has become embedded in labour contracts. It follows that the effects of final-offer arbitration need to be analysed at the same time as the impact of free agency. Thus, with respect to this latter point:

> . . . final offer arbitration . . . is widely believed to exhibit two character-
> istics. First, the series of offers and demands of the two parties are likely
> to be converging around the arbitrator's preferred award. This is claimed
> to promote a bargained settlement without recourse to arbitration.
> Second, and more important in this context, final offer arbitration is
> alleged to equalise bargaining power . . . [this] . . . should to some extent
> curtail attempts by clubs to extract monopsonistic returns from players.
>
> (Cairns *et al.*, 1986, p. 47)

It is interesting to note that the first point is supported by theory. Appendix 10.3 outlines a game theoretic model of final-offer arbitration, based on Farber (1980), which suggests that the differences in wage demands between players and teams varies inversely with the probability of the mean settlement of the arbitrator. As noted above, this implies that arbitration involves a degree of learning and that over time as the arbitrator starts to make more and more similar decisions then teams and players will take this into account in their wage offers. The impact of the arbitrator should thus increase over time. From the point of view of the decline in exploitation, however, the main point of interest here is the impact of free agency and final-offer arbitration on monsopsonistic exploitation.

To explore this issue, McDonald and Reynolds (1994, p. 443) use data from the 1986/87, season to specifically answer the question: '. . . have the new institutions of free agency and final offer arbitration brought baseball salaries into line with marginal revenue products?' Their paper, thus, is particularly worth discussing. Moreover, unlike the previous papers, it is based on publicly available data for all players on the major league roster and is sufficiently after the advent of the institutional changes to produce more plausible estimates of the outcomes of bargaining.

In the first stage of their analysis the authors made use of a refined Scully–Medoff econometric model to estimate player marginal revenue products. The second stage of their project involved them estimating regressions to explain the salaries of baseball players. Two insights are presented by the authors. Initially, excluding one–two year rookies from their sample, the independent variables used to explain the salaries of players included the players' career marginal revenue products, the (years) and (years)^2 of experience of the players – the latter being to capture the likely non-linear relationship between experience and salary – together with three dummy variables to measure the institutional features of the labour market. These included winning final-offer arbitration, losing final-offer arbitration and signing as a free agent that season.

The results show that career marginal revenue products significantly affect salaries and, importantly, that the effect of the marginal revenue product of pitchers was not significantly different from 1. This suggests that controlling for other characteristics of players, the true slope coefficient on this variable implies that a \$1 increase in marginal revenue product is associated with a \$1 increase in salary. Crucially, winning arbitration decisions and losing arbitration decisions are shown to have a statistically significant positive and negative affect on salaries respectively, '. . . confirming the general impression that players eligible for salary arbitration have little downside risk and good upside potential from arbitration' (McDonald and Reynolds, 1994, pp. 450–451).

Likewise the coefficients on the free agency variables were generally negative. This may seem surprising but this is readily explained for a number of reasons. The primary reason is that it is likely that arbitration 'ratchets-up' salaries to free agency levels in advance of players being eligible for free agency. Moreover, it seems likely that by the time players are well established as free agents they may well be beyond their peak.

Because the variables measuring the experience of players were highly significant, McDonald and Reynolds, secondly, re-estimate their regressions for the three classes of experience enshrined in baseball contracts: rookies, eligibility for final-offer arbitration and eligibility for free agency. Based on these subsets of data, player salaries were regressed upon career marginal revenue products – in the case of rookies, career marginal revenue products and winning or losing arbitration decisions – for those eligible for arbitration, and these variables plus free agency for free agents. The results from these regressions confirm that there is a stepwise climb in player salaries towards their marginal revenue products. For both pitchers and hitters the results imply that rookies receive the salary minimum and that the impact of marginal revenue product on salaries is very small. Winning final-offer arbitration adds significantly to player salaries. Players also receive much more of their marginal revenue product. Finally, by the time players become free agents, they receive their marginal revenue products but free agency *per se* reduces salaries. These results suggest that over time players receive their marginal revenue products controlling for the different contractual regimes they belong to. The results for the contractual regimes suggest that final-offer arbitration, rather than free agency produces the most bargaining power for players.

One potential problem with the above results is that the 1986/87 season is part of a period in baseball history, between 1986 and 1988, wherein baseball clubs are alleged to have conspired to supress free agent mobility and salaries. This was by not bidding for free agents unless former teams were no longer interested in the players. Bruggink and Rose (1990) hypothesise that this 'financial restraint hypothesis' would imply that free agents would receive lower salaries during the collusion years than before them. Using a Scully–Medoff model they estimated players' marginal revenue products for 1984 before the alleged collusion and for 1985 and 1986 in which grievances were filed by the Baseball Players' Association that collusion was taking place. Based on salary data and estimates of marginal revenue productivity of players, a salary/marginal revenue productivity ratio was calculated and averaged for each group of free agents, both before and during collusion, and then compared. Both a simple and a weighted-average ratio were calculated. In the latter case, the weights were based on the player's salary divided by the mean salary of the group of free agents. In the first calculations a drop in the salary/marginal revenue product ratio of 28% was calculated. In the latter case, a drop of 38% was calculated. These mean differences were significant in *t*-test comparisons. Not surprisingly, this may well be a reason why the impact of free agency in McDonald and Reynolds (1994) was identified as negative.

A related problem concerns the econometric specification used by McDonald and Reynolds (op. cit.). By including marginal revenue products and dummy variables, to control for differences in contractual regime, the results somewhat arbitrarily separate out what is likely to be an interactive process. If marginal revenue product determines salary, then this will be because of bargaining power. The authors thus appear to double control the effects of contractual status by separating out the regressions for each contractual regime and at the same time including the arbitration/free agent variables. A more plausible scenario might have been to interact the arbitration/free agent variables with marginal-revenue product, or indeed omit them.[5]

Nonetheless, a similar study by Marburger (1994), updating the results of Burgess and Marburger (1992), which also involves data from the 1986–88

---

[5] This would involve multiplying the dummy variables measuring the contractual regime with marginal revenue products. This new variable could then be included in the regressions and, if significant, the coefficient would indicate that marginal revenue products changed as a result of contractual regime.

period, provides evidence that is broadly supportive of the McDonald and Reynolds results. Marburger (1994) uses 1360 salary observations between 1991 and 1992 to estimate separate salary equations for the three classes of experience in baseball contracts. Somewhat differently from McDonald and Reynolds (op. cit.) and the Scully–Medoff approach, rather than identifying an explicit measure of the player's marginal revenue product, Marburger includes the player's performance characteristics directly in the salary equations estimated for each contractual regime, together with the number of years of experience and the number of years of experience squared in major league baseball. This means that marginal revenue products are not directly included in the salary equation and thus separate out any effects of contractual status on marginal revenue product.

To identify the relationships between levels of bargaining power and salaries, the average value of each player performance variable is substituted into each regression equation for each year of experience. The predicted salaries that are calculated on this basis produce a profile of average earnings of players, controlling for average performance, for each year of experience. Because these values are calculated for each type of contractual arrangement, then the results also control away any interaction between experience and bargaining power. For both hitters and pitchers, Marburger argues:

> . . . ineligible salaries increase with experience. Once the player reaches arbitration-eligibility, his salary increases significantly . . . a measure of the 'pure' bargaining power . . . [is that] . . . An average ineligible hitter with three years of experience has an expected (1992) salary of $438,000 whereas a comparable arbitration-eligible hitter with three years of experience can be expected to earn $675,000 . . . [thus] . . . Upon reaching arbitration-eligibility, the player's salary rises significantly, but not to the level of comparable free agents . . . whereas the level of monopsonistic exploitation is reduced sharply in the first year of eligibility, the level of exploitation continues to diminish with each year of experience. Finally, as a player reaches the transition between arbitration-eligibility and free agent eligibility, he can expect to earn roughly the same salary as comparable free-agent eligibles.
>
> (Marburger, pp. 438–439)

Marburger thus essentially confirms the findings of McDonald and Reynolds that final-offer arbitration is important in increasing player bargaining power. Moreover, he presents evidence that profiles the changes in bargaining power over salaries as experience increases. As Marburger also presents a more convincing separation of the effects of contractual eligibility and player characteristics, it suggests that McDonald and Reynolds' (1994) results are reasonably robust.

This is an important point for two reasons. First, in addition to exploring bargaining power generally, McDonald and Reynolds (1994) also present evidence to test a 'superstars' model. It was recognised in the bargaining model discussed earlier than particular star players might have more bargaining power than others. As such, one might expect salary gaps to widen under free agency conditions. Moreover, models of 'superstars' have been put forward by Rosen (1981) and McDonald (1988). In Rosen's model, differences in talent become exaggerated in income because of the joint consumption of media and mass audience combined with the imperfect substitution of 'stars' given consumer preferences. MacDonald (1988) extends this model to occupations characterised by uncertainty in individual performances. Success is thus rare and highly rewarded. McDonald and Reynolds (1994) test the predictions of these models by running a regression of salaries on career marginal revenue product and career marginal revenue product squared. This augmentation of the impact of marginal revenue product tests for the presence of 'convex', that is increasing, salaries for 'superstars'. In addition to these variables, dummy variables controlling for eligibility for arbitration and free agency are included. McDonald and Reynolds show that the squared marginal revenue product term is positive and significant, supporting the hypothesis of disproportionate returns relative to rookies. In addition the contractual variables are also positive and significant, which shows that experienced players have bargaining power as predicted.

Second, it was also hypothesed earlier that the movement towards free agency would be associated with an increase in contract lengths. Kahn (1993) provides evidence to support this hypothesis. Kahn takes data on salaries, contracts and player performance variables for all major league players for the period 1987–90.[6] Kahn estimates salary and contract duration equations by regressing each of these variables on dummy variables indicating the contractual status of the player, in the spirit of McDonald and Reynolds (1994), and a set of player performance and market variables. Kahn's results suggest that arbitration and free agency have similar salary effects but free agency alone raises the duration of contracts. This suggests that there is a degree of risk aversion in sporting labour markets.

Collectively, these results suggest that there is some validity and growing weight of evidence that, in baseball, experienced players are paid in accordance with their marginal revenue products following the breakdown in the monsopsonistic nature of baseball contracts. Moreover, contract duration is likely to increase with moves towards free agency. In contrast, younger inexperienced players are, however, still exploited. Moreover, the results suggest that it is the arbitration process that endows the players with bargaining power as much as the recognition of 'free agency'. These results would tend to suggest that the increase in players' salaries, with perhaps the exception of particular superstars, is not out of line with their contributions

[6] The sample of long-term contracts was extended to 1983–86.

to baseball revenue. As such claims that players' salaries are too high lack economic justification. It is clear that more work needs to be done on other sports to help to consolidate these findings. However, given the anecdotal similarity of the development of sporting labour markets discussed above, one might have some confidence in suggesting that similar results are likely to be found elsewhere. However, it is clear that the precise nature of the contractual arrangements of particular sporting contexts needs to be accounted for in any research.

Transfer fees

Despite the commensurate developments in sporting labour markets discussed earlier, unfortunately the confidentiality of player salaries in the main sports has restricted efforts in the UK and Europe to explore the labour market. Nonetheless, there is the beginning of a literature exploring the determination of transfer fees in association football. The literature is currently split on how best to characterise the transfer market. One strand of the literature emphasises bargaining. The other strand argues that the transfer market has evolved into the competitive model.

From a Nash-bargaining perspective, Carmichael and Thomas (1993) explore a data set of 214 observations on permanent transfers during the 1990/91 season. Data on transfer fees are regressed on player characteristics such as age, number of league appearances, goals and position. The player characteristics can be thought of as indicators of the 'human capital' of players that gives players bargaining power and, of course, is bargained over by clubs. (Appendix 10.2 outlines the main elements of human capital theory.) Buying club characteristics such as goal difference compared to the previous season, position in the league, size of gates and profits and divisional location and parallel variables for selling clubs are included to measure their bargaining power. The regression results indicate that as well as player characteristics, both buying club and selling club factors influence the determination of transfer fees. Consequently the authors argue that their results support a bargaining hypothesis. Moreover, they argue that the determinants of bargaining power are not symmetric. For buying clubs, attendance and success generate bargaining power. For selling clubs, divisional status is important.

More recently, Dobson and Gerrard (1997) explore a data-set of 1350 transfer fees over the six-season period 1990–96 to test for 'rent sharing' as an indication of bargaining. Once again transfer fees are regressed upon player characteristics and buying and selling club characteristics. The number of variables that proxy these characteristics is greater in this study. Players' ages, number of previous clubs, career appearances, goals scored, international appearances and positions are included in a variety of formulations. As far as buying and selling clubs are concerned, current and last season league position, goal differences, divisional status and gate attendance variables are used. Moreover, the passage of time is accounted for by including monthly and seasonal dummy variables.

Dobson and Gerrard (op. cit.) argue that all of the player characteristics are significant determinants of transfer fees. Moreover, the set of selling club variables are jointly significant determinants of fees. Of these, last season's relative positions and goal difference are individually significant. Most of the buying club characteristics are individually significant determinants of transfer fees. These results, it is argued, provide evidence of rent sharing through bargaining. The authors also show that rent sharing is common to three categories of fees, low, medium and high, but that the degree of rent sharing is not the same.[7] Consistent with the observations made earlier, in commenting on the baseball labour market, Dobson and Gerrard argue that the actual institutional mechanisms by which the degree of rent sharing takes place thus needs researching.

In contrast, and echoing arguments originally put forward in Simmons (1997), Carmichael *et al.* (1999) argue that the transfer market is competitive. This suggests that the institutional adjustments in the transfer market have been sufficiently radical to dissipate power in labour negotiations. They argue, for example, that there is freedom of contract in association football, that there are many buyers and sellers in an international market for association football players, that there is a comprehensive but informal network on player quality, and that player performance is easily monitored. This competitive hypothesis implies that only player and selling club characteristics should enter the regression equation looking to explain transfer fee determination.

Carmichael *et al.*'s (op. cit.) difference of opinion over the appropriate theoretical characterisation of the labour market carries over to concerns with the econometric approach of Dobson and Gerrard (1997). For example, Carmichael *et al.* argue that buying club characteristics are likely to be jointly determined with the transfer fee as only wealthy clubs would be able to afford the higher fees. Thus, in an argument mirroring early criticism of Scully's early work, Carmichael *et al.* (op. cit.) argue that Dobson and Gerrard's (1997) work is likely to be affected by simultaneous equation bias and a two-stage least squares regression approach needs adopting. This said, Carmichael *et al.* also argue that selling club characteristics, which they include in their analysis, will also be jointly determined by player characteristics in part. This is an issue that they argue needs correcting in future literature.

More importantly, the main problem that Carmichael *et al.* (1999) identify with the bargaining literature is that it will be characterised by sample-selection bias. One of the assumptions made in all labour market literature is that the employment of labour will only take place where the newly bargained

---

[7] In the former case, the joint significance of the buying club characteristics is tested using an *F*-test for each of the sub-samples. In the latter case, a Chow test is conducted for parameter constancy.

wage is greater than the reservation wage of workers – the wage at which sufficient incentive to work is reached. This implies that the probability of employment is correlated with the size of the wage but only the wage offers of those working can be observed. Ordinary least squares estimates of wage equations will thus suffer from 'omitted variable bias' – that is, biased and inconsistent estimates. Once again a statistical problem, rather like the problems in Scully's original work, arises. In the transfer bargaining context this is because only data on transfer fees of players actually transferring clubs, because the fees received are higher than the 'reservation fee', are available. Only a minority of players in any given season transfer between clubs.

To overcome this statistical problem another 'two-stage' econometric model is employed by the authors. The 'Heckman two-step method' is used to, first, model the probability of workers taking a job – or players moving between clubs in this case. In the second stage, information on the factors likely to promote a transfer are included in a modified regression to explain transfer fees. This modified regression model allows for the covariance between the error terms of the probability-of-transfer equation and the simple transfer fee equation.[8] An interesting implication of this statistical correction is that it precludes the authors including buying club character-istics in their regression analysis. The statistical procedure essentially requires data on the same variables to model the probability of players transferring as well as determining their fee. It follows that one cannot, logically, have data on 'buying clubs' for players that do not move. In essence this precludes a direct test of the bargaining model.

Carmichael *et al.* (1999) analyse 2029 observations on professional foot-ballers during the 1993/94 season. Of this sample, 240 transferred between clubs and the remainder stayed with their club. Basically, the same set of variables is used to model both the probability of players transferring and the determination of the transfer fee. This is with the exception of the correction for the sample selection problem noted above, and a number of variables that might influence the likelihood of players transferring but not their fee. These include previous loans of the player, previous transfers and whether the club has changed manager, been promoted or relegated. The key variables measuring player characteristics include age, current and previous appear-ances, international appearances, goals scored and position played. Variables are also included to measure selling club status. These are divisional status and a ratio of goals scored for and against the club.

The main results of the study indicate that the transfer market is not random and that some players are much more likely than others to transfer

---

[8] In their analysis the authors also used Tobit as well as OLS estimates of transfer fees. This was because 42 of the transferred players were free transfers. The Tobit model allows for this 'truncation' in the dependent variable of a regression model. Observant readers will recall that Kuypers (1996) made use of this model when estimating a model of the demand for professional team sports on a sample that included clubs regularly selling out.

between clubs. This is particularly the case for experienced goal scorers who have been on loan. This suggests that standard regression estimates would have been subject to sample selection bias. Using the two-step approach to correct for this bias, the authors conclude that all of the player characteristics, with the exception of position, are statistically significant determinants of transfer fees along with the clubs' characteristics.

These results leave the literature on transfer fees in association football in a divisive state. Carmichael *et al.* (1999) argue that the bargaining approach suffers from sample selection problems, and that their results suggest that the market is now fully competitive. In contrast, Dobson and Gerrard (1997) argue that Carmichael *et al.*'s (op. cit.) results suffer from omitted variable problems because buying club characteristics are, of necessity, excluded. This suggests that: 'Disentangling the impacts of selling and buying club and human capital characteristics on both transfer fees and club attendances and finances remains an issue for further research' (Carmichael *et al.*, 1999, p. 129).

Of course this applies to both transfer fees and salary determination. Only data availability can solve the latter problem.

Despite these gaps in the literature on association football, however, coupled with the extensive work done in the US on baseball, it seems clear that professional team sports labour markets have evolved considerably from their previous monsopsony character. A clear research agenda for the future involves identifying the institutional mechanisms that lend themselves to bargaining power and investigating whether or not bargaining power has sufficiently equalised to argue that markets are now best characterised as competitive, either in terms of the outcomes, that is players receiving their marginal revenue products, or as a description of the labour market itself.

Implications of free agency for league policy

In this section we briefly re-consider the more indirect implications of free agency in the labour market for league policy. Some of the themes discussed in Chapter 4 are revisited following our detailed review of sporting labour markets.

The first point to note concerns whether or not the increased salary levels are justified. It is clear now that one's views on this issue really depend on one's views of the economic process. As implied in the competitive model, the conventional economic wisdom suggests that the fact that player salaries have increased will not, ultimately, affect the clubs' willingness or ability to hire players *per se*. This will depend on the demand for the sport and, as indicated last chapter, competition does not imply that clubs are not viable. All that happens in the move from monopsonistic to competitive markets is that revenues are redistributed from team owners to players. There are, of course, counter arguments to this.

As discussed earlier in this chapter, one argument that has been put forward for labour market restrictions, such as the reserve clause, is the need to fund training and development programmes. In economics terms, this suggests that players, possess 'human capital' that clubs have invested in through the provision of training facilities. Suffice it to note here that the above discussion of the move towards free agency in sporting labour markets implies that this has not, in either economic or legal terms, been seen to be a justifiable argument. Nonetheless in as much that some resources are transferred from clubs to players, and to the extent that training facilities are a genuine concern of clubs, this will reduce the incentives of clubs to invest in youth and development programmes. In contrast the onus will be on players to pay for the development of their skills themselves. Moreover, as also identified above, it will provide an incentive for clubs to issue longer contracts to players to offset training costs already sunk into current signings, for example, on players emerging from rookie status. Additionally it will limit clubs' exposure to competitive bidding for players' services.

Another aspect of increased bargaining power that is interesting in discussing league policy is the likely widening salary dispersion between top and bottom clubs. This will occur in a bargaining framework for much the same reasons discussed above for individual players. More talented, expensive players will cluster into more financially successful clubs, thus reinforcing their position in a virtuous circle. One can now understand why the funding arrangements of the Premier League, for example, are seen as so threatening to competitive balance. This is because of the two-fold impact of greater disparity of revenue sharing and the dynamics of the labour market that have been set in motion. This is particularly when coupled with the decline of transfer fees being recycled to smaller clubs, as noted by Dobson and Goddard (1998). More generally, however, as discussed in Chapter 4, the evidence seems to support the 'Coase theorem', that in sporting leagues resources have always seemed to gravitate towards their most valuable use. The implication is that labour market policies are likely to impact upon transfers of wealth but that this will not necessarily affect competitive balance.

Likewise, to the extent that price rises have taken place in, for example, football (Dobson and Goddard, 1995), it is clear that if players receive their marginal revenue products then price 'hikes' must be seen as an attempt to increase club profits. While this may be viewed as a response to increases in players' salaries, there is little empirical evidence to support a relationship between player salaries and ticket prices and, moreover, from the discussion above it cannot be justified on an economic basis (Sanderson and Seigfried, 1997). As discussed in Chapter 4, therefore, it remains that any regulations on labour markets, justified on the basis of being important for league development, need to be carefully articulated in terms of how competitive balance will be affected in leagues. More research rather than assertion also needs to be directed towards exploring exactly what the notion of competitive balance means. While this is an aspiration often talked about, it is clear that the evidence to date suggests that it is more an accepted than demonstrated 'truth'. Necessarily, moreover, any development of sporting leagues will be affected by emergent regulatory regimes.

Conclusions

In this chapter we have examined the key institutional changes that have taken place in both US and European sporting labour markets. The changes involve the movement to free agency in both US and UK sports. The 1995 Bosman ruling made by the European Court of Justice was also explored. It was argued that these developments reflect increased player power in the labour market. As a result players are now more able to bargain over their salaries and contracts. To provide an economic understanding of these processes, the chapter also explored bargaining theory and examined the application of this theory to sporting markets. It was argued that there is evidence in the US that player salaries are now more in line with marginal revenue products, that typical contract lengths have increased and there has been a widening dispersion of salaries. In the UK, transfer fee determination was discussed and it was noted that there are differences of opinion as to the correct characterisation of the labour market. Finally it was noted that the implications of increased player power for league policy really hinge upon players transferring wealth back to themselves and away from clubs. Labour market restrictions are probably indefensible in terms of policies to safeguard competitive balance in leagues. This implies that the other options, discussed in Chapter 4, remain the most salient for league management policies. As discussed in Chapter 8, moreover, targeting sources of revenues directly, that are increasingly generated by television contracts, may be more apposite.

Appendix 10.1: The Nash bargaining model

The Nash bargaining solution assumes that the product of the incremental gains to utility is maximised in striking a bargain. If we define M as the player's marginal revenue product, $W0$ as the player's monopsonistic wage and W the wage that players seek to achieve above $W0$, then the joint utility function for the team and the player, under the assumption that £1 = 1 unit of utility, as in the text, can be written as:

$$U = (M - W)(W - W0). \tag{10.1.1}$$

Clearly $M - W$ is the share of funds the club wishes to maximise. $W - W0$ is the share of funds the player wishes to maximise. This specification implies that W is the variable that will determine the impact on utility as it must lie between M and $W0$. Using calculus, the first-order derivative of the utility function will identify the necessary conditions for overall utility to be maximised. Thus, differentiating U with respect to W yields:

$$\delta U/\delta W = M - 2W + W0. \tag{10.1.2}$$

Setting this derivative equal to zero to identify the necessary condition for utility to be maximised yields:

$$0 = M - 2W + W0. \tag{10.1.3}$$

Rearranging this equation yields the prediction that:

$$W = (M + W0)/2. \tag{10.1.4}$$

This equation implies, as discussed in the text, that the new bargained wage will lie halfway between the marginal revenue product of the player and the monopsonistic wage.

To explore the more general case we can argue that the player does not necessarily identify £1 with 1 unit of utility. If this is the case the player's utility G will be a function of the wages he receives and (10.4.1) can be rewritten as:

$$U = (M - W)(G(W) - G(W0)). \tag{10.1.5}$$

Differentiating this function with respect to W yields:

$$\delta U/\delta W = M(\delta G/\delta W) - W(\delta G/\delta W) - G(W) + G(W0). \tag{10.1.6}$$

To identify the necessary conditions for a maximum this equation can be set equal to 0. Rearranging this condition implies that the newly bargained wage will be equal to:

$$W = M - [(G(W) - G(W0))/(\delta G/\delta W)]. \tag{10.1.7}$$

The top line of the term in square brackets will be positive because W will lie above $W0$ – or there would be no bargain – and hence the player's total utility will be higher in the case of W than $W0$. The bottom line of the term in square brackets will also be positive because it is the marginal utility of the player's wage and this is positive by assumption. This suggests that the overall term in square brackets is positive. Thus the newly bargained wage, W, will lie somewhere below the marginal revenue product of the player and the monopsonistic wage, $W0$.

Appendix 10.2: Human capital theory: investment in training

The human capital approach is probably the most widely used in valuing education and training. It views training and education as investment in the individual's stock of production capabilities, analogous to the treatment of advertising as an investment in the firm's stock of goodwill. Whether to invest in an individual would be determined by discounting a stream of expected future cash flows at a rate of discount applicable to other assets in the same category of risk. The decision to purchase a player obviously may be modelled in the same way; whether the team is buying or training players, it is investing resources in them. Future cash flows are 'discounted' relative to cash in hand because of the risk that they might not be received and the inconvenience of having to wait for them; £1 in the hand always beats an IOU for the same amount.

In most investment projects, the costs (cash outflows) precede the expected inflows. Somehow these estimated inflows must be added, and the sum of the outflows subtracted, to find out if the investment will bring in more money than it takes out. A standard method of evaluating the return on a project is to compute its net present value (*NPV*). To do this one computes the sum of all the net (in minus out) cash flows over the anticipated lifetime of the project, every cash flow being discounted to reflect the waiting time. If the *NPV* of an investment is zero, the implication is that its rate of return is exactly equal to the required rate of return. If positive, the rate of return exceeds the required (minimum acceptable) rate. The greater the (positive) *NPV* of a project, the more likely it will be undertaken. Profit maximising investors would select the investment with the largest *NPV*, then that with the second largest *NPV* and so on. The appropriate discount rate equals the investor's desired rate of return on the investment, taking into account the attached risk. Formally the *NPV* may be expressed

$$NPV_0 = \sum_1^T (I - O)_i/(1 + d)^i + RV_T/(1 + d)^T. \tag{10.2.1}$$

(10.2.1) says that the *NPV* now (period 0) of a project having a life expectancy of *T* periods comprises two elements. First, the sum (Σ) of all the net cash flows (Inflow minus Outflow) from period 1 (next year, say) to year *T*, when one expects the stream of earnings to stop. Each net cash flow is discounted at rate *d*, *d* being expressed as the required percentage return divided by 100 – if the investor seeks 5% a year *d* = 0.05. Indexing (powering) the discount component (1 + *d*) causes today's valuation of a future £1 to diminish as the time until receipt increases. *Ceteris paribus*, the higher the discount rate, the faster the present value declines. Note that if *d* = 0, implying that the investor is equally happy with money in ten years as with money today, you can simply add up all the revenues and subtract all the costs to obtain *NPV*; but this is very unrealistic.

Second, the residual value – if any – at year *T*, which again must be appropriately discounted. The residual value might be a scrap or secondhand value in the case of a machine, or zero in the case of a leasehold property when the lease expires. If deciding whether to buy a player, *RV* would be the expected transfer value at the next change of club. If deciding whether to invest in further training of a player already on the staff, *RV* would be the *change* in the transfer value brought about by the *additional* training. Notice it is not easy to decide how long the stream of returns continues, or to predict the future cash flows. Economists and accountants provide theoretical approaches to the valuation of projects; to paraphrase Keynes, they offer ways to look at the world. They cannot decide whether team *X* should buy pitcher *Y*, but they can suggest to team *X* how it might go about making the decision.

To illustrate the process of computing the *NPV* using (10.2.1), in a familiar context, consider whether student *A* should invest in three-year full-time degree *B*. *A* faces reasonably knowable cash outflows over the immediate period, tuition fees and textbooks for example; also living costs – but as *A* needs food, fuel, transport, clothing and shelter even if not at university, it makes no sense to count all of these as 'costs'.

Student *A* might more reasonably compute the excess of these costs while studying relative to when at work and count the excess as part of the cost of education. Suppose this to be £2000 per year of study. Much more expensive (but not always appreciated by students) is the opportunity cost of income forgone as a direct result of not being in full-time employment; less if *A* works part-time. Although this does not involve an outflow of cash, it is still the major single component of most full-time students' costs; let this be £5000 per year of study (note the financial implications of having to re-take a year.) Finally the student may have acquired some debt that would not have been acquired had she been at work. Assume she has to repay £1500 a year (interest included) during her first two years of work.

Against these outflows must be balanced the more distant – hence more heavily discounted – inflows, measured as the expected difference between future labour incomes that result from having the degree and the labour incomes that would have accrued had student *A* not gone to university. Call this £3000 a year over an expected working life of 40 years.

Provided the investment shows a positive *NPV* at student *A*'s required rate of return, going to university is worthy of consideration – if there are superior investments she would prefer to undertake those. (10.2.2) is (10.2.1) applied to the case under review. It shows the *NPV* of degree *B* to student *A*, assuming that she expects to get about 10% return per annum – about the average of estimates of the private return to education in the UK,

$$NPV_0 = -\pounds7000/(1.1) - \pounds7000/(1.1)^2 - \pounds7000/(1.1)^3$$
$$+ \pounds1500/(1.1)^4 + \pounds1500/(1.1)^5 + \pounds3000/(1.1)^6$$
$$+ \pounds3000/(1.1)^7 + \ldots + \pounds3000/(1.1)^{43}. \qquad (10.2.2)$$

The main thing to notice about the equation is the effect of discounting upon the *PV* of future money. Obviously the *PV* of £3000 now is £3000, but six years hence it is down to £1693, while 43 years hence it is a mere £50. Had student *A* been content with a 5% rate of return, the *NPV* of the investment would have been considerably greater; for example the PV of £3000 in 43 years at 5% discount is £3000/(1.05)^{43} = £368, considerably above £3000/(1.1)^{43} = £50. *Ceteris paribus*, the lower the required rate of return, the more likely it is that investments will be undertaken. The calculations reveal that:

$$NPV = -\text{£}6364 - \text{£}5785 - \text{£}5259 + \text{£}1025 + \text{£}931 + \text{£}18130$$
$$= -\text{£}15452 + \text{£}18130 = \text{£}2678. \tag{10.2.3}$$

This implies that student A would earn £2678 over and above her minimum required rate of return of 10% per annum. Degree B is worthwhile considering from student A's perspective. She would not necessarily undertake the investment – a better one might be available, but it is worthwhile considering. A lower minimum acceptable rate of return, lower tuition fees or greater future earnings benefits would all make education even more attractive. Attending university might be more enjoyable to student A than working, in which case she will have to make a financial allowance for the non-pecuniary (consumption good) benefits of study; simple in theory, hard in practice. Student A, if her object was to maximise returns and if she were able to borrow unlimited amounts at given rates of interest, would invest in education up to the point where the NPV was zero; that is, where the rate of return on education exactly equalled the required rate of return (borrowing cost).

The rate of discount applied to an investment is the rate of return required by the investor for assuming the risk. To the extent that lenders (investors) are risk averse, they require a higher return – *ceteris paribus* – for bearing more risk. In the early summer of 1998, the annual interest yield on Russian government bonds reached 82%, whereas US bonds were paying about 5%. The 75% extra yield apparently required by buyers of Russian bonds represented a 'risk premium' – Russia was and remains politically and economically unstable. It is very difficult to enforce payment of taxes, so the main source of government revenue (other than the printing press) is unreliable. The bond market was pessimistic about Moscow's ability to pay the interest on its debt and in August 1998 Moscow suspended interest payments.

Investors in UK or US government fixed interest bonds have the knowledge that the annual coupon (interest) payment is fixed in money terms and that neither government is likely to be unable to meet its commitments. So the cash flows are relatively easy to compute, although the degree of risk and hence the appropriate discount rate are not so easy to evaluate. Currently (May 1999) interest yields on bonds are at their lowest in 50 years, helped by very low inflation. However, recovery in South East Asia and Latin America will bring about a rise in basic commodity prices. This is likely to feed through into price inflation in the US and Europe later in 1999, causing bond markets to seek higher yields in compensation. Bond prices will fall (bond yields and prices move in opposite directions). Stock markets should also fall – higher interest rates cause investors to apply higher discount rates to expected dividends on company shares, lowering *PV*s and by implication, share prices.

Investors in company shares have the more complex task of trying to predict future dividends per share; ordinary shares do not guarantee an annual monetary return. As companies (unlike governments) cannot put up taxes to pay dividends, they are, *ceteris paribus*, riskier borrowers. Hence shares generally provide higher returns than government bonds to compensate the lender for the extra risk. Buyers of bonds and shares who decide that they have made a mistake can usually sell securities fairly quickly, admittedly at an uncertain price, provided there is an active market in the issuer's (the government's or the company's) debt.

Holders of infrequently traded (usually small company) shares are likely to experience delay and also price risk; the eventual price may be either much higher or much lower than one had anticipated when deciding to sell. The shares are hard to value because there are no 'recent' share transactions to act as a guide. In contrast, if 10,000 Microsoft shares were sold at a given price five minutes ago, it is likely that the 25,000 you want to buy now will cost about the same and that you will take possession very rapidly.

Investing in the training of players is beset by problems similar to those faced by purchasers of small company shares. The future cash flows, the life expectation of the investment, the appropriate rate of discount and the player's future resale price are very hard to estimate – an association football player's career might be terminated by an accident on his first appearance, or he might develop into the next Pelé. Under perfect competition (perfect knowledge) investment in each player would be optimised – pushed to the level where every player's *NPV* was zero. It would be impossible to make more profit either by re-allocating investment among players or by re-allocating investment away from players to other assets. Market failure – lack of information – will prevent optimal allocation of investment among professional sports players.

So much for how perfectly competitive markets would determine the optimum allocation of resources to the training of professional sports men and women; thus far we have not asked who invests in training players under perfect competition. Those investing in non-human capital acquire assets (goodwill, technology or equipment) over which as owners they enjoy exclusive rights to the income streams generated – hence the incentive to invest. The firm, given perfect competition in all markets, invests to the point where the *NPV* on each asset is zero, ensuring optimal allocation of its resources. Firms do not own their employees and therefore cannot be certain of internalising the benefits of investments in individuals.

Labour economists, following Becker (1975), differentiate between 'general' and 'specific' training. The latter provides the employee with skills that raise in-house productivity, for example knowing the telephone extension of the marketing manager, but these skills do not affect their productivity and earning power with other firms. Hence specific skills do not command a premium wage outside the present employer's business and the worker has no incentive to finance their acquisition.

Literacy, numeracy, the ability to get up in the morning and come to work, the ability to drive a Formula One car, the ability to play rugby league, to extract teeth or to audit company accounts are all examples of 'general' or 'transferrable' skills. General training raises the (trained) worker's marginal product (hence their real wage) above that of untrained labour with the current employer and (crucially) with other employers. During general training the employee's marginal product and the real wage fall below the pre-training level; in the absence of other costs the amount of income sacrificed by the worker during training is the extent of their investment. Once training is complete, the firm pays the worker exactly the same wage that every other firm pays its skilled workers, otherwise the entire skilled workforce leaves. The property rights produced by general training are internalised in the worker; the employer has no incentive to contribute. The worker, their family or some other organisation must provide investment funds. A clear implication of Becker's analysis is that a wage below the worker's marginal product may be evidence that they are under-training rather than that they are a victim of exploitation.

Human capital theory predicts that firms confronted with skill shortages bid up wages relative to those of the unskilled and the otherwise skilled, in the expectation that by increasing expected returns, more people will be encouraged to invest in the skills in excess demand. It also predicts that professional sports players, whose most important skills are transferrable, would have to finance their own training. While there is plenty of evidence to support the former proposition, the latter is confronted by favourable and unfavourable evidence. In its favour sports players, like accountants, earn substantially less during training than they do once qualified. Also favourable to the hypothesis, players of individual sports such as golf and tennis seem by and large to finance their own training.

Unfavourably, team sport employers partly finance player training. A key issue to emerge in the wake of the Bosman case is that clubs argue that they had traditionally relied on receiving transfer fees when selling players to finance training; with the disappearance of the transfer fee, they alleged that investment in training would be curtailed. Observers concluded that as a result of the ruling clubs would want to lengthen player contracts in order to recoup training costs. In contrast, players would negotiate for shorter contracts as, once out of contract, they would be able to negotiate 'signing on' fees. Small clubs, which relied on finding, training and selling on young players, would lose a vital source of revenue. These observations seem at odds with Becker's model, according to which training should have been financed by the players all along, since it is general rather than specific. The traditional way to deal with the training anomaly is to attribute it to capital and labour market imperfections. Given perfectly competitive capital markets the player is able to borrow unlimited amounts at a given interest rate to invest in themself. They (likewise any potential lender) have all the information required to compute the *NPV* of proposed training (10.2.2). A perfectly competitive labour market would enable them to move instantly and without cost from their current team to any other, should the employer try to pay them less after 'graduation' than the 'going' rate for fully qualified players. They have no difficulty in making the optimal investment in their own training.

In life market imperfections play leading roles. First, imperfect information implies that neither they nor their employer nor any lending institution can calculate the *NPV* of their training without significant error. Second, lending institutions may be reluctant to finance human capital investment compared to their willingness to finance the acquisition of non-human assets such as property. The latter may be seized and sold to recover losses if the borrower defaults – not so human assets. In consequence intending sports professionals unable to finance training from their own, or family, resources may be constrained by failure in the capital market. Possible evidence of capital market failure is that in most countries the voluntary sector acting through private universities and amateur leagues, and the public sector operating via state schools, provide training for team sport players.

The private sector by means of sponsorships could be seen likewise – usually in connection with the joint aim of managing the firm's image. Also in the private sector employers in team sports provide training. From this perspective it may be seen as justifiable that the player pays for training through a combination of lower wages during training and a lengthy employment contract that offers the team the chance to recover training costs not recovered during training. Employment contracts may thus be seen as a beneficial device for helping team sport players obtain training despite capital market failure. Alternatively, contracts which permit the existing employer to extract a transfer fee from the next employer may be regarded as a device for capturing players' economic rents, and this is consistent with the Bosman ruling.

Appendix 10.3: A model of final-offer arbitration

In this model it is assumed that the club makes a wage offer to the player of Wc. The player makes a wage offer to the club of Wp. If x is the arbitrator's settlement, then, provided $Wc < Wp$ as implied in the need to go to arbitration, the arbitrator will choose Wc if $x < (Wp + Wc)/2$ or choose Wp if $x > (Wp + Wc)/2$. The intuition here is clear because the term $(Wp + Wc)/2$ is the midpoint of the difference of the salary offers $(Wp - Wc)$ with $Wc < Wp$.

If it is assumed that the arbitrator's settlement will reflect a cumulative probability function $F(x)$, with $f(x)$ implying the probability density function, then:

$$\text{Prob } \{Wc \text{ is chosen}\} = \text{Prob } \{x < (Wp + Wc)/2\} = F[(Wp + Wc)/2]$$

$$(10.3.1)$$

and:

$$\text{Prob } \{Wp \text{ is chosen}\} = \text{Prob } \{x > (Wp + Wc)/2\}$$
$$= 1 - F[(Wp + Wc)/2]. \tag{10.3.2}$$

The expected (probability weighted average) wage then becomes:

$$We = Wc. F[(Wp + Wc)/2] + Wp. [1 - F(Wp + Wc)/2], \tag{10.3.3}$$

or:

$$We = Wc. F[(Wp + Wc)/2) + Wp - WpF(Wp + Wc)/2], \tag{10.3.4}$$

remembering that the probability that Wp is chosen is 1 *minus* the probability that Wc is chosen, i.e. $1 - F$, so that $Wp \times 1 - F$ simply scales up or down this difference as $Wp - WpF$.

It is clear that the club would like to mimimise the wage imposed by the arbitrator and the player would like to maximise the wage imposed by the arbitrator. So, to identify the club's desired minimum wage, *given* a maximised value of the player's wage offer, analogous to the Cournot-Nash discussions of Chapters 3 and 10, calculus is used to obtain the necessary conditions for a minimum. Making use of the product and 'function of a function' rules of calculus, we derive the first-order condition by differentiating (10.3.3) with respect to Wc:

$$\delta We/\delta Wc = Wc. f(Wp + Wc)/2. (1/2) + F(Wp + Wc)/2$$
$$- Wp. f(Wp + Wc)/2. (1/2) = 0. \tag{10.3.5}$$

Rearranging (10.3.5) yields:

$$F(Wp + Wc)/2 = (Wp - Wc). f(Wp + Wc)/2. (1/2). \tag{10.3.6}$$

To identify the necessary conditions to maximise the player's offer, given the club's offer (10.3.3) is differentiated with respect to Wp for a *given* minimised value of the club's offer, similar manipulations yield:

$$\delta We/\delta Wp = Wc. f(Wp + Wc)/2. (1/2) + 1$$
$$- Wp. f(Wp + Wc)/2. (1/2) - F(Wp + Wc)/2 = 0, \tag{10.3.7}$$

rearranging (10.3.7) yields

$$1 - F(Wp + Wc)/2 = (Wp - Wc). f(Wp + Wc)/2. (1/2). \tag{10.3.8}$$

(10.3.6) and (10.3.8) define the desired states of the club and player respectively, given the other agents' behaviour. As the right-hand side of each of these expressions is identical, they imply:

$$F(Wp + Wc)/2 = 1 - F(Wp + Wc)/2, \qquad (10.3.9)$$

that implies:

$$F(Wp + Wc)/2 = 1/2. \qquad (10.3.10)$$

This implies that the average of the wage offers lies at the median of the arbitrator's probability function. Substituting (10.3.10) into any of the first-order conditions yields:

$$(Wp - Wc).\, f(Wp + Wc)/2.\, (1/2). = 1/2, \qquad (10.3.11)$$

dividing both sides by 1/2 implies:

$$(Wp - Wc) = 1/f(Wp + Wc)/2. \qquad (10.3.12)$$

This implies that the gap between the club's and player's preferred offers reflects the reciprocal of the value of the median of the density function of the arbitrator's preferred settlement. If the arbitrator's preferred settlement followed a normal distribution, then the median and mean (m) would coincide. In this case:

$$(Wp - Wc) = 1/f(m). \qquad (10.3.13)$$

(10.3.13) implies that the gap between the player's and club's wage offers narrows as the probability of the arbitrator's mean settlement rises. This suggests that final-offer arbitration will, over time, produce narrower and narrower dispersions of wage offers. (10.3.13), though static, carries a dynamic historical connotation. As discussed in the text, there is evidence that wage offers increasingly take into account the arbitrator's decisions.

Discussion questions

1. Advocate (General) Lenz's judgement in the Bosman case was initially received in England with some alarm by the soccer industry as potentially threatening competitive balance. With the benefit of hindsight, do you think that the concern was justified? Where might concern have been better directed?
2. Attempt to account for the explosive growth of team sport players' salaries since the 1970s. To what extent is there a consensus among economists both about the causes of the wage rise and about how to model it?

3.   How did McDonald and Reynolds (1994) and Marburger (1994) attempt to separate the effects of free agency and of final-offer arbitration on baseball players' salaries? Do their results seem to make sense?

4.   Dobson and Gerrard (1997) argue that the English premier league labour market is imperfect. Explain their model and the rationale behind their test for 'rent sharing'.

5.   Carmichael *et al.* (1999) argue that the English football players' labour market is effectively perfect.
    (a) How do they justify this assertion?
    (b) How do they explain the apparently contrary findings of Dobson and Gerrard?

6.   Do you expect that the rate of growth of players' wages will remain about the same or slow down, and why?

11 Conclusions

A brief review of chapters

In this book we have attempted to draw together some of the main issues relating to the economic analysis of professional team sports. We have examined the economic nature of the sporting league as a market in general and explored in some detail issues associated individually with the demand and supply of professional team sports.

In Chapter 2 we outlined some of the key economic theories and concepts that are referred to throughout the analysis. The chapter introduces the theme that there is a tension between the economic characterisation of professional team sports and usual economic policy recommendations because of the uncertainty of outcome hypothesis. We argue that this has generated a pre-occupation with institutional arrangements in professional team sports that lie outside economists' usual emphasis on free markets.

In Chapter 3 we argued that the precise economic characterisation of the objectives of professional team sports club owners remains unsettled. However, we have also argued that it probably does not matter too much what it is assumed they pursue, so long as economists are able to derive useful predictions about the markets in which they operate. Such predictions subsequently are explored in Chapter 4. Consequently, we focus on arguing that a cartel is probably a fair representation of the sports league. However, we do not imply that a natural monopoly thesis is redundant. We argue that one of the main reasons why, for example, Neale's (1964) predictions are consistent with the development of sporting leagues is that cartel behaviour will echo that of a monopoly. However, we argue that by adopting the cartel definition of sporting leagues the rationale for, and description of, the mechanisms by which leagues operate and develop is enhanced. Some broad empirical developments in leagues are sketched. These developments are particularly associated with the rise of television revenues in sport, which are further discussed in Chapter 8.

In examining the theoretical and empirical literature on league management policies, Chapter 4 concludes that the effects of policies aimed at affecting competitive balance are unlikely to be captured in models and manipulated in policies in a simple way. We argue that, following the discussions of Chapter 2, sporting leagues evolve and adjust institutionally through time. What may matter more than the hypothetically complete competitive balance implied in the literature is the perception or relative state of competitive balance. This implies that analysis should begin to focus more on the time profiles of competitive balance and league results and finances.

Chapter 5 begins a more detailed analysis of sporting leagues, by beginning to analyse the demand for professional team sports. Both the underlying economic theory of demand and the central statistical features employed by economists to measure the demand for professional team sports are outlined. They are illustrated with reference to an investigation into the demand for Scottish association football. Chapter 6 explores the empirical literature on the demand for professional team sports in more detail. We argue that as far as economic factors are concerned, while the traditional literature argued that market size was a ubiquitous determinant of demand, price and income effects were identified as weak influences. Moreover, as far as sporting factors are concerned, seasonal success, though not the traditional notion of uncertainty of outcome, and team and player qualities appear important determinants of demand. Recent developments in demand estimates for the long run are then discussed. We argue that the more recent long-run studies should be emphasised because of their appropriate econometric methodology and also because they reflect a changed emphasis from aggregating or averaging results across clubs over short time periods.

The fact that the uncertainty of outcome hypothesis appears to receive little support in the literature, together with the results of empirical work on the effects of league management policies, discussed in Chapter 4, prompts the discussion of Chapter 7. Here we re-examine some theoretical and empirical issues associated with the measurement of uncertainty of outcome in more detail. We conclude this chapter with the observation that there are several problems associated with any measurement of uncertainty of outcome. Nonetheless, the existent evidence suggests that the uncertainty of outcome hypothesis has been an overworked hypothesis in explaining the demand for professional team sports. Moreover, long-run domination in sports into a traditionally acceptable form of competition seems to have been the pattern in sports league development.

In contrast, in Chapter 8 we turn our attention to the television coverage of sport. A brief history of the origins of televised sport in the US and the UK is presented. Broad economic reasons explaining these developments are offered. We suggest that the evidence that is available implies that the impact of television coverage of traditional fixtures is not likely to affect attendance demand. However, the feedback effects of television through the financing and supply side of professional team sports could be profound. The advent of huge increases in television revenues in, for example, the UK has produced an 'exogenous' shock to historically more stable relationships. We argue that whatever the precise outcome, it is possible that such vast skewed television revenues will change the structure of leagues at a previously unknown speed. Competitive balance may thus change at a previously unknown speed, and despite the previous discussion in this book, may thus matter much more in the future than in the past.

Having once again alluded to the supply of professional team sports we then turn our attention to what we argue has been the main impact of league management. In Chapter 9 we outline some of the key economic concepts associated with the economic analysis of labour markets. In particular, the idealised labour market is outlined illustrating the close relationship between product and labour markets. The theory of monopsonistic competition that has figured prominently in the traditional literature is then outlined. The theory is exemplified by exploring, in some detail, some of the early studies of monopsonistic exploitation in US baseball. In Chapter 10 we examine the key institutional changes that have taken place in both US and European sporting labour markets. The changes involve the movement to free agency in both US and UK sports. The 1995 Bosman ruling made by the European Court of Justice is also explored. It is argued that these changes mean that players are now more able to bargain over their salaries and contracts. To provide an economic understanding of these processes, the chapter also explores bargaining theory and argues that there is evidence in the US that player salaries are now more in line with marginal revenue products, that typical contract lengths have increased and there has been a widening dispersion of salaries. In the UK, through discussing transfer fee deter-mination it is noted that there are differences of opinion as to the correct characterisation of the labour market. Finally, it was noted that the implications of increased player power for league policy really hinge upon players transferring wealth back to themselves and away from clubs.

It remains for us to offer, in perhaps an over-succinct fashion, what we perceive to be the main implications of the analysis of this book. We confine our comments to a discussion of the uncertainty of outcome hypothesis or the Louis–Schmeling hypothesis and future research.

Evaluation of the Louis–Schmeling paradox/uncertainty of outcome hypothesis

Throughout this book it has been argued that the uncertainty of outcome hypothesis, the Louis–Schmeling paradox in one of its earliest manifestations, has been identified as a central feature of professional team sports in sustaining effective sporting leagues. Consequently, sporting leagues can be understood as cartels whose economic organisation and policies of cross-subsidisation contrast with the economists' usual emphasis upon free markets. We argue that, although problematic in its measurement, the hypothesis is neither effectively targeted by these policies nor appears as important in understanding the long-term structure of the demand for professional team sports. It does appear to matter, however, in the very short run, for example associated with particular unique fixtures. In contrast, sporting leagues appear to develop in such a way that long-term domination is the norm. The impact of TV revenues could affect these relationships by changing the structure of demand and making it more short-term in focus and casual by nature.

More generally, the economic processes underlying the evolution of leagues prompted by such changes in financial regime, coupled with the clear indications from the labour market, where league management policies have had an observable impact, suggest that bargaining processes will be important in these developments. This has profound implications for league policy because it suggests that the effects of policies aimed at affecting competitive balance are unlikely to be captured in models and manipulated in policies in a simple way.

Implications for future research

The implications of these arguments suggest a number of research objectives. To this end, extending the models of sporting leagues to capture some of the institutional characteristics of professional team sports such as bargaining needs to occur. Importantly, this may imply some compromise with the emphasis of economic methodology outlined in the Introduction. This is because both interdisciplinary and more context-specific research would help to meet these objectives.

Related to this, effort should be made to conceptualise the evolving nature of uncertainty of outcome and competitive balance as it actually occurs. It follows that further work needs to be done in producing time-dependent measures of uncertainty of outcome or including them in time-series analysis of a more long-term nature. Perhaps of a more economic focus, this implies that further insights from the industrial organisation literature and game theory, as alluded to in Chapters 3, 7 and 9, should be sought, coupled with, for example, time-series econometric work. Anecdotally, for example, it could be argued that many markets in economics tend towards domination and market power. Such tendencies can be discerned in professional team sports, we would suggest, and focusing on them could proceed using similar models and analysis. In short we argue that re-focusing the economic analysis of professional team sports and combining this with insights from more context-specific analysis provides an exciting and interesting future research agenda.

Bibliography

Baimbridge, M. (1997) 'Match Attendance at Euro '96: was the crowd waving or drowning?' *Applied Economics Letters*, 9: 555–558.

Baimbridge, M., Cameron, S. and Dawson P. (1995) 'Satellite Broadcasting and Match Attendance: the case of rugby league', *Applied Economics Letters*, 2, 10: 343–346.

Baimbridge, M., Cameron, S. and Dawson, P. (1996) 'Satellite Television and the Demand for Football: A whole new ball game?' *Scottish Journal of Political Economy*, 43, 3: 317–333

Becker, G.S. (1975) *Human Capital: A Theoretical and Empirical Analysis*, second edition. New York: National Bureau of Economic Research.

Bird, P.J.W.N. (1982) 'The Demand for League Football', *Applied Economics*, 14, 6: 637–649.

Borland, J. (1987) 'The Demand for Australian Rules Football', *The Economic Record*, 63, 182: 220–230.

Borland, J. and Lye, J. (1992) 'Attendance at Australian Rules Football: a panel study', *Applied Economics*, 24, 9: 1053–1058.

Brown, T.M. (1952) 'Habit Persistence and Lags in Consumer Behaviour', *Econometrica*, 20, 3: 355–371.

Bruggink, T. and Rose, D.J. (1990) 'Financial Restraint on the Free Agent Labor Market for Major League Baseball: players look at strike three', *Southern Economic Journal*, 56, 4: 1029–1043.

Burgess, P.L. and Marburger, D.R. (1992) 'Bargaining Power and Baseball' in P.M. Sommer (ed.) *Diamonds are Forever: the Business of Baseball*. Washington, DC: Brookings Institution.

Cairns, J. (1988) 'Uncertainty of Outcome and the Demand for Football', University of Aberdeen Discussion Paper, 88-02.

Cairns, J. (1990) 'The Demand for Professional Team Sports', *British Review of Economic Issues*, 12, 28: 1–20.

Cairns, J., Jennett, N. and Sloane, P. J. (1986) 'The Economics of Professional Team Sports: a survey of theory and evidence,' *Journal of Economic Studies*, 13, 1: 3–80.

Campbell, A. and Sloane, P.J. (1997) 'The Implications of the Bosman Case for Professional Football', University of Aberdeen Discussion Paper, 02.

Carmichael, F. and Thomas, D. (1993) 'Bargaining in the Transfer Market: theory and evidence', *Applied Economics*, 25: 1467–1476.

Carmichael, F., Forrest, D. and Simmons R. (1999) 'The Labour Market in Association Football: who gets transferred and for how much', *Bulletin of Economic Research*, 51, 2: 125–150.

Carmichael, F., Millington, J. and Simmons, R. (1998) 'Elasticity of Demand for Rugby League Attendance and the impact of BSkyB', mimeo, University of Salford.

Cashmore, E.E. (1994) *And Then There Was Television*. London: Routledge.

Charemza, W. and Deadman, D.F. (1997) *New Directions in Econometric Practice*. Cheltenham: Edward Elgar.

Coase, R. (1960) 'The Problem of Social Cost', *Journal of Law and Economics*, 3, October: 1–44.

Cournot, A. (1838) *Researches into the Mathematical Principles of the Theory of Wealth*', English translation by N. Bacon. New York: Macmillan, 1893.

Court, A.T. (1939) 'Hedonic Price Indexes with Automotive Examples', in *The Dynamics of Automobile Demand*. New York: General Motors Corporation.

Cooke, A. (1994) *The Economics of Leisure and Sport*. London: Routledge.

Davies, B., Downward P.M. and Jackson, I. (1995a), 'The Demand for Rugby League: evidence from causality tests', *Applied Economics*, 27, 10: 1003–1007.

Davies, B., Downward P.M. and Jackson, I. (1995b), 'Cultural Determinants and the Demand for Professional Team Sports: a study of rugby league clubs', *Leisure Cultures: Values, Genders, Lifestyles*, L.S.A. Publications.

De Marchi, N. and Gilbert, C. (eds) (1989), *Oxford Economic Papers*, 41, Special Edition on Econometrics.

Demmert, H.G. (1973), *The Economics of Professional Team Sports*. Lexington, Mass.: D.C. Heath.

Dobson, S.M. and Gerrard, W. (1997) 'Testing for Rent-sharing in Football Transfer Fees: evidence from the English football league', Leeds University Business School Discussion Paper, E97-03.

Dobson, S.M. and Goddard, J.A. (1992) 'The Demand for Standing and Seated Accommodation in the English Football League', *Applied Economics*, 24, 10: 1155–1163.

Dobson, S.M. and Goddard, J.A. (1995) 'The Demand for Professional League Football in England and Wales, 1925–92', Discussion Paper, Department of Economics, University of Hull.

Dobson, S.M. and Goddard, J.A. (1996) 'The Demand for Football in the Regions of England and Wales', Discussion Paper, Department of Economics, University of Hull.

Dobson, S.M. and Goddard, J.A. (1998) 'Performance, Revenue and Cross Subsidisation in the Football League 1927–1994', *Economic History Review*, LI, 4: 763–785.

Drever, P. and McDonald, J. (1981) 'Attendances at South Australian Football Games', *International Review of Sports Sociology*, 16, 2: 103–113.

Dworkin, J.B. (1981) *Owners versus Players*. Boston: Auburn Books.

El Hodiri, M. and Quirk, J. (1971) 'An Economic Model of a Professional Sports League', *Journal of Political Economy*, 79, 6: 1302–1319.

Engle, R. and Granger, C.W.J. (1987) 'Co-integration and Error Correction: representation, estimation and testing', *Econometrica*, 55, 2: 256–278.

Farber, H.S. (1980) 'An Analysis of Final-offer Arbitration as a Conflict Resolution Device', *Journal of Conflict Resolution*, 35: 683–705.

Findlay, J., Holahan, W.L. and Oughton, C. (1999) 'Revenue Sharing from Broadcasting Football: the need for league balance', in S. Hamil, J. Michie and T. Sharot (eds) *The Business of Football: A Game of Two Halves*. London: Mainstream Publishing.

Fizel, J.L. and Bennett, R.W. (1989) 'The Impact of College Football Telecasts on College Football Attendance', *Social Science Quarterly*, 70, 4: 980–988.

Fort, R. and Quirk, J. (1995) 'Cross-subsidization, Incentives, and Outcomes in Professional Team Sports Leagues', *Journal of Economic Literature*, 33, 3: 1265–1299.

Friedman, M. (1953) 'The Methodology of Positive Economics' in *Essays in Positive Economics*. Chicago: University of Chicago Press.

Frindall, B. (1993) *The WISDEN book of Cricket Records*, third edition. London: Headline Book Publishing.

Gartner, M. and Pommerehene, W.W. (1978) 'Der Fussballzuschauer – ein Homo Oeconomicus?' *Jahrbuch fur Sozial Wissenschaft*, 29, 88–107.

Geddert, R.L. and Semple, R.K. (1985) 'Locating a Major Hockey Franchise: regional considerations', *Regional Sciences Perspectives*, 15, 1: 13–29.

Granger, C.W.J. and Newbold, P. (1974) 'Spurious Regressions in Econometrics', *Journal of Econometrics*, 2, 2: 110–120.

Gratton, C. and Taylor, P. (1985) *Sport and Recreation: An Economic Analysis*. London: E. and F. Spon.

Gwartney, J. and Howarth, C. (1974) 'Employer Costs and Discrimination: the case of baseball', *Journal of Political Economy*, 82, 4: 103–112.

Hamil, S., Michie, J. and Oughton, C. (eds) (1999) *The Business of Football: A Game of Two Halves*. London: Mainstream Publishing.

Hart, R.A., Hutton, J. and Sharot, T. (1975) 'A Statistical Analysis of Association Football Attendance', *Journal of the Royal Statistical Society; Series C (Applied Statistics)*, 24, 1: 17–27.

Hendry, D. (1992) *Econometrics: Alchemy or Science*. Oxford: Blackwell.

Hill, J.R. (1985) 'The Threat of Free Agency and Exploitation in Professional Baseball', *Quarterly Review of Economics and Business*, 25, 4: 68–82.

Hill, J.R. and Spellman, W. (1983) 'Professional Baseball: the reserve clause and salary structure', *Industrial Relations*, 22, 1: 1–19.

Hill, J.R., Madura, J. and Zuber, R.A. (1982) 'The Short Run Demand for Major League Baseball', *Atlantic Economic Journal*, 10, 2: 31–35.

Hynds, M. and Smith, I. (1994) 'The Demand for Test Match Cricket', University of St Andrews Working Paper.

Jennett, N. (1984) 'Attendances, Uncertainty of Outcome and Policy in Scottish League Football', *Scottish Journal of Political Economy*, 31, 2: 175–197.

Johansen, S. (1991) 'Estimation and hypothesis testing of cointegrating vectors in Gaussian autoregressive models', *Econometrics*, 59, 6: 1551–1580.

Jones, J.C.H. and Ferguson, D.G. (1988) 'Location and Survival in the National Hockey League', *Journal of Industrial Economics*, 36, 4: 443–457.

Kaempfer, W.H. and Pacey, P.L. (1986) 'Televising College Football: the complementarity of attendance and viewing', *Social Science Quarterly*, 67, 1: 176–185.

Kahn, L.M. (1993) 'Free Agency, Long Term Contracts and Compensation in Major League Baseball: estimates from panel data', *Review of Economics and Statistics*, 75: 157–164.

Kahn, L.M. and Sherer, P.O. (1988) 'Racial Differences in Professional Basketball Players' Compensation', *Journal of Labour Economics*, 6, 1: 40–61.

Koyck, L.M. (1954) *Distributed Lags and Investment Analysis*. Amsterdam: North Holland.

Kuypers, T. (1996) 'The Beautiful Game? An econometric study of why people watch English football', *University College London Discussion Papers in Economics*, 96–101.

Lancaster, K. (1966) 'A New Approach to Consumer Theory', *Journal of Political Economy*, 74, 2: 132–157.

Lee, S. (1999) 'The BSkyB Bid for Manchester United plc', in S. Hamil, J. Michie and C. Oughton (eds) *The Business of Football: A Game of Two Halves*. London: Mainstream Publishing.

Leibenstein, H. (1950) 'Bandwagon, Snob, and Veblen Effects in the Theory of Consumers' Demand', *Quarterly Journal of Economics*, 64, 1: 187–207.

McDonald, D.N. and Reynolds, M.O. (1994) 'Are Baseball Players Paid their Marginal Products?' *Managerial and Decision Economics*, 15, 5: 443–457.

MacDonald, G. (1988) 'The Economics of Rising Stars', *American Economic Review*, 78, 1: 155–166.

Mair, D. and Miller, A. (eds) (1992) *A Modern Guide to Economic Thought*. Aldershot: Edward Elgar.

Marburger, D.R. (1994) 'Bargaining Power and the Structure of Salaries in Major League Baseball', *Managerial and Decision Economics*, 15, 5: 433–441.

Marburger, D.R. (1997) 'Optimal Ticket Pricing for Performance Goods' *Managerial and Decision Economics*, 18: 375–381.

Mason, D.S. (1997) Revenue Sharing and Agency Problems in Professional Team Sport: the case of the National Football League, *Journal of Sports Management*, 11: 203–222.

Medoff, M. (1976) 'On Monopsonistic Exploitation in Professional Baseball', *Quarterly Review of Economics and Business* 16, 2: 113–121.

Nagel, E. (1963) 'Assumptions in Economic Theory', *American Economic Review*, 53 May: 211–219.

Neale, W.C. (1964) 'The Peculiar Economics of Professional Sport', *Quarterly Journal of Economics* 78, 1: 1–14.

Noll, R.G. (1974) 'Attendance and Price Setting' in R.G. Noll (ed.), *Government and the Sports Business*, Washington, DC: Brookings Institution.

Peel, D. and Thomas, D. (1988) 'Outcome Uncertainty and the Demand for Football: an analysis of match attendances in the English football league', *Scottish Journal of Political Economy*, 35, 3: 242–249.

Peel, D. and Thomas, D. (1997) 'Handicaps, Outcome Uncertainty and Attendance Demand', *Applied Economics Letters*, 4, 9: 567–570.

Peel, D. and Thomas, D. (1996) 'Attendance Demand: an investigation of repeat fixtures', *Applied Economics Letters*, 3, 6: 391–394.

Pesaran, M.H. and Smith, R. (1995) 'Estimating Long-run Relationships from Dynamic Heterogeneous Panels', *Journal of Econometrics*, 68, 1: 79–113.

Quirk, J. and Fort, R.D. (1992) *Pay Dirt the Business of Professional Team Sports*. Princeton: Princeton University Press.

Ramiondo, H.J. (1983) 'Free Agents' Impact on the Labor Market for Baseball Players', *Journal of Labor Research*, 4, 2: 183–193.

Rosen, S. (1981) 'The Economics of Superstars', *American Economic Review*, 71, 5: 845–858.

Rottenberg, S. (1956) 'The Baseball Players' Labour Market', *Journal of Political Economy*, 64, 3: 242–258.

Salomon Brothers (1997) 'UK Football Clubs: valuable assets?' *Global Equity Research: Leisure*. London: Salomon Brothers.

Sanderson, A.R. and Seigfried, J.Y. (1997) 'The Implications of Athlete Freedom to Contract: lessons from North America', *Institute of Economic Affairs*, 17, 3: 7–13.

Schollaert, P.T. and Smith, D.H. (1987) 'Team Racial Composition and Sports Attendance', *Sociological Quarterly*, 28, 1: 71–87.

Scully, G. (1974) 'Pay and Performance in Major League Baseball', *The American Economic Review*, 64, 6: 915–930.

Scully, G. (1989) *The Business of Major League Baseball*. Chicago: University of Chicago Press.

Scully, G. (1995) *The Market Structure of Sports*. Chicago: The University of Chicago Press.

Seigfried, J.Y. and Eisenberg, J.D. (1980) 'The Demand for Minor League Baseball', *Atlantic Economic Journal*, 8, 2: 59–69.

Seigfried, J.Y. and Hinshaw, C.E. (1979) 'The Effect of Lifting Television Blackouts in Professional Football No-shows', *Journal of the Economics of Business*, 32, 1: 1–13.

Simmons, R. (1996) 'The Demand for English League Football: a club-level analysis', *Applied Economics*, 28, 2: 139–155.

Simmons, R. (1997) 'Implications of the Bosman Ruling for Football Transfer Markets', *Institute of Economic Affairs*, 17, 3: 13–18.

Sloane, P.J. (1971) 'The Economics of Professional Football: the football club as a utility maximiser', *Scottish Journal of Political Economy*, 17, 2: 121–146.

Sloane, P.J. (1997) 'The Economics of Sport: an overview', *Institute of Economic Affairs*, 17, 3: 2–6.

Sommers, P. and Quinton, N. (1982) 'Pay and Performance in Major League Baseball: the case of the first family of free agents', *Journal of Human Resources*, 17, 3: 426–436.

Swales, A. (1996) *Golf Facts and Feats*. London: Guinness Publishing.

Szymanski, S. and Kuypers, T. (1999) *Winners & Losers*. London: Viking Press.

Szymanski, S. and Smith, R.P. (1997) 'The English Football Industry: profit, performance and industrial structure', *International Review of Applied Economics*, 11, 1, 135–154.

Thomas, D. (1997) 'The Rugby Revolution: new horizons or false dawn?, *Institute of Economic Affairs*, 17, 3: 19–24.

Thomas, S.M. and Jolson, M.A. (1979) 'Components of the Demand for Major League Baseball', *University of Michigan Business Review*, 31, 3: 1–6.

Vrooman, J.A. (1997) 'A General Theory of Professional Sports Leagues', *Southern Economic Journal*, 61: 971–990.

Waylen, P. and Snook, A. (1990) 'Patterns of Regional Success in the Football League, 1921 to 1987', *Area*, 22: 353–367.

Whannel, G. (1992) *Fields in Vision: Television, Sport and Cultural Transformation*. London: Routledge.

Whitney, J.D. (1988), 'Winning Games Versus Winning Championships: the economics of fan interest and team performance', *Economic Inquiry*, 26: 703–724.

Wilson, J. (1994) *Sport Society and the State: Playing by the Rules*. Iowa: Wayne State University Press.

Wilson, P. and Sim, B. (1995) 'The Demand for Semi-Pro League Football in Malaysia 1989–91: a panel data approach', *Applied Economics*, 27, 1: 131–138.

Zhang, J.J. and Smith, D.W. (1997) 'Impact of Broadcasting on the Attendance of Professional Basketball Games', *Sports Marketing Quarterly*, 6, 1: 23–29.

Zhang, J.J., Pease, D.G. and Smith, D.W. (1998) 'Relationship Between Broadcasting Media and Minor League Hockey Game Attendance', *Journal of Sports Management*, 12: 103–122.

Index